CHRISTIAN POLITICS;

AN

ESSAY ON THE TEXT OF PALEY.

CHRISTIAN POLITICS;

AN

ESSAY ON THE TEXT OF PALEY,

IN

THREE BOOKS;

BY THE

REV. HENRY CHRISTMAS, M.A.

F.R.S. F.S.A. F.R.G.S.

LATE OF ST. JOHN'S COLLEGE, CAMBRIDGE,
MEMBER OF THE ROYAL ACADEMY OF ARCHÆOLOGY OF MADRID,
MEMBER OF THE IMPERIAL SOCIETY OF ANTIQUARIES OF LA MORINIE,
AUTHOR OF "THE CRADLE OF THE TWIN GIANTS,"
"ECHOES OF THE UNIVERSE,"
"SHORES AND ISLANDS OF THE MEDITERRANEAN,"
ETC. ETC. ETC.

LONDON:

HOPE AND CO. 16, GREAT MARLBOROUGH STREET.

MDCCCLV.

TO

THE RIGHT HONORABLE

THE LORD VISCOUNT PALMERSTON, M.P.

My Lord,

I take the freedom of dedicating this book to your Lordship; because I believe your Politics to be Christian Politics;—because I believe that, as a patriotic statesman, the welfare of the country has ever been your highest aim;—because I believe that, while you have never given way to the mere demagogue, you have been always ready to concede what the People had a right to demand; and, lastly, because I believe that we are now engaged in what may be a long, dangerous, and expensive war, solely through neglecting your counsels.

I remain,

My Lord,

Your Lordship's most obedient Servant,

THE AUTHOR.

CONTENTS.

*The Chapters marked * are entirely original; † are partly so; ‡ are Paley's alone.*

BOOK I.
OF GOVERNMENT AND ITS FORMS.

	CHAPTER		PAGE
*	I.	Introductory..................................	1
*	II.	Of Power and Liberty in general..........	6
†	III.	Of the Origin of Civil Government........	11
*	IV.	Of the People as the alone Source of Power.	18
†	V.	How Subjection to Civil Government is maintained............................	24
†	VI.	The Duty of Submission to Civil Government explained............................	33
†	VII.	Of Expediency as the Foundation of a Subject's Obligation.....................	44
*	VIII.	Of Right as the Foundation of a Subject's Obligation............................	53
†	IX.	Of the Duty of Civil Obedience as stated in the Christian Scriptures...............	55
†	X.	Of Civil and Political Liberty...............	66
‡	XI.	Of Different Forms of Government.........	74
‡	XII.	Of the Theory of the British Constitution..	88
†	XIII.	Of the Practice of the British Constitution or the British Government.............	96
†	XIV.	Of the Representative System, and especially on that Form adopted in England....	114
*	XV.	Of the Progress of the Representative Principle............................	130
*	XVI.	Of Restrictions on Electors in the Choice of Representatives...................	140
*	XVII.	Of the Duration of Representative Assemblies and the Payment of Representatives............................	145

BOOK II.

OF LAW AND JUSTICE.

	CHAPTER		PAGE
†	I.	Of the Administration of Justice	154
‡	II.	Of Modes of Judicature	163
‡	III.	Of the Necessity for Legal Enactments	172
†	IV.	Of certain Anomalies in our Judicial System	184
‡	V.	Of Crimes and Punishments	189
†	VI.	Of Arguments in favour of Capital Punishments	195
‡	VII.	Of Aggravations and Mitigations	201
‡	VIII.	Of Fraudulent Crimes	204
‡	IX.	Of the presumed Necessity of frequent Executions	208
‡	X.	Of Reforming Punishments	211
‡	XI.	Of Inexpedient Punishments	215
*	XII.	Of Capital Punishments morally and politically considered	225
*	XIII.	Of Capital Punishments as supposed to be supported by Scripture	228
*	XIV.	Of the Noachic Precept as applied to Capital Punishment	239
*	XV.	Of the Practice of the Pre-mosaic World with respect to Capital Punishment	247
*	XVI.	Of the Mosaic Law of Capital Punishment	253
*	XVII.	Of the supposed Christian Sanction of Capital Punishment	259
*	XVIII.	Of Laws concerning Marriage, Divorce, &c.	275
*	XIX.	Of the Law of Primogeniture	289
*	XX.	Of Game Laws	292
*	XXI.	Of certain Redundant Legislations	297

BOOK III.

OF POLITICAL ECONOMY.

	CHAPTER		PAGE
†	I.	Of Population	300
†	II.	On Modes of Life as bearing on the Question of Population	310
†	III.	Of Provision and its Influence on Population	317
†	IV.	Of the Distribution of Provision	322
†	V.	Of Emigration	335
†	VI.	Of Colonization	338
*	VII.	Of Money and Currency	342
†	VIII.	Of Taxation	351
†	IX.	Of the Exportation of Provisions	372
†	X.	Of Labour	375
‡	XI.	Of Laws and Customs relating to Land	379
*	XII.	Of Free Trade and Restriction	385
†	XIII.	Of the Lawfulness of War	394
†	XIV.	Of the Conduct of War	410
†	XV.	Of Standing Armies	414

INTRODUCTION.

The causes which have led to the publication of this volume may be briefly stated.

No one can read the writings of Paley without feeling that his peculiar clearness of mind was transferred to his pages, and that, whether right or wrong, all he advanced was worthy of the most attentive consideration. Those who pursue the study of political science will find that Paley's views are represented to them whenever and wherever they seek for information—conveyed indeed in language less concise and intelligible, but made the basis of all, or nearly all, the works written since on the subject.

Yet, though Paley was undoubtedly far in advance of his own time, too far indeed for his own worldly interests, there are occasional proofs in his works that he did not always perceive the results to which his principles tended; and while we are at times struck with the largeness of his elementary views, we find the most startling, inadequate, and sometimes inconsistent consequences drawn from them.

The defects, however, of Paley's works are, for the most part, negative ones. He does *sometimes*, though *rarely*, advance propositions which we must, in the clearer light which we now enjoy, unhesitatingly condemn: but he frequently stops far short of the mark to which his steps appear to be tending, and to which his principles, if rightly carried out, would infallibly lead him.

Instead, therefore, of writing an entirely new book on Politics, considered as a Christian Science, I have decided to avail myself of that which Paley had already written; thinking it more honest to do this, than to disguise the statements and opinions of Paley in language of my own.

As a precedent to this, I have the example of Lord Brougham, who has treated in this way the Natural Theology of the same author, and has thus given to a meritorious book an additional base of popular favour, and rendered to the public, at the same time, a very important service.

The PRINCIPLES OF POLITICAL PHILOSOPHY, as it came from the hands of its author, formed but a small part of a single volume; the larger portion being occupied by the consideration of MORAL PHILOSOPHY. Confined thus for space, it was obviously impossible that all the weighty questions suggested by the subject could be discussed with that freedom and to that extent which their importance demanded; and those, therefore, were postponed which seemed the least interesting *in that day*, however intrinsically momentous they might be. This circumstance alone would render the work in some manner unsatisfactory; but, in addition to this, there are several topics on which Paley's judgment appears to have been warped by the prevailing opinions of his day; and there is much reason to believe that, had he lived a century earlier, or half a century later, his writings would have taken, in many respects, a loftier tone.

Many changes too have taken place in the political world since the publication of his PRINCIPLES OF POLITICAL PHILOSOPHY. Three French Revolutions and many others in Europe, together with the establishment, as a permanent polity, of the American Republic, have tended greatly to modify the opinions held by the generality of mankind as to the objects of government and the sources of power: while the alterations and amendments cautiously and successfully introduced into our own constitution have proved that changes are not always for the worse, even when they seem most opposed to the prejudices of former ages.

It is therefore with a degree of experience enlarged far more than in proportion to the time which has elapsed since Paley's work appeared, that the student of Christian Politics addresses himself now to his subject. Many things are now admitted as facts, which were then scarcely allowed as possibilities; and many principles might be maintained as conservative, as would then have been looked upon as most destructive.

But, in addition to these motives for taking up this subject, there is the further and higher one of applying to it the rules of Christianity, and of showing that what the theologian rightly counts most divine, is in perfect accordance with what the well-informed statesman reckons as most expedient; and of proving that the broadest assertions of civil and political freedom are in strict unison with a revelation which preaches to us " the glorious liberty of the children of God."

Legislation has taken many strides within these few years; but it has yet many more to take. We have many unnecessary laws; many excessive penalties; many useless restrictions; and till these are all done away, the code of our country will be imperfect. It *has been* a disgrace to us as a free and educated nation; it is still far behind the requirements of the time. If a new state were now to be founded, the duty of its first legislators would be to see that, while no interest was left unguarded, there should not be a single law passed which was not imperatively called for by the circumstances of the case. In an old, but rapidly advancing empire like our own, political growth is not less to be studied; and all that shackled the free progress of the national spirit must be unsparingly removed, however time-honored the abuse. Defective legislation, with all its evils, is better than redundant legislation; nor ought there to be a single provision remaining in our statute book which is not as necessary now as on the day when it was first promulgated.

It is impossible for a country to make much progress, without rendering a frequent revision of its laws necessary. The change in political circumstances, in popular feeling, the growth of education, the increase of wealth and luxury, all require corresponding changes in the legislative enactments of a nation. The statute necessary in one age becomes mischievous in the next: the penalty moderate at one period, becomes barbarous a century later. It is by such accommodations that our constitution has been made to last; and it must be by similar accommodations that its existence will be perpetuated.

The removal of *every needless* restriction is what a free people have a right to demand. The removal of every useless expense will follow as a matter of course; and it will be seen that the country which is governed upon the most correct philosophical principles, will be governed also with the strictest regard to public economy.

I put forth this work with the most loyal and dutiful feelings: I would advocate a strong government, for the very reasons that I would advocate a just one. The freedom of the subject can only be maintained by a powerful executive. Nor can any economy be called wise which reduces that power below the standard required for the energetic maintenance of public order.

But the times are long past in which mere prescription can take the place of argument, or authority trample upon right. Abuses must and will be reformed; and the only question, in an age like the present, is—shall we freely give up all that is contrary to justice and freedom, cause our practice to walk side by side with the theory of our constitution, or, keeping up a delusive peace, and mistaking sullen silence for contented acquiescence, fall suddenly into anarchy, from which it would indeed be difficult to rise again?

This question is receiving its answer day by day, in the safe and beneficial reforms which are going on around us. To aid the progress, is to add to the safety and to advance the happiness of the nation: to retard it, even in trifles, is to forsake the present and to renounce the future; it is to identify ourselves with the errors and barbarities of the past.

One part only of Paley's short treatise is omitted: it is that which treats of Religious Establishments, and of Toleration. The subject is one on which the author of the present work is preparing a volume: it is far too important to be dismissed with a brief notice here.

London, Oct. 1854.

CHRISTIAN POLITICS.

BOOK I.

CHAPTER I.

INTRODUCTORY.

POLITICS is the Science of Government. It teaches the duties which devolve on men as members of a state or polity; and if the state to which they belong is a *Christian state*, it may be denominated CHRISTIAN POLITICS. But what constitutes a Christian state? This question will be variously answered. One will reply, a Christian state is a state whose laws are in accordance with the spirit of Christianity. Another will say, it is one whose government is committed only to Christian men; a third will define it to be a state, the majority of whose subjects profess the Christian faith; while a fourth will consider the establishment of a Christian church essential to the right assumption of the title.

A little examination, however, will satisfy us that none of these definitions will exactly meet the circumstances of the case.

The principles of Christianity might be applied to the governments of Turks or Hindoos, and might recommend themselves by their natural adaptation to the exigences of mankind; a Christian minister might govern a pagan nation, under a pagan sovereign, according to his own views of right; he might amend the laws, remodel the institutions, and reform the spirit of the government; and yet it would be absurd to call the state a Christian state, because the principles of Christianity had been brought to bear on its institutions. Pagan Rome witnessed many such examples in her numberless provinces, and yet provinces and metropolis continued pagan still.

Let us take the second definition—Was Mexico a Christian state, or Peru, when the last of the Heathen Emperors was dethroned and their seats occupied by Cortes or Pizarro? Was Rome more Christian the day after Constantine declared himself a follower of the Cross than it had been the day before? The rulers of our vast Indian Empire are Christians, yet who would call India—British India— a Christian state, or even Calcutta a Christian city? It is possible then that a state may have laws in accordance with the spirit of Christianity, and be ruled by men professing the Christian faith, and yet not be entitled to the appellation of a *Christian State.*

Can it be said that a state is a Christian state, the majority of whose subjects profess the Christian faith? Hardly so; for then Turkey, with Moslem governors ruling according to Mohammedan laws, would be entitled to the designation, inasmuch as the professors of a corrupt and debased Christianity are said on the whole to outnumber the Islamite population.

The fourth definition is equally unsatisfactory, and indeed more so; for while it recognizes British India, with its few thousands of Christians, and its hundred millions of Idolaters as a *Christian* state, it excludes the United States of America.

While, however, none of these definitions will be found sufficient by itself, it is evident that in some combination of them resides that which may be called the Christianity of an empire. In England, they *all* exist. In France, the first, third, and fourth; America, the first and third only. Russia, Spain, Denmark, Sweden, Austria, are in the same condition as England; in Prussia, the second element is wanting, religious restrictions do not exist: but wherever we look, we shall find that a state to be called Christian must have two conditions of those above-mentioned; and the instance of America will suffice to show that a state has a right to the title, when,

1, The great majority of her subjects profess the Christian religion; and when,

2, Her laws are avowedly in accordance with the principles of Christianity.

It has been necessary to make these preliminary

observations; because we shall, in the course of this work, have to speak of a Christian state as something clearly defined; and of certain classes of laws as affecting the Christianity of the body politic.

Let it then be granted that in any land, our own for example, the great majority of citizens profess the Christian faith, and that our laws are, *as a whole*, avowedly in accordance with the spirit of Christianity, we assume a right to call our state a Christian state, and to apply to her constitution all the rules of Christian politics.

Now, Christianity recognizes the equality (by nature) of all men before God. This principle is so clearly laid down in Scripture, that it would be worse than idle to attempt to enforce it in a work which presupposes the truth of Christianity itself. Alike in origin—for God hath made of one blood all men that dwell on the earth; alike in a state of lapse—"for that all have sinned;" and alike in mortal destiny— "for it is appointed unto man once to die." God has given for *all* the revelation of a Saviour, and bestowed the earth in common upon the children of men.

The very first principle, therefore, of Christian politics is, that

1. All men are by nature equal in the sight of God.

From this we may deduce the following truths:

2. That all government is for the benefit of the governed, and not for that of the governors; except so far as those governors partake of the common prosperity.

3. That, when any government disregards this principle, and ceases to act for the advantage of the commonwealth, it has no longer any Christian right to existence.

4. That, as it is the right of every Christian to live under a Christian law, and the Christian law is *"a perfect law of liberty,"* all restriction, *however necessary*, and *however the necessity may arise*, is to be looked upon as *in itself* an evil.

5. That, in consequence of this last principle, it will follow that no Christian government should either make, continue, or allow to be made or continued, any restriction of what kind so ever, save on proof of its necessity.

As we proceed to the investigation of these preliminary principles, we shall see that, in a state of society like that which now prevails, the necessity of restriction takes a wide range, and assumes a vast variety of aspect; so that nothing would be more erroneous than to imagine the doctrines just laid down inimical to just or strong government, or in the slightest degree favourable to anarchy and confusion.

CHAPTER II.

OF POWER AND LIBERTY IN GENERAL.

Much labour has been wasted and much ability misemployed in attempting to discover the origin of civil government. To the believer in divine revelation one thing will be clear, that the parental authority expanded into the patriarchal, and that the Supreme Ruler himself interposed in cases of doubt and difficulty. He checked the spirit of revenge which would have slain the first-born of men, by establishing a special covenant with the first murderer. He revealed his will by a thousand unmistakeable signs and tokens, by dreams, visions, and miracles, by prophecy, and divinely inspired wisdom, and finally, established among one people a law and a polity perfectly adapted to its purpose, and based on a pure Theocracy.

That this Theocracy was soon only nominally so, is but too true, and its practical cessation is to be traced to that weakness of human nature which judges of authority not so much by its own weight and value as by the estimation in which it is held by other men. The Jews found despotism the established form of government in the nations around them, and, perceiving certain advantages connected therewith, they, too, "desired a king." The error into which they had fallen was sufficiently shown by the manner in which their request was granted, and the evil consequences of the change were further manifested; first, by a warlike and insecure government, under Saul: secondly, by a long series of misfortunes, national and personal, befalling the greatest king and most illustrious hero of ancient times, David: thirdly, by a splendid, but at last tyrannical and oppressive, rule under Solomon: fourthly, by the division of the great Israelitish Empire into comparatively insignificant kingdoms, unable to stand alone amidst the mightier monarchies around them: fifthly, by an uninterrupted succession of evil princes over the house of Israel, and a very large admixture of similar rulers among those of Judah: and, lastly, by the captivity and dispersion, first, of the ten, and afterwards of the two remaining tribes.

It would be absurd to pretend from this, as some do, that the monarchical form of government is displeasing to the Deity; but it does clearly demonstrate, that other forms may be equally and in some cases more acceptable to Him. It must be borne in mind, too, that very few arguments drawn from the *first* institutes of civil government will be found applicable in our times. Man was not created in a state of barbarism, nor has barbarism been the *universal* condition of the human race at any period of the world's history. When he sunk to it, he sunk gradually, and many centuries were occupied in the descent. Again, from the most barbarous nations of antiquity have sprung the most cultivated of modern days. As the polished empires of old retrograded, or at least continued stationary, and the modern ones advanced, we come to a point in which the amount of civilization may may be deemed equal, and their relative position is afterwards proceeding in an inverse order. It follows from this, that it must be a difficult task to trace the idea of civil government in any modern nation to its root, to show how far it springs from the exigences of barbarous times, and how far the notions which *then* prevailed were influenced by the traditions of a prior civilization. Thus much, however, may be said, that no man willingly surrenders any part of his right without an equivalent; and if I submit to any rule which circumscribes my otherwise unrestrained freedom of speech and action, I either do so because I am forced, or because I find my advantage to result from so doing. If I am forced, I am *so far* the victim of tyranny, whether it be of one or of many. If I willingly agree, then I exchange a certain portion of freedom for a certain portion of security. Now, as it will not be denied that the secure and undisputed holding of one acre is a more valuable possession than the uncertain occupation of two, and that the freeholder is, *cæteris paribus*, a richer man than the mere squatter, so it will be found that, by thus voluntarily yielding a portion of my liberty, I am a gainer in the amount of real freedom which I actually enjoy. The welfare of society at large requires that I should be restrained from any assault on the life, person, property, or reputation of my neighbour; and my own welfare requires, in like manner, that he should be similarly restrained with regard to me. If this restraint be necessary, there must be a power lodged somewhere in order to enforce its provisions and to punish its violations; and he who will not acquiesce in the existence of such a power, and towards whom therefore it becomes a tyranny, must seek out some perfectly savage state of life in which his own freedom, both for good and evil, may be perfectly unrestrained, and the freedom of others towards him equally so.

It may seem strange at first to call the restraint which we admit to be so necessary, a tyranny towards those who refuse to acquiesce in it; but the apparent anomaly will soon vanish when we consider that the person so placed is self-outlawed. Society is instituted for good purposes, and acquires a corporate right from the cession of those individual rights which formerly its members possessed. If, then, I suffer injury, and have ceded to the commonwealth the right of retaliation, I may move that commonwealth to act in my behalf. The man who takes the law and authority into his own hands and inflicts an injury on me, aims a blow *in his manner* not at *me* only, but at the commonwealth, which returns the blow *according to its own.*

This view of the case will be more clearly understood by calling to mind that the Christian law is a *perfect* law of liberty, and that God has by his own word taken away from us the right of revenging our own wrongs. "Dearly beloved, avenge not yourselves, but rather give place unto wrath; for it is written—vengeance is mine, I will repay, saith the Lord!" so that the work of retaliation is taken into the passionless hands of a pure Spirit, and by his providence delegated here on earth to the passionless hands of a disinterested government. It is on this ground that the Apostle states that "the Powers that be are ordained of God," and that "whosoever resisteth the power, resisteth the ordinance of God, and they that resist shall receive to themselves damnation." The words are a protest in favour of government *in general*, in favour of the existence of that wholesome restraint which secures life, fame, person, and property, and do not touch on the question of the lawfulness of resisting or overthrowing any particular government, when that government is no longer carrying out those purposes for which it was established.

CHAPTER III.

OF THE ORIGIN OF CIVIL GOVERNMENT.

THE reasons alleged in the last chapter will probably be held sufficient for attempting no lengthened analysis of the various opinions which have been maintained concerning the origin of civil government; yet, as that subject cannot be dismissed without *some* notice, and that given by Paley is both plain and lucid, we shall here introduce it. Government, at first, says that great writer, was either patriarchal or military; that of a parent over his family, or of a commander over his fellow warriors.

I. Paternal authority, and the order of domestic life, supplied the foundation of civil government. Did mankind spring out of the earth mature and independent, it would be found perhaps impossible to introduce subjection and subordination among them; but the condition of human infancy prepares men for society, by combining individuals into small communities, and by placing them from the beginning under direction and control. A family contains the rudiments of an empire. The authority of one over many, and the disposition to govern and to be governed, are in this way incidental to the very nature, and coeval, no doubt, with the existence of the human species.

Moreover, the constitution of families not only assists the formation of civil government, by the disposition which it generates, but also furnishes the first steps of the process by which empires have been actually reared. A parent would retain a considerable part of this authority after his children were grown up and had formed families of their own. The obedience of which they remembered not the beginning, would be considered as natural; and would scarcely, during the parent's life, be entirely or abruptly withdrawn.

Here, then, we see the second stage in the progress of dominion. The first was, that of a parent over his young children; this, that of an ancestor presiding over his adult descendants.

Although the original progenitor was the centre of union to his posterity, yet it is not probable that the association would be immediately or altogether dissolved by his death. Connected by habits of intercourse and affection, and by some common rights, necessities and interests, they would consider themselves as allied to each other in a nearer degree than to the rest of the species. Almost all would be sensible of an inclination to continue in the society in which they had been brought up; and experiencing, as they soon would do, many inconveniences from the absence of that authority which their common ancestor exercised, especially in deciding their disputes, and directing their operations in matters in which it was necessary to act in conjunction, they might be induced to supply his place by a formal choice of a successor; or rather might willingly, and almost imperceptibly, transfer their obedience to some one of the family, who, by his age or services, or by the part he possessed in the direction of their affairs during the life-time of the parent, had already taught them to respect his advice, or to attend to his commands; or, lastly, the prospect of these inconveniences might prompt the first ancestor to appoint a successor; and his posterity, from the same motive, united with an habitual deference to the ancestor's authority, might receive the appointment with submission. Here, then, we have a tribe or clan incorporated under one chief. Such communities might be increased by considerable numbers, and fulfil the purposes of civil union without any other or more regular convention, constitution, or form of government, than what we have described. Every branch which was slipped off from the primitive stock, and removed to a distance from it, would in like manner take root, and grow into a separate clan. Two or three of these clans were frequently, we may suppose, united into one. (Marriage, conquest, mutual defence, common distress, or more accidental conditions, might produce this effect.)

II. A second source of personal authority, and which might easily extend, or sometimes, perhaps, supersede, the patriarchal, is that which results from military arrangements. In wars, either of aggression or defence, manifest necessity would prompt those who fought on the same side to array themselves under one leader. And although their leader was advanced to this eminence for the purpose only, and during the operations of a single expedition, yet his authority would not always terminate with the reasons for which it was conferred. A warrior who had led forth his tribe against their enemies with repeated success, would procure to himself, even in the deliberations of peace, a powerful and permanent influence. If this advantage were added to the authority of the patriarchal chief, or favoured by any previous distinction of ancestry, it would be no difficult undertaking for the person who possessed it to obtain the almost absolute direction of the affairs of the community: especially if he was careful to associate to himself proper auxiliaries, and content to practise the obvious art of gratifying or removing those who opposed his pretensions.

But although we may be able to comprehend how, by his personal abilities or fortune, one man may obtain the rule over many, yet it seems more difficult to explain how empire became hereditary, or in what manner sovereign power, which is never acquired without great merit or management, learns to descend in a succession which has no dependence upon any qualities either of understanding or activity. The causes which have introduced hereditary dominion into so general reception in the world are principally the following: The influence of association, which communicates to the son a portion of the same respect which was wont to be paid to the virtues or station of the father; the greater envy with which all behold the exaltation of an equal, than the continuance of an acknowledged superiority; a reigning prince leaving behind him many adherents, who can preserve their own importance only by supporting the succession of his children: add to these reasons, that elections to the supreme power having, upon trial, produced destructive contensions, many states would take a refuge from a return of the same calamities in a rule of succession; and no rule presents itself so obvious, certain, and intelligible, as consanguinity of birth.

The ancient state of society in most countries, and the modern condition of some uncivilised parts of the world, exhibit that appearance which this account of the origin of civil government would lead us to expect. The earliest histories of Palestine, Greece, Italy, Gaul, Britain, inform us that these countries were occupied by many small independent nations, not much, perhaps, unlike those which are found at present amongst the savage inhabitants of North America, and upon the coast of Africa. These nations I consider as the amplifications of so many single families, or as derived from the junction of two or three families, whom society, in war or the approach of some common danger, had united.

Suppose a country to have been first peopled by shipwreck on its coasts, or by emigrants or exiles from some neighbouring country; the new settlers, having no enemy to provide against, and occupied with the care of their personal subsistence, would think little of digesting a system of laws, of contriving a form of government, or indeed of any political union whatever; but each settler would remain at the head of his own family, and each family would include all of every age and generation who were descended from him. So many of the families as were holden together after the death of the original ancestor, by the reasons and in the method above recited, would wax, as the individuals were multiplied, into tribes, clans, hordes, or nations, similar to those into which the ancient inhabitants of many countries are known to have been divided, and which are still found wherever the state of society and manners is immature and uncultivated.

Nor need we be surprised at the early existence in the world of some vast empires, or at the rapidity with which they advanced to their greatness, from comparatively small and obscure originals. Whilst the inhabitants of so many countries were broken into numerous communities, unconnected, and oftentimes contending with each other; before experience had taught these little states to see their own danger in their neighbour's ruin, or had instructed them in the necessity of resisting the aggrandizement of an aspiring power, by alliances, and timely preparations; in this condition of civil policy, a particular tribe, who by any means had got the start of the rest in strength or discipline, and happened to fall under the conduct of an ambitious chief, by directing their first attempts to the part where success was most secure, and by assuming, as they went along, those whom they conquered into a share of their future enterprises, might soon gather a force which would infallibly overbear any opposition which the scattered power and unprovided state of such enemies could make to the progress of their victories.

Lastly, our theory affords a presumption that the earliest governments were monarchies; because the government of families and of armies, from which, according to our account, civil government derived its institution and probably its form, is universally monarchical.

CHAPTER IV.

OF THE PEOPLE AS THE ONLY SOURCE OF POWER.

WHATEVER may have been the origin of civil government in ancient times, one thing is clear, that no theory framed from such premises can apply to ourselves. Change after change has taken place, revelation after revelation has been accomplished, each more firmly establishing the principle, *that the source of political power is in the people,* so that now it is *almost* universally admitted; and the very existence of representative government may be taken as a tacit concession of all that its supporters require.

The few who hesitate to give in their adhesion to this doctrine, are those who imagine that it detracts somewhat from the divine supremacy. Finding it written, that "the powers that be are ordained OF GOD," they deem it something like a contradiction in terms, to say, that "the powers that be" are also ordained OF THE PEOPLE. But this arises from a not unnatural fallacy. It is undoubtedly the will of God, and *His ordination* that there should be civil governors, and it is as unquestionably the will of man also; but God has left *His* ordination to be worked out by the free will of His intelligent creatures.

The old figment of the divine right of kings is scarcely susceptible of a single argument in its favour. Let us put a case: All the old theological advocates of legitimacy would agree that the "right divine" to govern in France was vested in Louis XVI, that it was not in any of the republican forms of the first revolution, that it was not in the Emperor Napoleon, crowned and anointed though he were, that it *was* again found under Louis XVIII and Charles X, that it once more disappeared from the nation when Louis Philippe ascended the throne, and has not been restored by the late republic or the present empire. One, therefore, of two consequences must follow: either that a state of complete anarchy was during so many years the divinely recognized state of France, and is so now, a state in which crime can receive no lawful punishment, and property no lawful protection,—or that God's law recognizes the existing authority, and commands obedience to be paid to it by all Christians.

There will scarcely be a doubt as to which side of the alternative we are bound to take; and if the unmistakeable voice OF THE POPULAR WILL were to establish a republic in this country to-morrow, it would be as much the duty of Christians to bow to its decision as it is now to pay a ready and happy obedience to the royal authority.

Nor does that authority lose anything thereby; on the contrary, it gains both in dignity and stability.

Who does not perceive that to be enthroned in the hearts of a mighty people, to be, in fact, the embodied expression of a magnificent national WILL, is to be, in the highest sense, *ordained* OF GOD? The sovereigns of this country ever have been so. John would have been driven from his kingdom by popular indignation, had his life lasted but a little longer. Charles I trampled upon the liberties of the subject, and all his high personal qualities could not save him from dethronement and death. James II attempted to introduce an alien and enslaving religion, and both he and his family were rejected by the nation.

But we go much further than this, and contend, that not only is this country ruled by the popular will, but all others in like manner; and that not only in our days, but from the remotest antiquity. The Emperor of all the Russias sits on his throne by precisely the same right, and is supported there by precisely the same power, as our own monarch. It scarcely admits of a doubt, that if the subjects of his vast and unwieldy empire were all polled on the question, it would indeed be a small minority that would not acquiesce in his rule, and vote for its continuance. Nor have we any right to invalidate their decision, by comparing their social and political state with our own; privileges which we value, would to them be worthless; as they advance to the position in which we are of civilization and refinement, they will progressively claim, obtain, and exercise like powers, assuming them as rights, and defending them from invasion.

Nothing is more common than to wonder at the long continuance of many tyrannical reigns, and nothing more unphilosophical. Perhaps the most popular of the Cæsars was Nero; months after his death, Otho could find no readier way of recommending himself to the Roman people, than a promise to take Nero for his model. The popularity of Henry VIII was, up to the very moment of his decease, almost unbounded; and it has been stated, by very competent authority, that no king of England since has attained a like amount, till the accession of the late justly beloved and lamented William IV.

In Spain, the two kings most decidedly the favorites of the people, were Philip II and Ferdinand VII; neither of them men likely to receive much praise from other nations, or from the thoughtful and considerate in their own. But the truth appears to be, that those sovereigns are most popular who are able to identify themselves with the national feeling of their times, to assimilate their own tastes and habits with those of the people over whom they rule. Nero was a complete type of the Roman of his day—cruel, vicious, insane, but still intensely Roman. Henry VIII was an Englishman alike in his words and actions, and all his vices and violences could not deprive him of the strongly marked national character. It must be remembered, also, that he was a prince of immense talent, splendid attainments, and the defender of his people against foreign domination. William IV was equally British with Henry VIII; and he presented the type of the national character under a most attractive aspect: the same observations may apply to the Spanish kings mentioned, and to the present Emperor of Russia.

If we turn our thoughts to more ancient times, we shall see reason to maintain the same doctrine. Nebuchadnezzar, doubtless, thought his power based on a divine foundation; but the safety of himself and his empire consisted in this, that his subjects thought so too: they cheerfully consented to his government, they felt it to be adapted to their wants, and had it been *oppressive* in any great degree, it could not have subsisted long. No nation, either ancient or modern, has ever been tyrannized over for any considerable time. Individual rights have been trampled upon, classes have been oppressed, laws have been disregarded, charters have been violated, kings have acted as though they had been in all respects above every legislature, human or divine. But they have avoided *universal tyranny;* or, if they have not, they have paid with their crowns and lives the penalties of their misdeeds. We cannot call a nation oppressed, because for centuries it has been under despotic rule; the subjects of a government alone can tell whether *to them* it be a tyranny or not; and if it be, they will not long suffer under its infliction. Neither can a government remain stationary while the people are advancing; or else that very rule which was mild, beneficent, and acceptable in the beginning of a century, will become oppressive and intolerable before its close: and the first French revolution stands on record as a fearful instance of what tremendous retribution a nation so misgoverned will exercise. It is quite true that in barbarous times there is comparatively little *sense of union* among the masses; they do not perceive their own strength; NOR DO THEY NOW! But this only acts in lengthening the period of transition, in putting off the day of atonement: it comes at last, and with convulsions only the more awful from the delay which has attended them.

If we can fancy a herd of tame lions, driven by a shepherd, and regulated by a few watch-dogs, we shall have some idea of the proportion of actual power in governments and their armies over the millions they rule. Let there be once *a common will in the commonwealth,* and there neither exists now, nor ever did exist, a power which could control it for a single second. We shall now be prepared to admit—I. That the rightful source of power is in the people; II. That the *actual* power is in their hands: and then the corollary will be self-evident, that if any nation be long misgoverned, they have no one to blame but themselves.

CHAPTER V.

HOW SUBJECTION TO CIVIL GOVERNMENT IS MAINTAINED.

PURSUING the train of thought with which the last chapter closed, we will now trace, with Paley, the manner in which subjection to civil government is maintained. Could we, says he, view our own species from a distance, or regard mankind with the same sort of observation with which we read the natural history, or remark the manners, of any other animal, there is nothing in the human character which would more surprise us, than the almost universal subjugation of strength to weakness;—than to see many millions of robust men, in the complete use and exercise of their personal faculties, and without any defect of courage, waiting upon the will of a child, a woman, a driveller, or a lunatic. And although, when we suppose a vast empire in absolute subjection to one person, and that one depressed beneath the level of his species by infirmities, or vice, we suppose, perhaps, an extreme case; yet in all cases, even in the most popular forms of civil government, *the physical strength resides in the governed.* In what manner opinion thus prevails over strength, or how power, which naturally belongs to superior force, is maintained in opposition to it; in other words, by what motives the many are induced to submit to the few; becomes an inquiry which lies at the root of almost every political speculation. It removes, indeed, but does not resolve the difficulty, to say that civil governments are now-a-days almost universally upholden by standing armies; for the question still returns: How are these armies themselves kept in subjection, or made to obey the commands, and carry on the designs, of the prince or state which employs them; and how are they permitted to be raised, trained, and paid for?

Now, although we should look in vain for any *single* reason which would account for the general submission of mankind to civil government, yet it may not be difficult to assign, for every class and character in the community, considerations powerful enough to dissuade *each* from any attempts to resist established authority. Every man has his motive, though not the same. In this as in other instances, the conduct is similar, but the principles which produce it extremely various.

There are three principal distinctions of character into which the subjects of a state may be divided: into those who obey from prejudice; those who obey from reason; and those who obey from self-interest.

I. They who obey from prejudice are determined

by an opinion of right in their governors; which opinion is founded upon *prescription*. In monarchies and aristocracies, which are hereditary, the prescription operates in favour of particular families; in republics and elective offices, in favour of particular forms of government, or constitutions. Nor is it to be wondered at, that mankind should reverence authority founded in prescription, when they observe that it is prescription which confers a title to almost everything else. The whole course, and all the habits, of civil life favour this prejudice. Upon what other foundation stands any man's right to his estate? The right of primogeniture, the succession of kindred, the descent of property, the inheritance of honours, the demand of tithes, tolls, rents, or services from the estates of others, the right of way, the powers of office and magistracy, the privileges of nobility, the immunities of the clergy, upon what are they founded (in the apprehension, at least, of the multitude) but upon prescription? To what else, when the claims are contested, is the appeal made? It is natural to transfer the same principle to the affairs of government, and to regard these exertions of power, which have been long exercised and acquiesced in, as so many *rights* in the sovereign; and to consider obedience to his commands, within certain accustomed limits, as enjoined by that rule of conscience which requires us to render to every man his due.

In hereditary monarchies, the *prescriptive title* is

corroborated, and its influence considerably augmented by an accession of religious sentiments, and by that sacredness which men are wont to ascribe to the persons of princes. Princes themselves have not failed to take advantage of this disposition, by claiming a superior dignity, as it were, of nature, or a peculiar delegation from the supreme Being. For this purpose, were introduced the title of Sacred Majesty, of God's Anointed, Representative, Vicegerent, together with the ceremonies of investitures and coronations, which are calculated, not so much to recognize the authority of sovereigns, as to consecrate their persons. Where a fabulous religion permitted it, the public veneration has been challenged by bolder pretensions. The Roman Emperors usurped the titles and arrogated the worship of gods. The mythology of the heroic ages, and many barbarous nations, was easily converted to this purpose. Some princes, like the heroes of Homer, and the founder of the Roman name, derived their birth from the gods; others, like Numa, pretended a supernatural communication with some divine being; and others, again, like the Incas of Peru, and the ancient Saxon Kings, extracted their descent from the deities of their country. The Lama of Thibet, at this day, is held forth to his subjects, not as the offspring or successor of a divine race of princes, but as the immortal God himself, the object at once of civil obedience and religious adoration. The instance is singular, and may be accounted the furthest point to which the abuse of human credulity has ever been carried. But, in all these instances, the purpose was the same—to engage the reverence of mankind, by an application to their religious principles.

The reader will be careful to observe that, in this article, we denominate every opinion, whether true or false, a prejudice, which is not founded upon argument, in the mind of the person who entertains it.

II. They who obey from *reason*, that is to say, from conscience as instructed by reasonings and conclusions of their own, are determined by the consideration of the necessity of some government or other; and the danger of re-settling the government of their country better, or at all, if once subverted or disturbed.

III. They who obey from *self-interest* are kept in order by want of leisure; by a succession of private cares, pleasures, and engagements; by contentment, or a sense of the ease, plenty, and safety, which they enjoy; or, lastly, by fear, foreseeing that they would bring themselves, by resistance, into a worse situation than their present, inasmuch as the strength of government, each discontented subject reflects, is greater than his own, and he knows not what others would join him.

This last consideration has often been called *opinion of power*, and we have seen in the last chapter somewhat of its natural limits.

This account of the principles by which mankind are retained in their obedience to civil government may suggest the following cautions:

I. Let civil governors learn hence to respect their subjects; let them be admonished, that *the physical strength lies in the governed;* that this strength wants only to be felt and roused, to lay prostrate the most ancient and confirmed dominion; that civil authority is founded in opinion; that general opinion, therefore, ought always to be treated with deference, and managed with delicacy and circumspection.

II. *Opinion of right,* always following the *custom,* being for the most part founded in nothing else, and lending one principal support to government, every innovation in the constitution, or, in other words, in the custom of governing, diminishes the stability of the government. Hence some absurdities are to be retained, and many small inconveniences endured in every country, rather than that the usage should be violated, or the course of public affairs diverted from their old and smooth channel. Even *names* are not indifferent. When the multitude are to be dealt with, there is a *charm* in sounds. It was upon this principle that several statesmen of those times advised Cromwell to assume the title of king, together with the ancient style and insignia of royalty. The minds of many, they contended, would be brought to acquiesce in the authority of a king, who suspected the office, and were offended with the administration, of a protector. Novelty reminded them of usurpation. The adversaries of this design opposed the measure, from the same persuasion of the efficacy of names and forms, jealous lest the veneration paid to these should add an influence to the new settlement which might ensnare the liberty of the commonwealth.

The Roman emperors, again, exercised a power far greater than that which had been enjoyed by the kings of Rome; but so great was the hatred entertained by the Roman people to the regal title, that the sovereigns of the then world wore for centuries the radiated crown peculiar to the gods—before they dared to assume the *diadem*, a simple fillet of white ribbon, the ancient and unmistakeable symbol of kingly power. Caligula did at one period of his reign purpose to call himself king; but, despot as he was, he was dissuaded from the measure.

Government may be too secure. The greatest tyrants have been those whose titles were the most unquestioned. Whenever, therefore, the opinion of right becomes too predominant and superstitious, it is abated by *breaking the custom*. Thus the Revolution broke the *custom* of *succession*, and thereby moderated, both in the prince and the people, those lofty notions of hereditary right which in the one were become a continual incentive to tyranny, and disposed the other to invite servitude, by undue compliances and dangerous concessions*.

---

* Paley, as will be seen in the subjoined note, recommends rulers to keep their subjects in ignorance of their own power.

From all this will be seen the duty of enlightening and educating the people, in order that they may see the necessity of civil government, and the tremendous evils of anarchy.

Nor will the duty be less apparent on the part of government to recommend itself to a reasoning people by a reasonable course of action; to an advancing people, by a proportionate advance in the spirit of its own measures.

---

and to maintain, for this purpose, a want of communication among them; but this advice is equally futile, dangerous, and criminal. In proportion as knowledge in general advances, in like manner will that of political right and political power make progress. No authority of government *can* stay it, so that the attempt must be futile; no authority *ought* to stay it, so that the attempt would be criminal; and the moment the eyes of the people were opened to the nature of the design, the government guilty of so nefarious an attempt would be hurled from its position, and consigned to the execration and contempt of posterity.

" As ignorance of union, and want of communication, appear amongst the principal preservatives of civil authority, it behoves every state to keep its subjects in this want and ignorance, not only by vigilance in guarding against actual confederacies and combinations, but by a timely care to prevent great collections of men of any separate party of religion, or of like occupation or profession, or in any way connected by a participation of interest or passion, from being assembled in the same vicinity. A Protestant establishment in this country may have little to fear from its Popish subjects, scattered as they are throughout the kingdom, and intermixed with the

Such has been for many years the *general* spirit of the British Government; and to this cause may it be attributed, that, in times of severe national affliction and persecution, there have been, comparatively speaking, few outbreaks among the people; and in times, when the rest of Europe has been politically shaken to its foundation, our own empire has escaped the shock.

Protestant inhabitants, which yet might think them a formidable body, if they were gathered together in one country. The most frequent and desperate riots are those which break out amongst men of the same profession, as weavers, miners, sailors. This circumstance makes a mutiny of soldiers more to be dreaded than any other insurrection. Hence also one danger of an overgrown metropolis, and of those great cities and crowded districts into which the inhabitants of trading countries are commonly collected. The worst effect of popular tumults consists in this, that they discover to the insurgents the secret of their own strength, teach them to depend upon it against a future occasion, and both produce and diffuse sentiments of confidence in one another, and assurances of mutual support. Leagues thus formed and strengthened may overawe or overset the power of any state; and the danger is greater, in proportion as, from the propinquity of habitation and intercourse of employment, the passions and counsels of a party can be circulated with ease and rapidity. It is by these means, and in such situations, that the minds of men are so affected and prepared, that the most dreadful uproars often arise from the slightest provocations. When the train is laid, a spark will produce the explosion."

This whole passage would gladly have been omitted; but such doctrine on such authority cannot be passed over in silence.

CHAPTER VI.

THE DUTY OF SUBMISSION TO CIVIL GOVERNMENT EXPLAINED.

The subject of this chapter is sufficiently distinguished from the subject of the last; as the motives which actually produce civil obedience may be, and often are, very different from the reasons which make that obedience a duty.

In order to prove civil obedience to be a moral duty, and an obligation upon the conscience of the subject, it hath been usual with many political writers (at the head of whom we find the venerable name of Locke) to state a compact between the citizen and the state, as the ground and cause of the relation between them; which compact, binding the parties for the same general reason that private contracts do, resolves the duty of submission to civil government into the universal obligation of fidelity in the performance of promises. This compact is twofold: First. An express compact by the primitive founders of the state, who are supposed to have convened for the declared purpose of settling the terms of their political union, and a future constitution of government. The whole body is supposed, in the first place, to have unanimously consented to be bound by the resolutions of the majority; that majority, in the next place, to have fixed certain fundamental regulations; and then to have constituted, either in one person, or in an assembly (the rule of succession, or appointment, being at the same time determined), a *standing legislature*, to whom, under these pre-established restrictions, the government of the state was thence forward committed, and whose laws the several members of the convention were, by their first undertaking, thus personally engaged to obey. This transaction is sometimes called the *social compact*, and these supposed original regulations compose what are meant by the *constitution*, the *fundamental laws of the constitution;* and form on one side, in cases of royalty, the *inherent, indefeasible prerogative of the crown;* and on the other, unalienable, imprescriptible *birthright* of the subject.

Secondly. A *tacit* or *implied* compact, by all succeeding members of state, who, by accepting its protection, consent to be bound by its laws; in like manner as whoever *voluntarily enters* into a private society is understood, without any other or more explicit stipulation, to promise a conformity with the rules and obedience to the government of that society, as the known conditions upon which he is admitted to a participation of its privileges.

[To understand Paley's reasoning against this theory, the theory itself must first be rightly understood. It is not a mere *general* compact, one implied by the circumstances of a majority having acquiesced in it, and founded on the principle that the majority *must* in all such cases decide for the minority, a compact capable of perpetual change as the changing events of the time demand progress or amendment; but a social agreement, requiring the consent of *each individual subject,* descending to *forms* of government, and vesting *these* with the character of fundamental and immutable principles.]

This account of the subject, although specious, and patronized by names the most respectable, appears to labour under the following objections: that it is founded upon a supposition, false in fact, and leading to dangerous conclusions.

No social compact, similar to what is here described, was ever made or entered into in reality; no such original convention of the people was ever actually holden, antecedent to the existence of civil government in that country. It is to suppose it possible to call savages out of caves and deserts, to deliberate and vote upon topics which the experience, and studies, and refinements, of civil life alone suggest. Therefore no government in the universe *began* from this original. Some imitation of a social compact may have taken place at a *revolution*. The last age was witness to a transaction which bears the nearest resemblance to this political idea of any of which history has preserved the account or memory:

I refer to the establishment of the United States of North America. We saw the *people* assembled to elect deputies for the avowed purpose of framing the constitution of a new empire. We saw this deputation of the people deliberating and resolving upon a form of government, erecting a permanent legislature, distributing the functions of sovereignty, establishing and promulgating a code of fundamental ordinances, which were to be considered, by succeeding generations, not merely as laws and acts of the state, but as the very terms and conditions of the confederation; as binding, not only upon the subjects and magistrates of the state, but as limitations of power which were to control and regulate the future legislature. Yet even here, much was presupposed. In settling the constitution, many important parts were presumed to be already settled. The qualifications of the constituents who were admitted to vote in the electing of members of congress, as well as the mode of electing the representatives, were taken from the old forms of government. That was wanting, from which every social union should set off, and which alone makes the resolution of the society the act of the individual —the unconstrained consent of all to be bound by the decision of the majority; and yet, without this previous consent, the revolt, and the regulations which followed it, were compulsory upon dissentients.

But the original compact, we are told, is not proposed as a *fact*, but as a fiction, which furnishes a commodious explication of the mutual rights and duties of sovereigns and subjects. In answer to this representation of the matter, we observe that the original compact, if it be not a fact, is nothing; can confer no actual authority upon laws or magistrates; nor afford any foundation to rights, which are supposed to be real and existing. But the truth is, that in the books, and in the apprehension of those who deduce our civil rights and obligations *a pactis*, the original convention is appealed to and treated of as a reality. Whenever the disciples of this system speak of the constitution; of the fundamental articles of the constitution; of laws being constitutional or unconstitutional; of inherent, unalienable, inextinguishable rights, either in the prince or the people; or indeed of any laws, usages, or civil rights, as transcending the authority of the subsisting legislature, or possessing a force and sanction superior to what belong to the modern acts and edicts of the legislature, they secretly refer us to what passed at the original convention. They would teach us to believe that certain rules and ordinances were established by the people, at the same time that they settled the charter of government, and the powers as well as the form of the future legislature; that this legislature consequently, deriving its commission and existence from the consent and act of the primitive assembly (of which indeed it is only the standing deputation), continues subject, in the exercise of its offices, and as to the extent of its power, to the rules, reservations, and limitations which the same assembly then made and prescribed to it.

"As the first members of the state were bound
"by express stipulation to obey the government
"which they had erected, so the succeeding inha-
"bitants of the same country are understood to
"promise allegiance to the constitution and govern-
"ment they find established, by accepting its protec-
"tion, claiming its privileges, and acquiescing in its
"laws; more especially by the purchase or inherit-
"ance of lands, to the possession of which, allegiance
"to the state is annexed, as the very service and con-
"dition of the tenure." Smoothly as this train of argument proceeds, little of it will endure examination. The native subjects of modern states are not conscious of any stipulation with the sovereigns, of ever exercising an election whether they will be bound or not by the acts of the legislature, of any alternative being proposed to their choice, of a promise either required or given; nor do they apprehend that the validity or authority of the laws depends at all upon *their* recognition or consent. In all stipulations, whether they be expressed or implied, private or public, formal or constructive, the parties stipulating must both possess the liberty of assent and refusal, and also be conscious of this liberty; which cannot with truth be affirmed of the subjects of civil government, as government is now, or ever was,

actually administered. This is a defect which no arguments can excuse or supply; all presumptions of consent, without this consciousness, or in opposition to it, are vain and erroneous. Still less is it possible to reconcile with any idea of stipulation the practice, in which all European nations agree, of founding allegiance upon the circumstance of nativity; that is, of claiming and treating as subjects all those who are born within the confines of their dominions, although removed to another country in their youth or infancy. In this instance, certainly, the state does not presume a compact. Also if the subject be bound only by his own consent, and if the voluntary abiding in the country be the proof and intimation of that consent, by what arguments should we defend the right, which sovereigns universally assume, of prohibiting the departure of their subjects out of the realm*?

Again, when it is contended that the taking and

---

* Paley says, "when they please;" but it is to be observed, that this right only exists when necessity requires its exercise. A sovereign, or rather a government, has a right to prevent men flying from the kingdom or republic in order to escape punishment, or to elude the fulfilment of obligations; but then it must be done by rightful powers of law; otherwise the act becomes one of tyranny, and no right for it exists at all. It is therefore a fallacy to assume that any sovereign possesses the " right of prohibiting, *when he pleases*, the departure of his " subjects out of the realm."

holding possession of land amounts to an acknowledgment of the sovereign, and a virtual promise of allegiance to his laws, it is necessary to the validity of the argument to prove, that the inhabitants, who first composed and constituted the state, collectively possessed a right to the soil of the country; a right to parcel it out to whom they pleased, and to annex to the donation what conditions they thought fit. How came they by this right? An agreement amongst themselves would not confer it: that could only adjust what already belonged to them. A society of men vote themselves to be the owners of a region of the world; does that vote, unaccompanied especially with any culture, inclosure, or proper act of occupation, make it theirs? does it entitle them to exclude others from it, or to dictate the conditions upon which it shall be enjoyed? Yet this original collective right and ownership is the foundation for all the reasoning by which the duty of allegiance is inferred from the possession of land.

The theory of government which affirms the existence and the obligation of a social compact, would, after all, merit little discussion, and, however groundless and unnecessary, should receive no opposition from us, did it not appear to lead to conclusions unfavourable to the improvement, and to the peace, of human society.

1st. Upon the supposition that government was first erected by, and that it derives all its just authority from, resolutions entered into by a convention of the people, it is capable of being presumed, that many points were settled by that convention anterior to the establishment of the subsisting legislature, and which the legislature, consequently, has no right to alter, or interfere with. These points are called the *fundamentals* of the constitution; and as it is impossible to determine how many, or what they are, the suggesting of any such serves extremely to embarrass the deliberations of the legislature, and affords a dangerous pretence for disputing the authority of the laws. It was this sort of reasoning (so far as reasoning of any kind was employed in the question) that produced in this nation the doubt, which so much agitated the minds of men in the reign of the second Charles, whether an Act of Parliament could of right alter or limit the succession of the Crown.

2dly. If it be by virtue of such a compact that the subject owes obedience to civil government, it will follow, that he ought to abide by the form of goverment which he finds established, be it ever so absurd or inconvenient. He is bound by his bargain. It is not permitted to any man to retreat from his engagement, merely because he finds the performance disadvantageous, or because he has an opportunity of entering into a better. This law of contracts is universal; and to call the relation between the sovereign and the subjects a contract, yet not to apply to it the rules, or allow of the effects of a contract, is an arbitrary use of names, and an unsteadiness in reasoning, which can teach nothing. Resistance to the *encroachments* of the supreme magistrate may be justified upon this principle; recourse to arms, for the purpose of bringing about an amendment of the constitution, never can. No form of government contains a provision for its own dissolution; and few governors will consent to the extinction, or even to any abridgment, of their own power. It does not therefore appear, how despotic governments can ever, in consistency with the obligation of the subject, be changed or mitigated. Despotism is the constitution of many states; and whilst a despotic prince exacts from his subjects the most rigorous servitude, according to this account, he is only holding them to their agreement. A people may vindicate, by force, the rights which the constitution has left them: but every attempt to narrow the prerogative of the crown, by *new* limitations, and in opposition to the will of the reigning prince, whatever opportunities may invite, or success follow it, must be condemned as an infraction of the compact between the sovereign and the subject.

3dly. Every violation of the compact on the part of the governor releases the subject from his allegiance, and dissolves the government. I do not perceive how we can avoid this consequence, if we found the duty of allegiance upon compact, and confess any analogy between the social compact and other contracts.

In private contracts, the violation and non-performance of the conditions, by one of the parties, vacates the obligation of the other. Now the terms and articles of the social compact being no where extant or expressed; the rights and offices of the administrator of an empire being so many and various; the imaginary and controverted line of his prerogative, being so liable to be overstepped in one part or other of it; the position, that every such transgression amounts to a forfeiture of the government, and consequently authorizes the people to withdraw their obedience, and provide for themselves by a new settlement, would endanger the stability of every political fabric in the world, and has in fact always supplied the disaffected with a topic of seditious declamation. If occasions have arisen, in which this plea has been resorted to with justice and success; they have been occasions in which a revolution was defensible upon other and plainer principles. The plea itself is at all times captious and unsafe.

These arguments are amply sufficient to overthrow the notion of any such compact as that which has been described. A more general kind of compact will be shown in the next two chapters to be perfectly coincident and consistent with the rule there laid down by Paley, that the chief ground of the subject's obligation is THE WILL OF GOD AS COLLECTED FROM EXPEDIENCY.

CHAPTER VII.

OF EXPEDIENCY AS THE FOUNDATION OF A SUBJECT'S OBLIGATION.

REJECTING the intervention of such a compact as has been imagined, as unfounded in its principle, and dangerous in the application, we assign for the only* ground of the subject's obligation, THE WILL OF GOD —and first, AS COLLECTED FROM EXPEDIENCY.

[Some philosophers would call this "THE PRINCIPLE OF PROMOTING THE GREATEST HAPPINESS OF "THE GREATEST NUMBER," or more briefly, "the greatest happiness principle."]

The steps by which the argument proceeds are few and direct. "It is the will of God that the hap-"piness of human life be promoted;" this is the first step, and the foundation not only of this, but of every moral conclusion. "Civil society conduces to that end;" this is the second proposition. "Civil soci-"eties cannot be upholden, unless in each the interest "of the whole society be binding upon every part and "member of it;" this is the third step, and conducts us to the conclusion, namely, "That so long as the

---

* Paley says the *chief* ground.

"interest of the whole society requires it, that is, so
"long as the established government cannot be resisted
"or changed without public inconveniency, it is the
"will of God (which *will* universally determines our
"duty) that the established government be obeyed,"
and no longer.

It is a principle of Christian ETHICS that our duty is determined by the Divine WILL, and we must here *assume* it as a principle of Christian POLITICS. But further, it is a rule of Christian METAPHYSICS, that the Divine will is our ONLY standard of right; whatever, therefore, is proved to be the Divine will, is proved to be not only expedient, but necessary.

This principle being admitted, the justice of every particular case of resistance is reduced to a computation of the quantity of the danger and grievance on the one side, and of the probability and expense of redressing it on the other.

But who shall judge this? We answer, "Every "man for himself." In contentions between the sovereign power and the subject, the parties acknowledge no common arbitrator; and it would be absurd to refer the decision to *those* whose conduct has provoked the question, and whose own interest, authority, and fate are immediately concerned in it. The danger of error and abuse is no objection to the rule of expediency, because every other rule is liable to the same or greater; and every rule that can be propounded upon the subject (like all rules indeed which appeal to, or bind, the conscience) must in the application depend upon private judgment. It may be observed, however, that it ought equally to be accounted the exercise of a man's own private judgment, whether he be determined by reasonings and conclusions of his own, or submit to be directed by the advice of others, provided he be free to choose his guide.

We proceed to point out some easy but important inferences, which result from the substitution of *public expediency* into the place of all implied compacts, promises, or conventions whatsoever.

I. It may be as much a duty at one time to resist government, as it is at another to obey it; to wit, whenever more advantage will, in our opinion, accrue to the community from resistance, than mischief.

II. The lawfulness of resistance, or the lawfulness of a revolt, does not depend alone upon the grievance which is sustained or feared, but also upon the probable expense and event of the contest. They who concerted the Revolution in England were justified in their counsels; because, from the apparent disposition of the nation and the strength and character of the parties engaged, the measure was likely to be brought about with little mischief or bloodshed; whereas it might have been a question with many friends of their country, whether the injuries then endured and threatened would have authorized the renewal of a doubtful civil war.

III. Irregularity in the first foundation of a state,

or subsequent violence, fraud, or injustice in getting possession of the supreme power, are not sufficient reasons for resistance, after the government is once peaceably settled. No subject of the British empire conceives himself engaged to vindicate the justice of the Norman claim or conquest, or apprehend that his duty in any manner depends upon that controversy. So, likewise, if the house of Lancaster, or even the posterity of Cromwell, had been at this day seated upon the throne of England, we should have been as little concerned to inquire how the founder of the family came there. No civil contests are so futile, although none have been so furious and sanguinary, as those which are excited by a disputed succession.

IV. Not every invasion of the subject's rights, or liberty, or of the constitution; not every breach of promise, or of oath; not every stretch of prerogative, abuse of power, or neglect of duty, by the chief magistrate, or by the whole or any branch of the legislative body, justifies resistance; unless these crimes draw after them public consequences of sufficient magnitude to outweigh the evils of civil disturbance. Nevertheless, every violation of the constitution ought to be watched with jealousy, and resented as *such*, beyond what the quantity of estimable damage would require or warrant; because a known and settled usage of governing affords the only security against the enormities of uncontrolled dominion, and because this security is weakened by every encroachment which is made without opposition, or opposed without effect.

V. No usage, law, or authority whatever, is so binding, that it need or ought to be continued, when it may be changed with advantage to the community. The family of the prince, the order of succession, the prerogative of the crown, the form and parts of the legislature, together with the respective powers, office, duration, and mutual dependency of the several parts, are all only so many *laws*, mutable like other laws, whenever expediency requires, either by the ordinary act of the legislature, or, if the occasion deserve it, by the interposition of the people. These points are wont to be approached with a kind of awe; they are represented to the mind as principles of the constitution settled by our ancestors, and, being settled, to be no more committed to innovation or debate: as foundations never to be stirred, as the terms and conditions of the social compact, to which every citizen of the state has engaged his fidelity, by virtue of a promise which he cannot now recall. Such reasons have no place in our system: to us, if there be any good reason for treating them with more deference and respect than other laws, it is either the advantage of the present constitution of government (which reason must be of different force in different countries), or because in all countries it is of importance that the form and usage of governing be acknowledged and understood, as well by the governors as by the governed, and because the seldomer it is changed, the more perfectly it will be known by both sides.

VI. As all civil obligation is thus resolved into expediency, what, it may be asked, is the difference between the obligation of an Englishman and a Russian? or why, since the obligation of both appears to be founded in the same reason, is a Russian bound in conscience to bear anything from his sovereign which an Englishman would not be bound to bear from his? Their conditions may differ, but their *rights*, according to this account, should seem to be equal; and yet we are accustomed to speak of the *rights* as well as of the happiness of a free people, compared with what belong to the subjects of absolute monarchies; how, you will say, can this comparison be explained, unless we refer to a difference in the compacts by which they are respectively bound? This is a fair question, and the answer to it will afford a farther illustration of our principles. We admit, then, that there are many things which a Russian is bound in conscience, as well as by coercion, to endure at the hands of his prince, to which an Englishman would not be obliged to submit; but we assert, that it is for these two reasons alone: first, because the same act of the prince is not the same grievance, where it is agreeable to the constitution, and where it infringes it—(this assumes that the constitution of Russia is as expedient for that country as our own constitution is for

England); secondly, because redress in the two cases is not equally attainable. Resistance cannot be attempted with equal hopes of success, or with the same prospect of receiving support from others, where the people are reconciled to* the authority exercised over them, as where they are alarmed by innovation. In this way, and no otherwise, the subjects of different states possess different civil rights; the duty of obedience is defined by different boundaries; and the point of justifiable resistance placed at different parts of the scale of suffering: all which is sufficiently intelligible without such a social compact as has been supposed.

VII. "The interest of the whole society is binding on every part of it." No rule, short of this, will provide for the stability of civil government, or for the peace and safety of social life. Wherefore, as individual members of the state are not permitted to pursue their private emolument to the prejudice of the community, so it is equally a consequence of this rule, that no particular colonies, provinces, towns, or districts, can justly concert measures for their separate interest, which shall appear at the same time to diminish the *sum* of public prosperity. I do not mean that it is necessary to the justice of a measure that it profit each and every part of the community—(for as the happiness of the whole may be increased, whilst

---

* "Their sufferings."—Paley.

that of some parts is diminished, it is possible that the conduct of one part of an empire may be detrimental to some other part, and yet just, provided one part gain more in happiness than the other part loses, so that the common weal be augmented by the change); but what I affirm is, that these counsels can never be reconciled with the obligations resulting from civil union, which cause the *whole* happiness of the society to be impaired for the conveniency of a *part*. This conclusion is applicable to the question of right between Great Britain and her revolted colonies. Had I been an American, I should not have thought it enough to have had it even demonstrated that a separation from the parent state would produce effects beneficial to America. My relation to that state imposed upon me a farther inquiry; namely, whether the whole happiness of the empire was likely to be promoted by such a measure: not indeed the happiness of every part; that was not necessary, nor to be expected; but whether what Great Britain would lose by separation was likely to be compensated to the joint stock of happiness by the advantages which America would receive from it. The contested claims of sovereign states, and their remote dependencies, may be submitted to the adjudication of this rule with mutual safety. A public advantage is measured by the advantage which each individual receives, and by the number of those who receive it. A public evil is compounded of the same proportions. Whilst, therefore, a colony is small, or a province thinly inhabited, if a competition of interests arise between the original country and their acquired dominions, the former ought to be preferred; because it is fit that, if one must necessarily be sacrificed, the less give place to the greater. But when, by an increase of population, the interest of the provinces begins to bear a considerable proportion to the *entire* interest of the community, it is possible that they may suffer so much by their subjection, that not only theirs, but the whole happiness of the empire, may be obstructed by their union. The rule and principle of the calculation being still the same, the *result* is different: and this difference begets a new situation, which entitles the subordinate parts of the states to more eqnal terms of confederation, and, if these be refused, to independency.

CHAPTER VIII.

OF RIGHT AS THE FOUNDATION OF A SUBJECT'S OBLIGATION.

It is susceptible of proof, that whatever is *really* expedient, is right; and that no line of conduct can be politically right, and morally wrong: but it may tend to clear away some preliminary difficulties, if we apply these principles to the positions laid down in the last chapter. And here, reserving the express commands of Scripture to another occasion, we may observe that the natural equality of mankind before God, invests every man with certain rights, which, although not inalienable, are yet sacred. No government could have been established at all, even in the rudest form, and among the most barbarous nations, without the *cession* of *some* of these rights; and as we have already seen that no man parts with any portion of his liberty without an equivalent, so there must have been an implied compact, however simple, to establish a civil rule at all. We do not contend for any elaborate constitution, for any refined stipulations, for any philosophical safe-guards for the liberty of the subject; but merely for an exchange of liberty, or some portion of it, on one side, for security and protection on the other. Thus there arises a series of *rightful* obligations, of correlative duties; and as the natural equality of mankind before God continues during all the progress of advancing civilization, so do the correlative duties, both of governors and governed, take their tone from the varied position and increasing civilization of nations. That which is a good, and *therefore* an expedient, constitution for one people, would be altogether unfit for another. China and America, Russia and England, *could not* be governed by the same system of laws: and in like manner the same country requires a different spirit of administration at different eras. An implied compact therefore exists, founded on this natural equality, and not the less real because unwritten, which, rejecting, as we saw in a former chapter, the prescribing of forms under which government should be carried on, stipulates on the one side for *good* government—that is, government adapted to the people and the age; and on the other side, promises obedience to a rule so constituted.

To accept any other theory, would be to suppose that God had deliberately submitted the many to the few, and had given to kings " a right divine to govern " wrong."

But the right and the expediency will be found to coalesce; those very measures which promote the greatest happiness of the greatest number, will be found most in accordance with the rules laid down in the Word of God.

This short chapter will serve as an introduction to that portion of the subject.

CHAPTER IX.

OF THE DUTY OF CIVIL OBEDIENCE, AS STATED IN THE CHRISTIAN SCRIPTURES*.

The only passages of Scripture which have been seriously alleged in the controversy, or which it is necessary for us to state and examine, are the two following; the one extracted from St. Paul's Epistle to the Romans, the other from the First General Epistle of St. Peter.

Romans viii, 1—7. "Let every soul be subject "unto the higher powers; For there is no power but "of God; the powers that be are ordained of God. "Whosoever therefore resisteth the power, resisteth "the ordinance of God: and they that resist, shall

---

* We affirm, Paley asserts, that, as to the *extent* of our civil rights and obligations, *Christianity* hath left us where she found us: that she hath neither altered nor ascertained it; that the New Testament contains not one passage which, fairly interpreted, affords either argument or objection applicable to any conclusions upon the subject that are deduced from the law and religion of nature.

That this is not *strictly* correct, we shall see in the course of this chapter.

"receive to themselves damnation. For rulers are not a terror to good works, but to the evil. Wilt thou then not be afraid of the power? Do that which is good, and thou shalt have praise of the same: for he is the minister of God to thee for good. But if thou do that which is evil, be afraid: for, he beareth not the sword in vain: for, he is the minister of God, a revenger to *execute* wrath upon him that doeth evil. Wherefore ye must needs be subject, not only for wrath, but also for conscience sake. For, for this cause pay ye tribute also: for they are God's ministers, attending continually upon this very thing. Render therefore to all their dues; tribute to whom tribute is due, custom to whom custom, fear to whom fear, honour to whom honour."

I, Peter ii, 13—18. "Submit yourselves to every ordinance of man, for the Lord's sake; whether it be to the King as supreme; or unto Governors, as unto them that are sent by him for the punishment of evil-doers, and for the praise of them that do well. For so is the will God, that with well-doing ye may put to silence the ignorance of foolish men; as free, and not using your liberty for a cloke of maliciousness, but as the servants of God."

To comprehend the proper import of these instructions, let the reader reflect, that upon the subject of civil obedience there are two questions; *the first*, whether to obey government be a moral duty and obligation upon the conscience at all? *the second*, how far, and to what cases, that obedience ought to extend? that these two questions are so distinguishable in the imagination, that it is possible to treat of the one, without any thought of the other, and lastly, that if expressions which relate to one of these questions be transferred and applied to the other, it is with great danger of giving them a signification very different from the author's meaning. This distinction is not only possible, but natural. If I met with a person who appeared to entertain doubts whether civil obedience were a moral duty which ought to be voluntarily discharged, or whether it were not a mere submission to force, like that which we yield to a robber who holds a pistol to our breast, I should represent to him the use and offices of civil government, the end and the necessity of civil subjection; or, if I preferred a different theory, I should explain to him the social compact, urge him with the obligation and the equity of his implied promise and tacit consent to be governed by the laws of the state from which he received protection; or I should argue, perhaps, that Nature herself dictated the law of subordination, when she planted within us an inclination to associate with our species, and framed us with capacities so various and unequal. From whatever principle I set out, I should labour to infer from it this conclusion: "That " obedience to the state is to be numbered amongst " the relative duties of human life, for the trans- " gression of which we shall be accountable at the "tribunal of Divine justice, whether the magistrate "be able to punish us for it or not;" and being arrived at this conclusion, I should stop, having delivered the conclusion itself, and throughout the whole argument expressed the obedience, which I inculcated, in the most general and unqualified terms; all reservations and restrictions being superfluous and foreign to the doubts I was employed to remove.

If, in a short time afterwards, I should be accosted by the same person with complaints of public grievances, of exorbitant taxes, of acts of cruelty and oppression, of tyrannical encroachments upon the ancient or stipulated rights of the people, and should be consulted whether it were lawful to revolt, or justifiable to join in an attempt to shake off the yoke by open resistance; I should certainly consider myself as having a case and question before me very different from the former. I should now define and discriminate. I should reply, that if public expediency be *the foundation*, it is also *the measure*, of civil obedience; that the obligation of subjects and sovereigns is reciprocal; that the duty of allegiance, whether it be founded in utility or compact, is neither unlimited nor unconditional; that peace may be purchased too dearly; that patience becomes culpable pusillanimity, when it serves only to encourage our rulers to increase the weight of our burden, or to bind it faster; that the submission which surrenders the liberty of a nation, and entails slavery upon future generations, is enjoined by no law of rational morality; finally, I should instruct the inquirer to compare the peril and expense of his enterprise with the effects it was expected to produce, and to make choice of the alternative, by which not his own present relief or profit, but the whole and permanent interest of the state, was likely to be best promoted. If any one who had been present at both these conversations, should upbraid me with change or inconsistency of opinion, should retort upon me the passive doctrine which I before taught, the large and absolute terms in which I then delivered lessons of obedience and submission, I should reply, that the only difference which the language of the two conversations presented was, that I added now many exceptions and limitations, which were omitted or unthought of then: that this difference arose naturally from the two occasions, such exceptions being as necessary to the subject of our present conference, as they would have been superfluous and unseasonable in the former.

Now the difference in these two conversations is precisely the distinction to be taken in interpreting those passages of Scripture concerning which we are debating. They inculcate the *duty*, they do not describe the *extent* of it. They enforce the obligation by the proper sanctions of Christianity, without intending either to enlarge or contract, without considering indeed the limits by which it is bounded. This is also the method in which the same apostles enjoin the duty of servants to their masters, of children to their parents, of wives to their husbands: "Servants, be "subject to your masters."—"Children, obey your "parents in all things."—"Wives, submit yourselves "unto your own husbands." The same concise and absolute form of expression occurs in all these precepts: the same silence, as to any exceptions or distinctions; yet no one doubts but that the commands of masters, parents, and husbands, are often so immoderate, unjust, and inconsistent with other obligations, that they both may and ought to be resisted. In letters or dissertations written professedly upon separate articles of morality, we might with more reason have looked for a precise delineation of our duty, and some degree of modern accuracy in the rules which were laid down for our direction; but in these short collections of practical maxims which compose the conclusion, or some small portion, of a doctrinal or perhaps controversial epistle, we cannot be surprised to find the author more solicitous to impress the duty, than curious to enumerate exceptions.

The consideration of this distinction is alone sufficient to vindicate these passages of Scripture from any explanation which may be put upon them, in favour of an unlimited passive obedience. But if we be permitted to assume a supposition, which many commentators proceed upon as a certainty, that the first Christians privately cherished an opinion that their conversion to Christianity entitled them to new immunities, to an exemption, as of *right* (however they might give way to necessity), from the authority of the Roman sovereign, we are furnished with a still more apt and satisfactory interpretation of the apostles' words. The two passages apply with great propriety to the refutation of this error: they teach the Christian convert to obey the magistrate "for the "Lord's sake;"—"not only for wrath, but for con- "science sake;"—"that the powers that be," even the present rulers of the Roman empire, though heathens and usurpers, seeing they are in possession of the actual and necessary authority of civil government, " are ordained of God;" and, consequently, entitled to receive obedience from those who profess themselves the peculiar servants of God, in a greater (certainly not in a less) degree than from any others. They briefly describe the office of " civil governors, " the punishment of evil-doers, and the praise of them " that do well;" from which description of the use of government, they justly infer the duty of subjection; which duty, being as extensive as the reason upon which it is founded, belongs to Christians no less than to the heathen members of the community. If it be admitted, that the two apostles wrote with a view to this particular question, it will be confessed that their words cannot be transferred to a question totally different from this, with any certainty of carrying along with us their authority and intention. There exists no resemblance between the case of a primitive convert, who disputed the jurisdiction of the Roman government over a disciple of Christianity, and *his* who, acknowledging the general authority of the state over all its subjects, doubts whether that authority be not, in some important branch of it, so ill-constituted or abused, as to warrant the endeavours of the people to bring about a reformation by force. Nor can we judge what reply the apostles would have made to this second question, if it had been proposed to them, from anything they have delivered upon the first; any more than, in the two consultations above described, it could be known before-hand what I would say in the latter, from the answer which I gave to the former.

The only defect in this account is, that neither the Scriptures, nor any subsequent history of the early ages of the church, furnish any direct attestation of the existence of such disaffected sentiments amongst the primitive converts. They supply indeed some circumstances which render probable the opinion, that extravagant notions of the political rights of the Christian state were at that time entertained by many proselytes to the religion. From the question proposed to Christ, "Is it lawful to give tribute unto "Cæsar?" it may be presumed that doubts had been started in the Jewish schools concerning the obligation, or even the lawfulness, of submission to the Roman yoke. The accounts delivered by Josephus, of various insurrections of the Jews of that and the following age, excited by this principle, or upon this pretence, confirm the presumption. Now, as the Christians were at first chiefly taken from the Jews, confounded with them by the rest of the world, and, from the affinity of the two religions, apt to intermix the doctrines of both, it is not to be wondered at that a tenet so flattering to the self-importance of those who embraced it should have been communicated to the new institution. Again, the teachers of Christianity, amongst the privileges which their religion conferred upon its professors, were wont to extol the "*liberty* " into which they were called,"—"in which Christ " had made them free." This liberty, which was intended of a deliverance from the various servitude in which they had heretofore lived, to the domination of sinful passions, to the superstition of the Gentile idolatry, or the encumbered ritual of the Jewish dispensation, might by some be interpreted to signify an emancipation from all restraint which was imposed by an authority merely human. At least, they might be represented by their enemies as maintaining notions of this dangerous tendency. To some error or calumny of this kind, the words of St. Peter seem to allude:—"For so is the will of God, that with well- " doing ye may put to silence the ignorance of foolish " men; as free, and not using your liberty for a cloke " of maliciousness (i. e. sedition), but as the servants " of God." After all, if any one think this conjecture too feebly supported by testimony to be relied upon in the interpretation of Scripture, he will then revert to the considerations alleged in the preceding part of this chapter.

What Christianity does ascertain is:

1. That Rulers are the ministers of God *for good*. When therefore the Ruler ceases to be a minister *for good*, he ceases to have any divine claim on our obedience. The magistrate who commanded the early Christians to worship the genius of the emperor was met with a flat refusal.

2. He is the Minister of God, so that his will and ours are alike referable to the will of the Common Superior. This distinction is throughout kept in view by the apostles, and their own practice was to yield a conditional obedience.

From thence it will follow that the ascertained will of God, as it is the measure of the ruler's right, so it is to be that of the subject's obedience.

After so copious an account of what we apprehend to be the general design and doctrine of these much-agitated passages, little need be added in explanation of particular clauses. St. Paul has said, "Whosoever "resisteth the power, resisteth the ordinance of God." This phrase, "the ordinance of God," is by many so interpreted as to authorize the most exalted and superstitious ideas of the regal character. But, surely, such interpreters have sacrificed truth to adulation. For, in the first place, the expression, as used by St. Paul, is just as applicable to one kind of government, and to one kind of succession, as to another;—to the elective magistrates of a pure republic, as to an absolute hereditary monarch. In the next place, it is not affirmed of the supreme magistrate exclusively, that *he* is the ordinance of God; the title, whatever it imports, belongs to every inferior officer of the state as much as to the highest. The divine right of *kings* is, like the divine right of other magistrates, the law of the land, or even actual and quiet possession of their office,—a right ratified, we humbly presume, by the divine approbation, so long as obedience to their authority appears to be necessary or conducive to the common welfare.—Rulers, however designated, are established for the *public* benefit, and not for their own private advantage. Hence it is that they are rightly called the servants of the public; they *command* individuals, but they are bound to *obey* the common or national will.

Just as the officer of a corporation is the servant of the body corporate, but in *no* sense the servant of any individual member: so, and even in a larger sense, the sovereign, though personally subject to no man, is yet the servant of the nation at large. Princes are ordained of God by virtue only of that general decree by which he assents, and adds the sanction of his will, to every law of society which promotes his own purpose, the communication of human happiness; according to which idea of their origin and constitution (and without any repugnancy to the words of St. Paul), they are by St. Peter denominated the *ordinance of man*.

CHAPTER X.

OF CIVIL AND POLITICAL LIBERTY.

Civil Liberty is not being restrained by any law but what conduces in a greater degree to the public welfare.

To do what we will, is natural liberty: to do what we will, consistently with the interest of the community to which we belong, is civil liberty; that is to say, the only liberty to be desired in a state of civil society.

I should wish, no doubt, to be allowed to act in every instance as I pleased; but I reflect that the rest also of mankind would then do the same: in which state of universal independence and self-direction, I should meet with so many checks and obstacles to my own will, from the interference and opposition of other men's, that not only my happiness, but my liberty, would be less than whilst the whole community were subject to the dominion of equal laws.

The boasted liberty of a state of nature exists only in a state of solitude. In every kind and degree of union and intercourse with his species, it is possible that the liberty of the individual may be augmented by the very laws which restrain it; because he may gain more from the limitation of other men's freedom, than he suffers by the diminution of his own. Natural liberty is the right of common upon a waste; civil liberty is the safe, exclusive, unmolested enjoyment of a cultivated enclosure.

The definition of civil liberty, above laid down, imports that the laws of a free people impose no restraints upon the private will of the subject, which do not conduce in a *greater degree* to the public happiness; by which it is intimated, first, that restraint itself is an evil; secondly, that this evil ought to be overbalanced by some public advantage; thirdly, that the proof of this advantage lies upon the legislature; fourthly, that a law being found to produce no sensible good effects, is a sufficient reason for repealing it, as adverse and injurious to the rights of a free citizen, without demanding specific evidence of its bad effects. This maxim might be remembered with advantage in a revision of many laws of this country; especially of the game laws; of the poor laws, so far as they lay restrictions upon the poor themselves; of the laws against Papists and Dissenters; and, amongst people enamoured to excess and jealous of their liberty, it seems a matter of surprise that this principle has been so imperfectly attended to.

The degree of actual liberty always bearing, according to this account of it, a reversed proportion to the number and severity of the restrictions, which are either useless, or the utility of which does not outweigh the evil of the restraint, it follows that every nation possesses some, no nation perfect, liberty: that this liberty may be enjoyed under *every* form of government: that it may be impaired, indeed, or increased, but that it is neither gained, nor lost, nor recovered, by any single regulation, change, or event whatever: that, consequently, those popular phrases which speak of a free people; of a nation of slaves; which call one revolution the era of liberty, or another the loss of it; with many expressions of a like absolute form; are intelligible only in a comparative sense.

Hence also we are enabled to apprehend the distinction between *personal* and *civil* liberty. A citizen of the freest republic in the world may be imprisoned for his crimes; and though his personal freedom be restrained by bolts and fetters, so long as his confinement is the effect of a beneficial public law, his civil liberty is not invaded*. And if this be true of the

---

* If this instance appear dubious, the following, says Paley, will be plainer. A passenger from the Levant, who, upon his return to England, should be conveyed to a lazaretto by an order of quarantine, with whatever impatience he might desire his enlargement, and though he saw a guard placed at the door to oppose his escape, or even ready to destroy his life if he attempted it, would hardly accuse government of encroaching upon his civil freedom; nay, might perhaps rather congratulate himself, that he had at length set his foot again in the land of liberty.

coercion of a prison, that it is compatible with a state of civil freedom, it cannot with reason be disputed of those more moderate constraints which the ordinary operation of government imposes upon the will of the individual. It is not the rigour, but the inexpediency, of laws and acts of authority which makes them tyrannical.

There is another idea of civil liberty, which, though neither so simple nor so accurate as the former, agrees better with the signification which the usage of common discourse, as well as the example of many respectable writers upon the subject, has affixed to the term. This idea places liberty in security; making it to consist, not merely in an actual exemption from the constraint of useless and noxious laws and acts of dominion, but in being free from the *danger* of having any such hereafter imposed or exercised. A very able writer* calls this security " *poli-* " *tical* LIBERTY." A Russian, at the present day, may have as much personal liberty as an Englishman. Nay, he may have as much civil liberty; for civil liberty is that which remains to the subject when

---

The manifest expediency of the measure not only justifies it, but reconciles the most odious confinement with the perfect possession and the loftiest notions of civil liberty.

The instance is *now* an unfortunate one; all quarantine regulations being ascertained to be useless, and CONSEQUENTLY tyrannical restrictions.

* Dymond Essays, 4th edition, p. 105.

those restrictions necessary for the common welfare have been laid upon him; but no one can contend that he has as much *political* liberty. This is a right of *communities*, which they have sometimes resigned by their own act, but which they are at all times entitled to demand, even from the best actual governments. Thus, speaking of the political state of Europe, we are accustomed to say of Sweden, that she lost her liberty by the revolution which took place in that country in the middle of the last century; and yet we are assured that the people continued to be governed by the same laws as before, or by others which were wiser, milder, and more equitable. What then had they lost? They had lost the power and functions of their diet; the constitution of their states and orders, whose deliberation and concurrence were required in the formation and establishment of every public law; and thereby had parted with the security which they possessed against any attempts of the crown to harass its subjects by oppressive and useless exertions of prerogative. The loss of this security we denominate the loss of liberty. They had changed, not their laws, but their legislature; not their enjoyment, but their safety; not their present burthens, but their prospects of future grievances; and this we pronounce a change from the condition of freedom to that of slaves. In like manner, in our own country, the Act of Parliament, in the reign of Henry the Eighth, which gave to the king's proclamation the force of law, has properly been called a complete and formal surrender of the liberty of the nation; and would have been so, although no proclamation were issued in pursuance of these new powers, or none but what was recommended by the highest wisdom and utility. The security was gone. Were it probable that the welfare and accommodation of the people would be as studiously and as providently consulted in the edicts of a despotic prince, as by the resolutions of a popular assembly, then would an absolute form of government be no less free than the purest democracy. The different degree of care and knowledge of the public interest which may reasonably be expected from the different form and composition of the legislature, constitutes the distinction, in respect of liberty, as well between these two extremes, as between all the intermediate modifications of civil government.

The definitions which have been framed of civil liberty, and which have become the subject of much unnecessary altercation, are most of them adapted to to this idea. Thus one political writer makes the very essence of the subject's liberty to consist in his being governed by no laws but those to which he hath actually consented; another is satisfied with an indirect and virtual consent; another, again, places civil liberty in the separation of the legislative and executive offices of government; another, in the being governed by *law*—that is, by known, pre-constituted, inflexible rules of action and adjudication; a fifth, in the exclusive right of the people to tax themselves by their own representatives; a sixth, in the freedom and purity of elections of representatives; a seventh, in the control which the democratic part of the constitution possesses over the military establishment. Concerning which, and some other similar accounts of civil liberty, it may be observed, that they all labour under one inaccuracy; viz. that they describe not so much liberty itself, as the safe-guards and preservatives of liberty. For example: a man's being governed by no laws but those to which he has given his consent, were it practicable, is no otherwise necessary to the enjoyment of civil liberty, than as it affords a probable security against the dictation of laws imposing superfluous restrictions upon his private will. This remark is applicable to the rest. The diversity of these definitions will not surprise us, when we consider that there is no contrariety or opposition amongst them whatever; for by how many different provisions and precautions civil liberty is fenced and protected, so many different accounts of liberty itself, all sufficiently consistent with truth and with each other, may, according to this mode of explaining the term, be framed and adopted.

Truth cannot be offended by a definition, but propriety may. In which view, those definitions of liberty ought to be rejected, which, by making that essential to civil freedom which is unattainable in experience, inflame expectations which can never be gratified, and disturb the public content with complaints which no wisdom or benevolence of government can remove.

It will not be thought extraordinary that an idea which occurs so much oftener as the subject of panegyric and careless declamation, than of just reasoning or correct knowledge, should be attended with uncertainty and confusion; or that it should be found impossible to contrive a definition which may include the numerous, unsettled, and ever-varying significations which the term is made to stand for, and at the same time accord with the condition and experience of social life.

Of the two ideas that have been stated of civil liberty, whichever we assume, and whatever reasoning we found upon them, concerning its extent, nature, value, and preservation, this is the conclusion: that *that* people, government, and constitution, is the *freest*, which makes the best provision for the enacting of expedient and salutary laws, and for the removal of all which are found to be either hurtful or useless.

CHAPTER XI.

OF DIFFERENT FORMS OF GOVERNMENT.

As a series of appeals must be finite, there necessarily exists in every government a power from which the constitution has provided no appeal; and which power, for that reason, may be termed absolute, omnipotent, uncontrollable, arbitrary, despotic; and is alike so in all countries.

The person or assembly in whom this power resides is called the *sovereign,* or the supreme power of the state.

Since to the same power universally appertains the office of establishing public laws, it is called also the *legislature* of the state.

A government receives its denomination from the form of the legislature; which form is likewise what we commonly mean by the *constitution* of a country.

Political writers enumerate three principal forms of government; which, however, are to be regarded rather as the simple forms, by some combination and intermixture of which all actual governments are composed, than as any where existing in a pure and elementary state. These forms are—

I. Despotism, or absolute MONARCHY, where the legislature is in a single person.

II. An ARISTOCRACY, where the legislature is in a select assembly, the members of which either fill up by election the vacancies in their own body, or succeed to their places in it by inheritance, property, tenure of certain lands, or in respect of some personal right or qualification.

III. A REPUBLIC, or Democracy, where the people at large, either collectively or by representation, constitute the legislature.

The separate advantages of MONARCHY are—unity of council, activity, decision, secrecy, despatch; the military strength and energy which result from these qualities of government; the exclusion of popular and aristocratical contentions; the preventing, by a known rule of succession, of all competition for the supreme power; and thereby repressing the hopes, intrigues, and dangerous ambition of aspiring citizens.

The mischiefs, or rather the dangers, of MONARCHY are—tyranny, expense, exaction, military domination; unnecessary wars, waged to gratify the passions of an individual; risk of the character of the reigning prince; ignorance, in the governors, of the interests and accommodation of the people, and a consequent deficiency of salutary regulations; want of constancy and uniformity in the rules of government, and, proceeding from thence, insecurity of person and property.

The separate advantages of an ARISTOCRACY consist in the wisdom which may be expected from experience and education. A permanent council naturally possesses experience; and the members who succeed to their places in it by inheritance, will probably be trained and educated with a view to the stations which they are destined by their birth to occupy.

The mischiefs of an ARISTOCRACY are—dissensions in the ruling orders of the state; which, from the want of a common superior, are liable to proceed to the most desperate extremities; oppression of the lower orders by the privileges of the higher, and by laws partial to the separate interest of the lawmakers.

The advantages of a REPUBLIC are—liberty, or exemption from needless restrictions; equal laws, regulations adapted to the wants and circumstances of the people, public spirit, frugality, averseness to war; the opportunities which democratic assemblies afford to men of every description of producing their abilities and counsels to public observation, and the exciting thereby, and calling forth to the service of the commonwealth, the faculties of its best citizens.

The evils of a REPUBLIC are—dissension, tumults, faction; the attempts of powerful citizens to possess themselves of the empire; the confusion, rage, and clamour, which are the inevitable consequences of assembling multitudes, and of propounding questions of state to the discussion of the people; the delay and disclosure of public counsels and designs; and the imbecility of measures retarded by the necessity of obtaining the consent of numbers; lastly, the oppression of the provinces which are not admitted to a participation in the legislative power.

A *mixed* government is composed by the combination of two or more of the simple forms of government above described; and in whatever proportion each form enters into the constitution of a government, in the same proportion may both the advantages and evils which we have attributed to that form be expected; that is, those are the uses to be maintained and cultivated in each part of the constitution, and these are the dangers to be provided against in each: Thus, if secrecy and despatch be truly enumerated amongst the separate excellences of regal government, then a mixed government, which retains monarchy in one part of its constitution, should be careful that the other estates of the empire do not, by an officious and inquisitive interference with the executive functions, which are, or ought to be, reserved to the administration of the prince, interpose delays, or divulge what it is expedient to conceal. On the other hand, if profusion, exaction, military domination, and needless wars, be justly accounted natural properties of monarchy, in its simple, unqualified form, then are these the objects to which, in a mixed government, the aristocratic and popular parts of the constitution ought to direct their vigilance; the dangers against which they should raise and fortify their barriers. These are departments of sovereignty over which a power of inspection and control ought to be deposited with the people.

The same observation may be repeated of all the other advantages and inconveniences which have been ascribed to the several simple forms of government; and affords a rule whereby to direct the constitution, improvements, and administration, of mixed governments,—subjected, however, to this remark, that a quality sometimes results from the conjunction of two simple forms of government which belongs not to the separate existence of either: thus corruption, which has no place in an absolute monarchy, and little in a pure republic, is sure to gain admission into a constitution which divides the supreme power between an executive magistrate and a popular council.

An *hereditary* MONARCHY is universally to be preferred to an *elective* monarchy. The confession of every writer on the subject of civil government, the experience of ages, the example of Poland, and of the papal dominions, seem to place this amongst the few indubitable maxims which the science of politics admits of. A crown is too splendid a prize to be conferred upon merit: the passions or interests of the electors exclude all consideration of the qualities of the competitors. The same observation holds concerning the appointment to any office which is attended with a great share of power or emolument. Nothing is gained by a popular choice, worth the dissensions, tumults, and interruption of regular industry, with which it is inseparably attended. Add to this, that a king, who owes his elevation to the event of a contest, or to any other cause than a fixed rule of succession, will be apt to regard one part of his subjects as the associates of his fortune, and the other as conquered foes. Nor should it be forgotten, amongst the advantages of an *hereditary* monarchy, that, as plans of national improvement and reform are seldom brought to maturity by the exertions of a single reign, a nation cannot attain to the degree of happiness and prosperity to which it is capable of being carried, unless a uniformity of counsels, a consistency of public measures and designs, be continued through a succession of ages. This benefit may be expected with greater probability where the supreme power descends in the same race, and where each prince succeeds, in some sort, to the aim, pursuits, and disposition of his ancestor, than if the crown, at every change, devolve upon a stranger, whose first care will commonly be to pull down what his predecessor had built up; and to substitute systems of administration which must, in their turn, give way to the more favorite novelties of the next successor.

ARISTOCRACIES are of two kinds. First, where the power of the nobility belongs to them in their collective capacity alone; that is, where, although the government reside in an assembly of the order, yet the members of that assembly separately and individually possess no authority or privilege beyond the rest of the community:—this describes the ancient constitution of Venice. Secondly, where the nobles are severally invested with great personal power and immunities, and where the power of the senate is little more than the aggregated power of the individuals who compose it:—this is the constitution of ancient Poland. Of these two forms of government, the first is more tolerable than the last; for although the members of a senate should, many, or even all of them, be profligate enough to abuse the authority of their stations in the prosecution of private designs, yet, not being all under a temptation to the same injustice, not having all the same end to gain, it would still be difficult to obtain the consent of a majority to any specific act of oppression which the iniquity of an individual might prompt him to propose: or, if the will were the same, the power is more confined; one tyrant, whether the tyranny reside in one single person or a senate, cannot exercise oppression at so many places at the same time as it may be carried on by the dominion of a numerous nobility over their respective vassals and dependants. Of all species of domination, this is the most odious; the freedom and satisfaction of private life are more constrained and harassed by it, than by the most vexatious laws, or even by the lawless will of an arbitrary monarch, from whose knowledge, and from whose injustice, the greatest part of his subjects are removed by their distance, or concealed by their obscurity.

Europe exhibits more than one modern example, where the people, aggrieved by the exactions, or provoked by the enormities, of their immediate superiors, having joined with the reigning prince in the overthrow of the aristocracy, deliberately exchanging their condition for the miseries of despotism. About the middle of the seventeenth century, the commons of Denmark, weary of the oppression which they had long suffered from the nobles, and exasperated by some recent insults, presented themselves at the foot of the throne with a formal offer of their consent to establish unlimited dominion in the King. The revolution in Sweden, at a still later period, brought about with the acquiescence, not to say the assistance, of the people, owed its success to the same cause; namely, to the prospect of deliverance that it afforded from the tyranny which their nobles exercised under the old constitution. In England, the people beheld the depression of the barons, under the house of Tudor, with satisfaction, although they saw the crown acquiring thereby a power which no limitations that the constitution had then provided were likely to confine. The lesson to be drawn from such events is this: that a mixed government, which admits a patrician order into its constitution, ought to circumscribe the personal privileges of the nobility, especially claims of hereditary jurisdiction and local authority, with a jealousy equal to the solicitude with which it wishes its own preservation: for nothing so alienates the minds of the people from the government under which they live, by a perpetual sense of annoyance and inconvenience, or so prepares them for the practices of an enterprising prince or a factious demagogue, as the abuse which almost always accompanies the existence of separate immunities.

Amongst the inferior, but by no means inconsiderable, advantages of a DEMOCRATIC constitution, or of a constitution in which the people partake of the power of legislation, the following should not be neglected:

I. The direction which it gives to the education, studies, and pursuits of the superior orders of the community. The share which this has in forming the public manners and national character, is very important. In countries, in which the gentry are excluded from all concern in the government, scarcely any thing is left which leads to advancement, but the profession of arms. They who do not addict themselves to this profession (and miserable must that country be which constantly employs the military service of a great proportion of any order of its subjects!) are commonly lost by the mere want of object and destination; that is, they either fall, without reserve, into the most sottish habits of animal gratification, or entirely devote themselves to the attainment of those futile arts and decorations which compose the business and recommendations of a court: on the other hand, where the whole, or any effective portion of civil power is possessed by a popular assembly, more serious pursuits will be encouraged; purer morals, and a more intellectual character, will engage the public esteem; those faculties which qualify men for deliberation and debate, and which are the fruit of sober habits, of early and long-continued application, will be roused and animated by the reward, which, of all others, most readily awakens the ambition of the human mind—political dignity and importance.

II. Popular elections procure to the common people courtesy from their superiors. That contemptuous and overbearing insolence, with which the lower orders of the community are wont to be treated by the higher, is greatly mitigated where the people have something to give. The assiduity with which their favour is sought, upon these occasions, serves to generate settled habits of condescension and respect; and, as human life is more embittered by affronts than injuries, whatever contributes to procure mildness and civility of manners toward those who are most liable to suffer from a contrary behaviour, connects, with the pride, in a great measure, the evil of inequality, and deserves to be accounted among the most generous institutions of social life.

III. The satisfaction which the people in free governments derive from the knowledge and agitation of political subjects; such as the proceedings and debates of the senate; the conduct and characters of ministers; the revolutions, intrigues, and contentions of parties; and, in general, from the discussion of public measures, questions, and occurrences. Subjects of this sort excite just enough of interest and emotion to afford a moderate engagement to the thoughts, without rising to any painful degree of anxiety, or ever leaving a fixed oppression upon the spirits; and what is this but the end and aim of all those amusements which compose so much of the business of life and of the value of riches? For my part (and I believe it to be the case with most men who are arrived at the middle age, and occupy the middle classes of life), had I all the money which I pay in taxes to government, at liberty to lay out upon amusement and diversion, I know not whether I could make choice of any in which I could find greater pleasure than what I receive from expecting, hearing, and relating public news; reading Parliamentary debates and proceedings; canvassing the political arguments, projects, predictions, and intelligence, which are conveyed by various channels to every corner of the kingdom. These topics, exciting universal curiosity, and being such as almost every man is ready to form and prepared to deliver his opinions about, greatly promote and, I think, improve conversation. They render it more rational and more innocent; they supply a substitute for drinking, gaming, scandal, and obscenity. Now the secrecy, the jealousy, the solitude, and precipitation of despotic governments, exclude all this. But the loss, you say, is trifling. I know that it is possible to render even the mention of it ridiculous, by representing it as the idle employment of the most insignificant part of the nation, the folly of village statesmen and coffee-house politicians; but I allow nothing to be trifling which ministers to the harmless gratification of multitudes; nor any order of men to be insignificant, whose number bears a respectable proportion to the sum of the whole community.

We have been accustomed to an opinion that a REPUBLICAN form of government suits only with the affairs of a small state: which opinion is founded in the consideration, *that unless the people, in every district of the empire,* be admitted to a share in the national representation, the government is not, as to them, a Republic; that elections, where the constituents are numerous and dispersed through a wide extent of country, are conducted with difficulty, or rather, indeed, managed by the intrigues and combination of a few, who are situated near the place of election, each voter considering his single suffrage as too minute a portion of the general interest to deserve his care or attendance, much less to be worth any opposition to influence and application; that, whilst we contract the representation within a compass small enough to admit of orderly debate, the interest of the constituent becomes too small,—of the representative, too great. It is difficult also to maintain any connexion between them. He who represents two hundred thousand, is necessarily a stranger to the greatest part of those who elect him; and when his interest amongst them ceases to depend upon an acquaintance with their persons and character, or a care and knowledge of their affairs; when such a representative finds the treasures and honours of a great empire at the disposal of a few, and himself one of the few; there is little reason to hope that he will not prefer to his public duty those temptations of personal aggrandizement which his situation offers, and which the price of his vote will always purchase. All appeal to the people is precluded by the impossibility of collecting a sufficient proportion of their force and numbers. The factions and the unanimity of the senate are equally dangerous. Add to these considerations, that in a democratic constitution the mechanism is too complicated, and the motions too slow, for the operations of a great empire, whose defence and government require execution and despatch, in proportion to the magnitude, extent, and variety of its concerns. There is weight, no doubt, in these reasons; but much of the objection seems to be done away by the contrivance of a *federal* republic, which, distributing the country into districts of a commodious extent, and leaving to each district its internal legislation, reserves to a convention of the states the adjustment of their relative claims; the levying, direction, and government of the common force of the confederacy; the requisition of subsidies for the support of this force; the making of peace and war; the entering into treaties; the regulation of foreign commerce; the equalization of duties upon imports, so as to prevent defrauding the revenue of one province by smuggling articles of taxation from the borders of another; and likewise so as to guard against undue partialities in the encouragement of trade. To what limits such a republic might, without inconvenience, enlarge its dominions, by assuming neighbouring provinces into the confederation; or how far it is capable of uniting the liberty of a small commonwealth with the safety of a powerful empire; or whether, amongst co-ordinate powers, dissensions and jealousies would not be likely to arise, which, for the want of a common superior, might proceed to fatal extremities; are questions upon which the records of mankind do not authorize us to decide with tolerable certainty. The experiment is about to be tried in America upon a large scale.

[This experiment has now been tried with complete success in the United States of America; but, as it has failed as signally in the Republics formed in the provinces once subject to the Spanish crown, it would appear that a Republic is adapted only to those who, like the Anglo-Saxon race, have long been accustomed to free institutions and representative government.]

CHAPTER XII.

OF THE THEORY OF THE BRITISH CONSTITUTION.

By the CONSTITUTION of a country, is meant so much of its law as relates to the designation and forms of the legislature; the rights and functions of the several parts of the legislative body; the construction, office, and jurisdiction of courts of justice. The constitution is one principal division, section, or title, of the code of public laws; distinguished from the rest only by the superior importance of the subject of which it treats. Therefore the terms *constitutional* and *unconstitutional* mean legal and illegal. The distinction and the ideas which these terms denote, are founded in the same authority with the law of the land upon any other subject, and to be ascertained by the same inquiries. In England, the system of public jurisprudence is made up of acts of parliament, of decisions of courts of law, and of immemorial usages: consequently, these are the principles of which the English constitution itself consists, the sources from which all our knowledge of its nature and limitations is to be deduced, and the authorities to which all appeal ought to be made, and by which every constitutional doubt and question can alone be decided. This plain and intelligible definition is the more necessary to be preserved in our thoughts, as some writers upon the subject absurdly confound what is constitutional with what is expedient; pronouncing forthwith a measure to be unconstitutional which they adjudge in any respect to be detrimental or dangerous; whilst others, again, ascribe a kind of transcendent authority or mysterious sanctity to the constitution, as if it were founded on some higher original than that which gives force and obligation to the ordinary laws and states of the realm, or were inviolable on any other account than its intrinsic utility. An act of parliament in England can never be unconstitutional, in the strict and proper acceptation of the term; in a lower, it may; viz. when it militates with the spirit, contradicts the analogy, or defeats the provision of other laws, made to regulate the form of government. Even that flagitious abuse of their trust, by which a parliament of Henry the Eighth conferred upon the king's proclamation the authority of law, was unconstitutional only in this latter sense.

Most of those who treat of the British constitution, consider it as a scheme of government formally planned and contrived by our ancestors, in some certain era of our national history, and as set up in pursuance of such regular plan and design. Something of this sort is secretly supposed, or referred to, in the expression of those who speak of the "principle of the constitution," of bringing back the constitution to its "first principles," of restoring it to its "original purity" or "primitive model." Now, this appears to me an erroneous conception of the subject. No such plan was ever formed, consequently no such first principles, original model, or standard, exist: I mean, there never was a date or point of time in our history, when the government of England was to be set up anew, and when it was referred to any single person, or assembly, or committee, to frame a charter for the future government of the country; or when a constitution so prepared and digested was by common consent received and established. In the time of the civil wars, or rather between the death of Charles the First and the restoration of his son, many such projects were published, but none were carried into execution. The Great Charter and the Bill of Rights were wise and strenuous efforts to obtain security against certain abuses of regal power, by which the subject had been formerly aggrieved: but these were, either of them, much too partial modifications of the constitution to give it a new original. The constitution of England, like that of most countries of Europe, hath grown out of occasion and emergency; from the fluctuating policy of different ages; from the contentions, successes, interests, and opportunities, of different orders and parties of men in the community. It resembles one of those old mansions, which, instead of being built all at once, after a regular plan, and according to the rules of architecture at present established, has been reared in different ages of the art, has been altered from time to time, and has been continually receiving additions and repairs suited to the taste, fortune, or convenience of its successive proprietors. In such a building, we look in vain for the elegance and proportion, for the just order and correspondence of parts, which we expect in a modern edifice; and which external symmetry, after all, contributes much more, perhaps, to the amusement of the beholder, than the accommodation of the inhabitant.

In the British, and possibly in all other constitutions, there exists a wide difference between the actual state of the government and the theory. The one results from the other; but still they are different. When we contemplate the *theory* of the British government, we see the king invested with the most absolute personal impunity; with a power of rejecting laws which have been resolved upon by both houses of Parliament; of conferring, by his charter, upon any set or succession of men he pleases the privilege of sending representatives into one house of Parliament, as, by his immediate appointment, he can place whom he will in the other. What is this, a foreigner might ask, but a mere circuitous despotism? Yet, when we turn our attention from the legal extent, to the actual exercises of royal authority in England, we see these formidable prerogatives dwindle into mere ceremonies; and, in their stead, a sure and commanding influence, of which the constitution, it seems, is totally ignorant, growing out of that enormous patronage which the increased territory and opulence of the empire have placed in the disposal of the executive magistrate.

Upon questions of reform, the habit of reflection to be encouraged is a sober comparison of the constitution under which we live; not with models of speculative perfection, but with the actual chance of obtaining a better. This turn of thought will generate a political disposition, equally removed from that puerile admiration of present establishments which sees no faults and can endure no change, and that distempered sensibility which is alive only to perceptions of inconvenience, and is too impatient to be delivered from the uneasiness which it feels, to compute either the peril or expense of the remedy. Political innovations commonly produce many effects beside those that are intended. The direct consequence is often the least important. Incidental, remote, and unthought-of evil, or advantages, frequently exceed the good that is designed, or the mischief that is foreseen. It is from the silent and unobserved operation, from the obscure progress of causes set at work for different purposes, that the greatest revolutions take their rise. When Elizabeth, and her immediate successor, applied themselves to the encouragement and regulation of trade by many wise laws, they knew not that, together with wealth and industry, they were diffusing a consciousness of strength and independency, which would not long endure, under the forms of a mixed government, the dominion of arbitrary princes. When it was debated whether the Mutiny Act, the law by which the army is governed and maintained, should be temporary or perpetual, little else probably occurred to the advocates of an annual bill, than the expediency of retaining a control over the most dangerous prerogatives of the crown—the direction and command of a standing army; whereas, in its effect, this single reservation has altered the whole frame and quality of the British constitution. For since, in consequence of the military system which prevails in neighbouring and rival nations, as well as on account of the internal exigences of government, a standing army has become essential to the safety and administration of the empire; it enables Parliament, by discontinuing this necessary provision, so to enforce its resolutions upon any other subject, as to render the king's dissent to a law, which has received the approbation of both houses, too dangerous an experiment any longer to be advised. A contest between the King and Parliament cannot now be persevered in without a dissolution of the government. Lastly, when the constitution conferred upon the crown the nomination to all employments in the public service, the authors of this arrangement were led to it by the obvious propriety of leaving to a master the choice of his servants, and by the manifest inconveniency of engaging the national council, upon every vacancy, in those personal contests which attend elections to places of honor and emolument. Our ancestors did not observe that this disposition added an influence to the regal office, which, as the number and value of public employments increased, would supersede, in a great measure, the forms, and change the character, of the ancient constitution. They knew not what the experience and reflection of modern ages have discovered, that patronage universally is power; that he who possesses, in a sufficient degree, the means of gratifying the desires of mankind after wealth and distinction, by whatever checks and forms his authority may be limited or disguised, will direct the management of public affairs. Whatever be the mechanism of the political engine, he will guide the motion. These instances are adduced in order to illustrate the proposition which we laid down, that, in politics, the most important and permanent effects have, for the most part, been incidental and unforeseen; and this proposition we inculcate, for the sake of the caution which teaches that changes ought not to be adventured upon without a *comprehensive* discernment of the consequences,—without a knowledge as well of the remote tendency, as of the immediate design. The courage of a statesman should resemble that of a commander; who, however regardless of personal danger, never forgets that, with his own, he commits the lives and fortunes of a multitude; and who does not consider it as any proof of zeal and valour to stake the safety of *other* men upon the success of a perilous or desperate enterprise.

There is one end of civil government peculiar to a good constitution; namely, the happiness of its subjects: there is another end essential to a good government, but common to it with many bad ones,— its own preservation. Observing that the best form of government would be defective, which did not provide for its own permanency, in our political reasonings we consider all such provisions as expedient; and are content to accept as a sufficient ground for a measure, or law, that it is necessary or conclusive to the preservation of the constitution. Yet, in truth, such provisions are absolutely expedient, and such an excuse final, only whilst the constitution is worth preserving; that is, until it can be changed for a better. I premise this distinction, because many things in the English, as in every constitution, are to be vindicated and accounted for solely from their tendency to maintain the government in its present state, and the several parts of it in possession of the powers which the constitution has assigned to them; and because I would wish it to be remarked, that such a consideration is always subordinate to another —the value and usefulness of the constitution itself.

CHAPTER XIII

OF THE PRACTICE OF THE BRITISH CONSTITUTION OR THE BRITISH GOVERNMENT.

The *Government of England*, which has been sometimes called a mixed government, sometimes a limited monarchy, is formed by a combination of the three regular species of government—the monarchy, residing in the King; the aristocracy, in the House of Lords; and the republic, being represented by the House of Commons. The perfection intended by such a scheme of government is, to unite the advantages of the several simple forms, and to exclude the inconveniences. To what degree this purpose is attained or attainable in the British constitution, wherein it is lost sight of or neglected, and by what means it may in any part be promoted with better success, the reader will be enabled to judge, by a separate recollection of these advantages and inconveniences, as enumerated in the preceding chapter, and a distinct application of each to the political condition of this country. We will present our remarks upon the subject in a brief account of the expedients by which the British constitution provides

1st. For the interest of its subjects.

2ndly. For its own preservation.

The contrivances for the first of these purposes are the following:

In order to promote the establishment of salutary public laws, every citizen of the state is capable of becoming a member of the senate; and every senator possesses the right of propounding to the deliberation of the legislature whatever law he pleases.

Every district of the empire enjoys the privilege of choosing representatives, informed of the interests, and circumstances, and desires of their constituents, and entitled by their situation to communicate that information to the national council. The meanest subject has some one whom he can call upon to bring forward his complaints and requests to public attention.

By annexing the right of voting for members of the House of Commons to different qualifications in different places, each order and profession of men in the community became, according to the theory in vogue before the Reform Act, virtually represented; that is, men of all orders and professions, statesmen, courtiers, country gentlemen, lawyers, merchants, manufacturers, soldiers, sailors, interested in the prosperity, and experienced in the occupation, of their respective professions, obtained seats in Parliament.

The elections, at the same time, are so connected with the influence of landed property as to afford a certainty that a considerable number of men of great estates will be returned to Parliament; and are also so modified, that men the most eminent and successful in their respective professions are the most likely, by their riches, or the weight of their stations, to prevail in these competitions.

The number, fortune, and quality, of the members; the variety of interests and characters amongst them; above all, the temporary duration of their power, and the change of men which every new election produces; are so many securities to the public, as well against the subjection of their judgment to any external dictation, as against the formation of a junto in their own body, sufficiently powerful to govern their decisions.

The representatives are so intermixed with the constituents, and the constituents with the rest of the people, that they cannot, with a partiality too flagrant to be endured, impose any burden upon the subject in which they do not share themselves; nor scarcely can they adopt an advantageous regulation, in which their own interests will not participate of the advantage.

The proceedings and debates of Parliament, and the parliamentary conduct of each representative, are known by the people at large.

The representative is so far dependent upon the constituent, and political importance upon public favour, that a senator most effectually recommends himself to eminence and advancement in the state, by contriving and patronizing laws of public utility.

When intelligence of the condition, wants, and occasions of the people, is thus collected from every quarter; when such a variety of invention, and so many understandings are set at work upon the subject; it may be presumed that the most eligible expedient, remedy, or improvement, will occur to some one or other; and when a wise counsel, or beneficial regulation, is once suggested, it may be expected, from the disposition of an assembly so constituted as the British House of Commons is, that it cannot fail of receiving the approbation of a majority.

To prevent those destructive contentions for the supreme power, which are sure to take place where the members of the state do not live under an acknowledged head, and a known rule of succession; to preserve the people in tranquillity at home, by a speedy and vigorous execution of the laws; to protect their interests abroad, by strength and energy in military operations, by those advantages of decision, secrecy, and despatch, which belong to the resolutions of monarchical counsels: for these purposes, the constitution has committed the executive government to the administration and limited authority of an hereditary king.

In the defence of the empire; in the maintenance of its power, dignity, and privileges, with foreign nations; in the advancement of its trade by treaties and conventions; and in the providing for the general administration of municipal justice, by a proper choice and appointment of magistrates; the inclination of the king and of the people usually coincides; in this part, therefore, of the regal office, the constitution entrusts the prerogative with ample powers.

The dangers principally to be apprehended from regal government, relate to the two articles, taxation and punishment. In every form of government from which the people are excluded, it is the interest of the governors to get as much, and of the governed to give as little, as they can: the power also of punishment, in the hands of an arbitrary prince, oftentimes becomes an engine of extortion, jealousy, and revenge. Wisely, therefore, hath the British constitution guarded the safety of the people, in these two points, by the most studious precautions.

Upon that of *taxation*, every law which, by the remotest construction, may de deemed to levy money upon the property of the subject, must originate, that is, must first be proposed and assented to, in the House of Commons; by which regulation, accompanying the weight which that assembly possesses in all its functions, the levying of taxes is almost exclusively reserved to the popular part of the constitution, who, it is presumed, will not tax themselves, nor their fellow-subjects, without being first convinced of the necessity of the aids which they grant.

The application also of the public supplies is watched with the same circumspection as the assessment. Many taxes are annual, the produce of others is mortgaged, or appropriated to specific services; the expenditure of all of them is accounted for to the House of Commons; as computations of the charge of the purpose for which they are wanted are previously submitted to the same tribunal.

In the infliction of *punishment*, the power of the crown, and of the magistrate appointed by the crown, is confined by the most precise limitations: the guilt of the offender must be pronounced by twelve men of his own order, indifferently chosen out of the county where the offence was committed; the punishment, or the limits to which the punishment may be extended are ascertained, and affixed to the crime, by laws which know not the person of the criminal.

And whereas the arbitrary or clandestine seizure and confinement of the person is the injury most to be dreaded from the strong hand of the executive government, because it deprives the prisoner at once of protection and defence, and delivers him into the power, and to the malicious or interested designs of his enemies; the constitution has provided against this danger with extreme solicitude. The ancient writ of habeas-corpus, the Habeas-corpus Act of Charles the

Second, and the practice and determinations of our sovereign courts of justice founded upon these laws, afford a complete remedy for every conceivable case of illegal imprisonment*.

Treason being that charge, under colour of which the destruction of an obnoxious individual is often sought; and government being at all times more im-

---

* Upon complaint in writing by, or on behalf of, any person in confinement, to any of the four courts of Westminster Hall, in term time, or to the Lord Chancellor, or one of the Judges, in the vacation; and upon a probable reason being suggested to question the legality of the detention, a writ is issued to the person in whose custody the complainant is alleged to be, commanding him within a certain limited and short time to produce the body of the prisoner, and the authority under which he is detained. Upon the return of the writ, strict and instantaneous obedience to which is enforced by very severe penalties, if no lawful cause of imprisonment appear, the court or judge before whom the prisoner is brought, is authorized and bound to discharge him; even though he may have been committed by a secretary, or other high officer of state, by the privy-council, or by the king in person; so that no subject of this realm can be held in confinement by any power, or under any pretence whatever, provided he can find means to convey his complaint to one of the four courts of Westminster Hall, or, during their recess, to any of the judges of the same, unless all these several tribunals agree in determining his imprisonment to be legal. He may make application to them in succession, and if one out of the number be found, who thinks the prisoner entitled to his liberty, that one possesses authority to restore it to him.

mediately a party in the prosecution; the law, beside the general care with which it watches over the safety of the accused, in this case, sensible of the unequal contest in which the subject is engaged, has assisted his defence with extraordinary indulgences. By two statutes, enacted since the Revolution, every person indicted for high treason shall have a copy of his indictment, a list of the witnesses to be produced, and of the jury empanelled, delivered to him ten days before the trial; he is also permitted to make his defence by counsel,—privileges which are not allowed to the prisoner in a trial for any other crime; and, what is of more importance to the party than all the rest, the testimony of two witnesses, at the least, is required to convict a person of treason; whereas, one positive witness is sufficient in almost every other species of accusation.

We proceed, in the second place, to inquire in what manner the constitution has provided for its own preservation; that is, in what manner each part of the legislature is secured, in the exercise of the powers assigned to it, from the encroachments of the other parts. This security is sometimes called the *balance of the constitution:* and the political equilibrium, which this phrase denotes, consists in two contrivances—a balance of power, and a balance of interest. By a balance of power is meant, that there is no power possessed by one part of the legislature, the abuse or excess of which is not checked by some antagonist power residing in another part. Thus the power of the two houses of Parliament to frame laws, is checked by the king's negative; that if laws subversive of regal government should obtain the consent of Parliament, the reigning prince, by interposing his prerogative, may save the necessary right and authority of his station. On the other hand, the arbitrary application of this negative is checked by the privilege, which Parliament possesses, of refusing supplies to the exigencies of the king's administration. The constitutional maxim, "that the king can do no wrong," is balanced by another maxim, not less constitutional, "that the illegal commands of the king do not justify those who assist, or concur, in " carrying them into execution:" and by a second rule, subsidiary to this, "that the acts of the crown " acquire not any legal force, until authenticated by " the subscription of some of its great officers." The wisdom of this contrivance is worthy of observation. As the king could not be punished without a civil war, the constitution exempts his person from trial or account; but lest this impunity should encourage a licentious exercise of dominion, various obstacles are opposed to the private will of the sovereign, when directed to illegal objects. The pleasure of the crown must be announced with certain solemnities, and attested by certain officers of state. In some cases, the royal order must be signified by a secretary of state; in others, it must pass under the privy seal;

and in many, under the great seal. And when the king's command is regularly published, no mischief can be achieved by it, without the ministry and compliance of those to whom it is directed. Now all who either concur in an illegal order, by authenticating its publication with their seal or subscription, or who assist in carrying it into execution, subject themselves to prosecution and punishment for the part they have taken; and are not permitted to plead or produce the command of the king, in justification of their obedience*.

But further, the power of the crown to direct the military force of the kingdom is balanced by the annual necessity of resorting to Parliament for the maintenance and government of that force. The power of the king to declare war is checked by the privilege

---

* Amongst the checks which Parliament holds over the administration of public affairs, I forbear to mention the practice of addressing the king, to know by whose advice he resolved upon a particular measure, and of punishing the authors of that advice for the counsel they had given. Not because I think this method either unconstitutional or improper; but for this reason: that it does not so much subject the King to the control of Parliament, as it supposes him to be already in subjection. For if the King were so far out of the reach of the resentment of the House of Commons, as to be able with safety to refuse the information requested, or to take upon himself the responsibility inquired after, there must be an end of all proceedings founded in this mode of application.

of the House of Commons to grant or withhold the supplies by which the war must be carried on. The king's choice of his ministers is controlled by the obligation he is under of appointing those men to offices in the state, who are found capable of managing the affairs of his government with the two houses of Parliament. Which consideration imposes such a necessity upon the crown, as hath in a great measure subdued the influence of favouritism; insomuch, that it is become no uncommon spectacle in this country to see men promoted by the king to the highest offices and richest preferments which he has in his power to bestow, who have been distinguished by their opposition to his personal inclinations.

By the *balance of interest* which accompanies and gives efficacy to the *balance of power*, is meant this: that the respective interests of the three estates of the empire are so disposed and adjusted, that whichever of the three shall attempt any encroachment, the other two will unite in resisting it. If the King should endeavour to extend his authority, by contracting the power and privileges of the Commons, the House of Lords would see their own dignity endangered by every advance which the crown made to independency upon the resolutions of Parliament. The admission of arbitrary power is no less formidable to the grandeur of the aristocracy than it is fatal to the liberty of the republic; that is, it would reduce the nobility from the hereditary share they possess in the national councils, in which their real greatness consists, to the being made a part of the empty pageantry of a despotic court. On the other hand, if the House of Commons should intrench upon the distinct province, or usurp the established prerogative of the crown, the House of Lords would receive an instant alarm from every new stretch of popular power. In every contest in which the king may be engaged with the representative body, in defence of his established share of authority, he will find a sure ally in the collective power of the nobility.

An attachment to the monarchy, from which they derive their own distinction; the allurements of a court, in the habits and with the sentiments of which they have been brought up; their hatred of equality, and of all levelling pretensions which may ultimately affect the privileges, or even the existence, of their order: in short, every principle and every prejudice which are wont to actuate human conduct, will determine their choice to the side and support of the crown. Lastly, if the nobles themselves should attempt to revive the superiorities which their ancestors exercised under the feudal constitution, the king and the people would alike remember how the one had been insulted and the other enslaved by that barbarous tyranny: they would forget the natural opposition of their views and inclinations, when they saw themselves threatened with the return of a domination which was odious and intolerable to both.

It has been attempted of late, and especially by the admirers of pure republican institutions, to refute this doctrine of a balance in the constitution, by an appeal to recent facts. All real power, say they, is in the House of Commons; and if *they* resolve on a measure, the other branches of the constitution have no *real power* to resist it. They instance the carrying of the Reform Bill, the repeal of the corn laws, and similar events—in which the inclination as well as the judgment of the hereditary portion of the legislature was in opposition to the popular will, but in which that popular will triumphed nevertheless. To which it may be replied, that it is not the *intention* of the British constitution to prevent the fulfilment of any determination which the people have formed, and that, when that determination is known, it becomes the *duty* of the other parts of the legislature to give way to the popular resolution.

The British Constitution is neither absolutism, checked by aristocratic and democratic elements, nor an oligarchy, blended with royal and popular ingredients; but it is a COMMONWEALTH or REPUBLIC, tempered by monarchical and aristocratic institutions.

The great use therefore of the royalty and nobility in a constitution so framed is to ascertain and carry into execution the will of the nation, and the cases just instanced are precisely in point.

The House of Commons is an elected body; it is more accessible to disturbing forces than the Peerage.

A movement of mere agitation may, under many circumstances, be mistaken for an expression of national determination, and might be too hastily accepted as such, did not the legislature interpose a non-elected body, whose consent must *first* be obtained. This delay has in every instance been advantageous; for not only have popular measures been increased in wisdom and efficiency, by the thorough and searching examination which they receive, but they are ascertained to be popular measures before they are passed into laws; and the delay even of a year or two is of comparatively small moment when put into comparison with this certainty. Paley observes, that, in describing the British constitution, little notice has been taken of the House of Lords. The proper uses and designs of this part of the constitution are the following:—First, to enable the king, by his right of bestowing the peerage, to reward the servants of the public, in a manner most grateful to them, and at a small expense to the nation: secondly, to fortify the power and to secure the stability of regal government, by an order of men naturally allied to its interests: and thirdly, to answer a purpose, which, though of superior importance to the other two, does not occur so readily to our observation; namely, to stem the progress of popular fury. Large bodies of men are subject to sudden frenzies. Opinions are sometimes circulated amongst a multitude without proof or examination, acquiring confidence and reputation merely by being repeated from one to another; and passions founded upon these opinions, diffusing themselves with a rapidity which can neither be accounted for nor resisted, may agitate a country with the most violent commotions. Now, the only way to stop the fermentation is to divide the mass; that is, to erect different orders in the community, with separate prejudices and interests. And this may occasionally become the use of an hereditary nobility, invested with a share of legislation. Averse to those prejudices which actuate the minds of the vulgar; accustomed to condemn the clamour of the populace; disdaining to receive laws and opinions from their inferiors in rank; they will oppose revolutions which are founded in the folly and violence of the lower part of the community. Were the voice of the people always dictated by reflection; did every man, or even one man in a hundred, think for himself, or actually consider the measure he was about to approve or censure; or even were the common people tolerably steadfast in the judgment which they formed, I should hold the interference of a superior order not only superfluous but wrong; for when every thing is allowed to difference of rank and education, which the actual state of these advantages deserves, that, after all, is most likely to be right and expedient, which appears to be so to the separate judgment and decision of a great majority of the nation; at least, that, in general, is right *for them*, which is agreeable to their fixed opinions and desires.

But when we observe what is urged as the public opinion, to be, in truth, the opinion only, or perhaps the feigned profession, of a few crafty leaders; that the numbers who join in the cry serve only to swell and multiply the sound, without any accession of judgment or exercise of understanding; and that oftentimes the wisest counsels have been thus everborne by tumult and uproar; we may conceive occasions to arise in which the commonwealth may be saved by the reluctance of the nobility to adopt the caprices or to yield to the vehemence of the common people. In expecting this advantage from an order of nobles, we do not suppose the nobility to be more unprejudiced than others; we only suppose that their prejudices will be different from, and may occasionally counteract, those of others.

If the personal privileges of the peerage, which are usually so many injuries to the rest of the community, be restrained, we see little inconveniency in the increase of its number: for it is only dividing the same quantity of power amongst more hands, which is rather favourable to public freedom than otherwise.

A subject which has been at various times much canvassed, is the propriety of conferring seats in the upper house on the prelates of the church. Paley says, "This admission of a small number of ecclesiastics into the House of Lords, is but an equitable compensation to the clergy for the exclusion of their order from the House of Commons. They are a set of men considerable by their number and property, as well as by their influence, and the duties of their station; yet, whilst every other profession has those amongst the national representatives, who, being conversant in the same occupation, are able to state, and naturally disposed to support, the rights and interests of the class and calling to which they belong, the clergy alone are deprived of this advantage; which hardship is made up to them by introducing the prelacy into Parliament; and if bishops, from gratitude or expectation, be more obsequious to the will of the crown than those who possess great temporal inheritances, they are properly inserted into that part of the constitution from which much or frequent resistance to the measures of government is not expected."

This is, however, hardly a fair view of the case; for, first, an *injustice* done to one man can hardly be compensated by a favour done to another.

Secondly, it is by no means self-evident that the rights and interests of the clergy *at large must* be supported by the Rulers of the clergy: and thirdly, the true theory is altogether overlooked, which is this, that by virtue of the Union between church and state, the church yields to the state the election of her chief ministers, and the state in return places those chief ministers in the legislature.

"I acknowledge," says Paley, "that I perceive no sufficient reason for exempting the persons of members of either house of Parliament from arrest for debt. The counsels or suffrages of a single senator, especially of one who, in the management of his own affairs, may justly be suspected of a want of prudence or honesty, can seldom be so necessary to those of the public as to justify a departure from that wholesome policy by which the laws of a commercial state punish and stigmatize insolvency. But, whatever reason may be pleaded for their *personal* immunity, when this privilege of Parliament is extended to domestics and retainers, or when it is permitted to impede or delay the course of judicial proceedings, it becomes an absurd sacrifice of equal justice to imaginary dignity." This absurdity is among those whose days are numbered, and a future generation will wonder that it subsisted so long.

We shall close this chapter with a few general observations. It is doubtless very humiliating to see that the wisest of constitutions, for so every Englishman considers that of his own country, should be only supported by *a balance*, which consists in opposing the frailties and selfishness of one class against the frailties and selfishness of another; but this recognition of widespread moral weakness is grounded on experience, and at the same time is consistent with a greater reliance on public virtue than exists in any nation on the face of the globe. It enlists self-love on the side of order, and makes the very faculties which would otherwise tend to oppression conducive to public liberty.

CHAPTER XIV.

ON THE REPRESENTATIVE SYSTEM, AND ESPECIALLY ON THAT FORM ADOPTED IN ENGLAND.

IF the whole world were composed of true Christians, the perfect law of liberty would universally prevail, and all human government would become unnecessary. There would be NO WAR, and *military establishments* with their expenses and evils would sink into disuetude. There would be NO CONTENTION, and the *civil law* with all its costly arrangements would be needless. There would be NEITHER FRAUD NOR VIOLENCE, and all *criminal jurisprudence* with its array of jails and gibbets would cease; taxation would no longer be required, and every man would be his own governor.

But as the state of society is such as to render this *perfect law* impracticable, we must be satisfied with a law embodying more or less of imperfection; but, at the same time, we must be fully aware that the government and constitution of that state is most perfect which approaches the nearest to the Christian standard.

The purest form of self-government is that in

which *every man* governs himself; and thus the whole body politic is governed by the whole body politic.

The next is that in which the whole people is still governed by the whole people, but by an intermediate action, each man governing his neighbour as well as himself by means of a representative system. A representative system is, however, a vast descent from the first-named form; because it supposes the existence of moral evil and the necessity of a coercive government—each subject delegating to his representative his respective share,—and each district or body represented, their entire and collected share of the executive and legislative power.

A perfect representation is that which embodies the will of the whole community, which leaves no man without the means of making his voice heard in the great council of his nation, and no interest unprotected there; and this, not with a perfect equality, but with an exact proportion to their relative importance. Men indeed should be equal, classes and interests unequal, in the council chamber, as they are in the world. This would at once point out universal suffrage as a necessary condition of perfect representation.

There is nothing, says Paley, in the British constitution so remarkable, as the irregularity of the popular representation. The House of Commons consists of five hundred and forty-eight members, of whom two hundred were elected by seven thousand constituents; so that a majority of these seven thousand, without any reasonable title to superior weight or influence in the state, might, under certain circumstances, decide a question against the opinion of as many millions. Or to place the same object in another point of view: if my estate be situated in one county of the kingdom, I possessed the ten thousandth part of a single representative; if in another, the thousandth; if in a particular district, I might be one in twenty who chose two representatives; if in a still more favoured spot, I might enjoy the right of appointing two myself. If I had been born, or dwelt, or had served an apprenticeship in one town, I was represented in the national assembly by two deputies in the choice of whom I exercised an actual and sensible share of power; if accident had thrown my birth, or habitation, or service, into another town, I had no representative at all, nor more power or concern in the election of those who make the laws by which I am governed, than if I was a subject of the Grand Signior: and this partiality subsisted without any pretence whatever of merit or propriety to justify the preference of one place to another. Or, thirdly, to describe the state of national representation as it existed in reality, it might have been affirmed, I believe, with truth, that about one-half of the House of Commons obtained their seats in that assembly by the election of the people; the other half, by purchase, or by the denomination of single proprietors of great estates.

This objection no longer exists to the same extent as before the Reform Act; but it is still the case, though in a minor degree. Small, insignificant towns are still represented; great and important ones, still unrepresented: here, a property qualification prevails; there, something akin to universal suffrage. Bribery and corruption, if diminished, are not suppressed, and the family influence of the aristocracy still places many members in the House of Commons.

This, says Paley, is a flagrant incongruity in the constitution; but it is one of those objections which strike most forcibly at first sight. The effect of all reasoning upon the subject is, to diminish the first impression; on which account it deserves the more attentive examination, that we may be assured, before we venture upon a reformation, that the magnitude of the evil justifies the danger of the experiment. And here we retain all the special pleading that follows; because Paley, seeing the mischiefs which would probably arise from any attempt *in his day* to reform the representation, has gathered together in a masterly way all the arguments for the policy of doing nothing; of being contented with things as they are; and of avoiding reform, lest it should lead to revolution; they are not the less valuable because they are old, for they have been reproduced a hundred times since, and to this day form the sub-stratum of every argument for resisting improvement. In a few remarks that follow, we would be understood, he says, in the first place, to decline all conference with those who wish to alter the form of government of these kingdoms. The reformers with whom we have to do, are they who, whilst they change this part of the system, would retain the rest. If any Englishman expect more happiness to this country under a republic, he may very consistently recommend a new modelling of elections to Parliament; because, if the King and House of Lords were laid aside, the present disproportionate representation would produce nothing but a confused and ill-digested oligarchy. In like manner we waive a controversy with those writers who insist upon representation as a *natural* right*; we consider it so far only as a right at all, as it conduces to public utility; that is, as it contributes to the establishment of good laws, or as it secures to the people the just administration of those laws†. These effects depend upon the disposition and abilities of

---

* If this right be *natural*, no doubt it must be equal; and the right, we may add, of one sex as well as the other. Whereas, every plan of representation that we have heard of, begins by excluding the votes of women; thus cutting off, at a single stroke, one half of the public from a right which is asserted to be inherent in all; a *right*, too, as some represent it, not only universal, but unalienable, and indefeasible, and imprescriptible.

† There is an error here; for political right does not depend upon public utility, but upon *national opinion* of public utility.

the national counsellors. Wherefore, if men the most likely by their qualifications to know and promote the public interest be actually returned to Parliament, it signifies little who return them. If the properest persons be elected, what matters it by whom they are elected? At least, no prudent statesman would subvert long-established or even settled rules of representation without a prospect of procuring wiser or better representatives. This, then, being well observed, let us, before we seek to obtain any thing more, consider duly what we already have. We *have* a House of Commons, composed of five hundred and forty-eight members; in which number are found the most considerable landholders and merchants of the kingdom; the heads of the army, the navy, and the law; the occupiers of great offices in the state; together with many private individuals, eminent by their knowledge, eloquence, or activity. Now, if the country be not safe in such hands, in whose may it confide its interests? If such a number of such men be liable to the influence of corrupt motives, what assembly of men will be secure from the same danger? Does any new scheme of representation promise to collect together more wisdom, or to produce firmer integrity? In this view of the subject, and attending not to ideas of order and proportion (of which many minds are much enamoured), but to effects alone, we may discover just excuses for those parts of the present representation which appear to a hasty observer most unexceptional and absurd. It should be remembered, as a maxim extremely applicable to this subject, that no order or assembly of men whatever can long maintain their place and authority, in a mixed government, of which the members do not individually possess a respectable share of personal importance. Now, whatever may be the defects of the present arrangement, it infallibly secures a great weight of property to the House of Commons, by rendering many seats in that house accessible to men of large fortunes, and to such men alone. By which means, those characters are engaged in the defence of the separate rights and interests of this branch of the legislature that are best able to support its claims. The constitution of most of the small boroughs, especially the burgage-tenure, contributes, though undesignedly, to the same effect; for the appointment of the representatives we find commonly annexed to certain great inheritances. Elections purely popular are in this respect uncertain; in times of tranquillity, the natural ascendancy of wealth will prevail; but when the minds of men are inflamed by political dissensions, this influence often yields to more impetuous motives. The variety of tenures and qualifications, upon which the right of voting is founded, appears to me a recommendation of the mode which now subsists, as it tends to introduce into Parliament a corresponding mixture of characters and professions. It has been long observed, that conspicuous abilities are most frequently found with the representatives of small boroughs. And this is nothing more than what the laws of human conduct might teach us to expect; when such boroughs are set to sale, those men are likely to become purchasers who are enabled by their talents to make the best of their bargain; when a seat is not sold, but given by the opulent proprietor of a burgage-tenure, the patron finds his own interests consulted by the reputation and abilities of the member whom he nominates*. If certain of the nobility hold the appointment of some part of the House of Commons, it serves to maintain that alliance between the two branches of the legislature which no good citizen would wish to see dissevered: it helps to keep the government of the country in the House of Commons, in which it would not perhaps long continue to reside, if so powerful and wealthy a part of the nation, as the peerage compose, were excluded from all share and interest in its constitution. If there be a few boroughs so circumstanced as to lie at the

---

* It is well observed by Dymond, that "what is really wanting in a legislator is not brilliant ability, but a sound, and an enlightened, and an upright mind. Nor is it to be forgotten that the splendid talents of those who seek to make the best of their bargain may be an evil rather than a good: the bargain, it is to be feared, will be a losing one to the public, and by him who makes the best, the public may lose the most."—Essays, 4th ed. p. 125.

disposal of the crown, whilst the number of such is known and small, they may be tolerated with little danger. For where would be the impropriety or the inconvenience, if the sovereign at once should nominate a limited number of his servants to seats in Parliament? or, what is the same thing, if seats in Parliament were annexed to the possession of certain of the most efficient and responsible offices in the state*? The present representation, after all these deductions, and under the confusion in which it confessedly lies, is still in such a degree popular, or rather the representatives are so connected with the mass of the community by a society of interests and passions, that the will of the people, when it is determined, permanent, and general, almost always at length prevails†.

Upon the whole, in the several plans which have been suggested of an equal or a reformed representa-

---

* This suggestion appears a very valuable one: for the introduction by the authority of the House of Commons itself of a few members under such circumstances could not be attended with any loss of, or danger to, the public liberty. But a short time since, a very valuable and efficient minister of the Crown was for some time without a seat in the House of Commons, and considerable detriment to the public service occurred thereby.

† Were there no other argument than this word "*almost,*" it would be sufficient to substantiate a claim for a full and perfect representation of the people.

tion, it will be difficult to discover any proposal that has a tendency to throw more of the business of the nation into the House of Commons, or to collect a set of men more fit to transact that business, or, in general, more interested in the national happiness and prosperity. One consequence, however, may be expected from these projects, namely, "less flexibility to the influence of the crown." And since the diminution of this influence is the declared and perhaps the sole design of the various schemes that have been produced, whether for regulating the elections, contracting the duration, or for purifying the constitution of Parliament, by the exclusion of placemen and pensioners, it is obvious, and of importance to remark, that the more apt and natural, as well as the more safe and quiet, way of obtaining the same end, would be by a direct reduction of the patronage of the crown, which might be effected to a certain extent without hazarding farther consequences. Superfluous and exorbitant emoluments of office may not only be suppressed for the present, but provisions of law be devised, which should for the future restrain within certain limits the number and value of the offices in the donation of the sovereign. But whilst we dispute concerning different schemes of reformation, all directed to the same end, a previous doubt occurs in the debate—whether the end itself be good or safe; whether the influence so loudly complained of can be destroyed, or even much diminished, without danger to the state. Whilst the zeal of some men beholds this influence with a jealousy which nothing but its entire abolition can appease, many wise and virtuous politicians deem a considerable portion of it to be as necessary a part of the British constitution as any other ingredient in the composition; to be that, indeed, which gives cohesion and solidity to the whole. Were the measures of government, say they, opposed from nothing but principle, government ought to have nothing but the rectitude of its measures to support them; but since opposition springs from other motives, government must possess an influence to counteract these motives, to produce not a bias of the passions, but a neutrality: it must have some weight to cast into the scale, to set the balance even*. It is the nature of power always to press upon the boundaries which confine it. Licentiousness, faction, envy, impatience of control, or inferiority; the secret pleasure of mortifying the great, or the hope of dispossessing them; a constant willingness to question and thwart whatever is dictated or even proposed by another; a disposition common to all bodies of men to extend the claims and authority of their orders; above all, that love of power, and of showing it,

---

* Carefully as what follows is written, it would be difficult to defend it against a charge of pleading for corruption. It is not a high Christian principle which requires power to *persuade* the *persuadeable* and to buy the buyable by means of any appeal to personal interests.

which resides more or less in every human breast, and which, in popular assemblies, is inflamed, like every other passion, by communication and encouragement: these motives, added to private designs and resentments, cherished also by popular acclamation, and operating upon the great share of power already possessed by the House of Commons, might induce a majority, or at least a large party of men in that assembly, to unite in endeavouring to draw to themselves the whole government of the state; or, at least, so to obstruct the conduct of public affairs, by a wanton and perverse opposition, as to render it impossible for the wisest statesman to carry forward the business of the nation in Parliament with such success or satisfaction.

Some passages of our national history afford grounds for these apprehensions. Before the accession of James the First, or, at least, during the reigns of his three immediate predecessors, the government of England was a government by force; that is, the king carried his measures in Parliament by *intimidation*. A sense of personal danger kept the members of the House of Commons in subjection. A conjunction of fortunate causes delivered at last the Parliament and nation from slavery. That overbearing system, which had declined in the hands of James, expired early in the reign of his son. After the Restoration, there succeeded in its place, and since the Revolution has been methodically pursued, the more successful expedient of *influence*. Now, we remember what passed between the loss of terror, and the establishment of influence. The transactions of that interval, whatever we may think of their occasion and effect, no friend of regal government would wish to see revived. But the affairs of this kingdom afford a more recent attestation to the same doctrine. In the British colonies of North America, the late assemblies possessed much of the power and constitution of our House of Commons. The king and government of Great Britain held no patronage in the country, which could create attachment and influence sufficient to counteract that restless, arrogating spirit, which, in popular assemblies, when left to itself, will never brook an authority that checks and interferes with its own. To this cause, excited perhaps by some unseasonable provocations, we may attribute, as to their true and proper original (we will not say the misfortunes, but) the changes that have taken place in the British empire. The admonition, which such examples suggest, will have its weight with those who are content with the general frame of the English constitution; and who consider stability amongst the first perfections of any government.

We protest, however, against any construction by which what is here said shall be attempted to be applied to the justification of bribery, or of any clandestine reward or solicitation whatever. The very secrecy of such negotiations confesses or begets a consciousness of guilt; which when the mind is once taught to endure without uneasiness, the character is prepared for every compliance: and there is the greater danger in these corrupt practices, as the extent of their operation is unlimited and unknown. Our apology relates solely to that influence which results from the acceptance or expectation of public preferments. Nor does the influence which we defend require any sacrifice of personal probity. In political, above all other subjects, the arguments, or rather the conjectures, on each side of a question, are often so equally poised, that the wisest judgments may be held in suspense: these I call subjects of *indifference*. But again, when the subject is not *indifferent* in inself, it will appear such to a great part of those to whom it is proposed, for want of information, or reflection, or experience, or of capacity to collect and weigh the reasons by which either side is supported. These are subjects of *apparent indifference*. This indifference occurs still more frequently in personal contests, in which we do not often discover any reason of public utility for the preference of one competitor to another. These cases compose the province of influence: that is, the decision in these cases will inevitably be determined by influence of some sort or other. The only doubt is, what influence shall be admitted. If you remove the influence of the crown, it is only to make way for influence from a different quarter. If motives of expectation and gratitude be withdrawn, other motives will succeed in their place, acting probably in an opposite direction, but equally irrelative and external to the proper merits of the question. There exist as we have seen, passions in the human heart which will always make a strong party against the executive power of a mixed government. According as the disposition of Parliament is friendly or adverse to the recommendation of the crown in matters which are really or apparently indifferent, as indifference hath been now explained, the business of the empire will be transacted with ease and convenience, or embarrassed with endless contention and difficulty. Nor is it a conclusion founded in justice, or warranted by experience, that because men are induced by views of interest to yield their consent to measures concerning which their judgment decides nothing, they may be brought by the same influence to act in direct opposition to knowledge and duty. Whoever reviews the operations of government in this country since the Revolution, will find few even of the most questionable measures of administration about which the best-instructed judgment might not have doubted at the time, but of which he may affirm, with certainty, that they were *indifferent* to the greatest part of those who concurred in them. From the success or the facility with which they who dealt out the patronage of the crown carried measures like these, ought we to conclude that a similar application of honors and emoluments would procure the consent of Parliament to counsels evidently detrimental to the common welfare? Is there not, on the contrary, more reason to fear that the prerogative, if deprived of influence, would not be long able to support itself? For when we reflect upon the power of the House of Commons to extort a compliance with its resolutions from the other parts of the legislature, or to put to death the constitution by a refusal of the annual grants of money to the support of the necessary functions of government; when we reflect also what motives there are, which, in the vicissitudes of political interests and passions, may one day arm and point this power against the executive magistrate; when we attend to these considerations, we shall be led, perhaps, to acknowledge, that there is not more of paradox than of probability in that important, but much-decried apophthegm, " that an independent parliament is " incompatible with the existence of the monarchy*."

---

* With an absolute monarchy, it undoubtedly is; and indeed with *any* monarchy less limited than our own. So long as the people are sovereign, and the chief magistrate the embodied and majestic expression of national will, so long the most perfect independence of Parliament is compatible with a *strong executive*, confided to the hands of the monarch: but when this constitutional order of things is changed, then the one party or the other *must* give way; and every day that passes makes it more clear where the power of the nation lies.

CHAPTER XV.

OF THE PROGRESS OF THE REPRESENTATIVE PRINCIPLE.

WE have now heard all that could be advanced in favour of the stationary policy, by one of the clearest-minded and most practical of philosophers. That the system worked to a *certain extent* well, with all its imperfections, must be admitted; but so far as it *did* work well, it was in despite of, and not because of, those imperfections. Since Paley wrote, many of the discrepancies between the theory and practice of the constitution have been removed; and their removal has only tended to make the great political machine work more easily and more effectually. If the people have rights, and are deprived of the exercise of those rights, it is no answer to their complaint to say that they are as well governed as though they did exercise them. If the theory of the constitution is that the people are represented in Parliament, they are not bound to be satisfied with the observation that, "provided the properest persons are chosen, what "matters it by whom they are elected;" and they are bound to see that the franchise be extended as far as possible. Now, as we saw in the last chapter, a perfect representative system involved *universal suffrage*. Why should not the theory and the practice of our constitution be made to coincide? This question we shall now proceed to consider: and first, what is meant by universal suffrage? for we do not understand it as some do, without any limitations. Christianity itself does not, we apprehend, confer political power on women. If it does subject them to the domestic government of their husbands, commanding them to "be obedient," and "to learn in silence with all subjection," it is manifestly inconsistent with this subjection that they should exercise political power. There are other reasons too, drawn from the nature of their positive duties, which maintain the same doctrine, and on which it is the less necessary to enlarge, as there are few of either sex who contend for an equality of political power. That there is an equality of political *rights*, we at once admit; but this does not imply an identity of political *duties*. There is, however, *one apparent* exception, and only apparent, because the real principles of the question are not touched. The highest office of the government is, by the laws of most civilized states, no longer confined to one sex. Whether the Salic law should be universally observed, was doubtless in the power as well as in the right of nations to decide; and in generally deciding against it, they have, it would appear, exercised a sound discretion: for, in many cases, the evils of a disputed succession have been thereby avoided, and the hereditary principle maintained: and as the person of the sovereign is by the constitution sacred, and the advisers of the crown responsible, there would be no advantage gained, and no principle supported, by the establishment of an opposite rule.

In discussing, therefore, the question of universal suffrage, we exclude women.

In the next place, we exclude all whom the laws consider as infants; for if, in the eye of the country, they are held incapable of managing their own affairs, much more must they be considered unqualified from managing those of the commonwealth.

Thirdly, criminals undergoing the actual punishment of their offences. It can hardly be contended that those whose evil deeds have brought them under the justice of the public, should at the same time be permitted to share in the direction of public affairs.

These three classes, then,—women, persons under age, and criminals,—will be generally looked on as unqualified with regard to the two first—disqualified as regards the third.

But there are two other classes concerning which a doubt may arise. First, those who *have been* convicted of crime—and secondly, those supported by the charity of the state. These two cases rest on widely different grounds. It may also be thought, concerning the first, that the nature of the crime should be taken into account, that the man convicted of burglary and the man convicted of poaching ought not, when the term of their punishment expires, to be looked upon as equals; but then it must be remembered that the state has already exacted from them a satisfaction to society proportionate to the amount of their guilt, and if it now sets them at large, and reconstitutes them members of society, it ought not to take from them the advantages of their restored condition.

I think it questionable whether the forfeiture of political privileges in perpetuity should be inflicted as a punishment for any crime, unless in cases where some other punishment of a disqualifying nature, such as imprisonment or transportation, was inflicted for life; and I hold this opinion both because it takes away a motive for reformation and a stimulus to good behaviour; and also because the enforcing of it would be attended with many difficulties, if universal suffrage prevailed.

On these grounds then I differ with those who would make the recorded conviction of *any* crime a ground of disfranchisement.

The case of those supported by public charity is somewhat more complicated. Their only *offence* is that heavy one of being poor; but then they have no stake in the commonwealth; they aid it not by their labours; they are, and the word must not be considered as a harsh one, a burden on the labours of others;

and as they are incapable, or supposed to be so, of supporting themselves, there appears no injustice in classing them with persons under age.

Universal suffrage then, according to the most rational mode of understanding it, appears to imply the investing with the elective franchise all men of full age, who are neither actually suffering for their offences, nor supported by the bounty of the state. It is obvious that this definition will include all soldiers and sailors, as such are undoubtedly maintaining themselves by their own exertions.

This, therefore, being the nature of universal suffrage, comes the further question: have the people of this country *a right* to it? The answer to this will depend on the result of certain preliminary inquiries. And first and chiefest, DO THEY DESIRE IT? If they do, they *have* a right to it; for no one will maintain that there is anything morally wrong in it, and it comes therefore into the category of those things in which the voice of the people is law. But it must be a *general* desire—not that of a few agitators or demagogues who may get up meetings and originate petitions. If this general desire does *not* exist, I may desire it for myself; I may be perfectly satisfied that it is necessary for the benefit of the nation; I may speak, and write, and agitate in favour of it, but I cannot say that I have *a right* to it; and yet I may be doing much to create a right.

Then there comes another query: Would the exercise of such a right, supposing it to exist, be beneficial to the country at large? In other words, are those whom it is now the fashion to call *"the masses"* prepared and qualified morally and mentally for such *a duty?* for now we have to look on the *duty* as well as the privilege; both constitute *a right*. These two questions do not so exactly coincide as some may suppose; for a right way may exist, and yet its exercise may be inexpedient. In the present instance, however, they seem to have the same common measure. If the privilege be generally desired, it becomes *a right*, and the fact of its being so desired, makes it expedient that it should be so exercised. A nation is very seldom wrong in that which it seeks, and *never* values political advantages for which it is not prepared. The Charter of Gul-Khaneh was absolutely forced upon the Turks by the present Sultan; and universal suffrage and a representative government would be a dead letter in Russia.

It will not be denied that the "masses" are advancing in intelligence; few will doubt that they are equally advancing in good order and right feeling; those who are best acquainted with them give them credit for much sincerity and single-mindedness; and the writer of these pages feels himself both qualified and bound to ratify the opinion.

So far as the fitness of the people to elect is concerned, I cannot see that the whole body are more unqualified now, than the voters of pot-walling* boroughs were before the passing of the Reform Act: on the contrary, I conceive them far more qualified; but there are many prejudices on the subject. One is, that the right and expediency of universal suffrage has been advocated by the agitators called Chartists, on whose theory we shall have presently to speak. Now it is clear that a truth is not less a truth because it may be advanced by unacceptable persons, and in a somewhat noisy and tumultuous way. If it be a right that the elective franchise should be co-extensive with the population of this country, the question must be examined on its own grounds, and without reference to monster meetings or monster processions. Let us then consider the objections.—First. It is said that improper persons would be chosen as representatives, and that revolution and anarchy would speedily be the result of its adoption. Recent events in France are pointed out to our notice as a proof that the objection is a sound one, and as a specimen of what we may expect among ourselves. To this it may be answered: That the French people have universal suffrage forced upon them, that they had

---

* Pot-walling boroughs were boroughs in which every person who "boiled his own pot," that is, had a fireplace of his own, had a vote. Taunton was one of these, and I have yet to learn that the representatives of Taunton were other than fit men.

not been gradually educated up to an appreciation of and a desire for it; that the country had been misgoverned for centuries; that real liberty is even now imperfectly understood; and finally, that the result of the French revolution has been the re-establishment, by popular vote, of the empire.

On the other hand, may be cited the example of America; where, in many states, universal suffrage prevails, and where it is said to have no evil effects: and the example will be the more powerful as it is that of an Anglo-Saxon and a Protestant nation.

There appears to be no ground whatever to suppose that working men would necessarily elect representatives of their own condition in life, merely because they were so; they have never evinced any tendency in that direction: nor again does it follow that a man should be disqualified as a representative because he labours with his hands. There have been men in the House of Commons who rose from the plough, and there are men engaged in every kind of handicraft now, who would be bright lights in our national senate.

On the whole, the objections to universal suffrage seem to me to be few now, and to be rapidly decreasing. If it should seem the will of the people to adopt it, we may lay aside all fear of its effects; and if the popular mind be advancing in that direction, then the franchise should be gradually extended. But it will be needful to look at the conditions which must attend a change so great as conferring the right of election on every adult male. National education must be extended; for if the safety of the commonwealth be jeopardized by the folly of its rulers, there will be a necessity of universal education entailed on a state conceding universal suffrage. It will be observed that nothing has been said concerning bribery; and this for the simple reason that, however much the poverty and ignorance of some voters may lay them open to the temptation of receiving a bribe, the numbers of every constituency will render the plan impossible: a few hundreds may be bribed; many thousands cannot. In cases where a few votes may decide an election, the majority must be comparatively a very small one; then bribery might be practicable; but very little injury would be done to the popular decision: and, besides, such cases would be of extreme rarity. The bribery oath might perhaps be dispensed with, and all its attendant penalties be expunged from the statute book.

And here, as incidental to the subject, we may make a few observations on secret voting. It is universally agreed, even by the warmest supporters of the ballot, that open voting is more in accordance with the frankness and boldness of the English character. We have a natural dislike to do secretly what we have a right to do openly; and those who join vote by ballot with universal suffrage seem to forget that the latter will *remove* the evils which the former only professes to rectify: intimidation may prevail now that the comparatively small number of voters renders each vote of great value; but it would no longer be practised at all, when it would have to be exercised against thousands at once, in order to be effectual. I am much inclined to think that thousands would never exercise the franchise at all, were they compelled to vote by ballot, who would cheerfully and proudly *record their votes.* These are reasons, among many others, which induce me to consider ballot-voting unnecessary where universal suffrage prevails. How far it may be advisable in the present state of affairs, is another question. It does not, however, seem to command any thing like universal approbation; and if the tendency of the public mind be towards throwing the franchise open to all, every step in that direction will render the ballot-box less necessary, as well as less agreeable.

CHAPTER XVI.

OF RESTRICTIONS ON ELECTORS IN THE CHOICE OF REPRESENTATIVES.

GOVERNMENT has not only limited the qualifications of those who elect, but of those who are to be elected. If I live in lodgings in one town, I have a vote;—in another, I have none, though I may have both intelligence, learning, practical wisdom, and, what the world values much more, wealth. Three candidates offer themselves; one is an able, philosophical, and wealthy man, patriotic and benevolent, but he is a Jew; another has all the same qualifications, save wealth, but he is a poor gentlemen, and has no landed estate; another is possessed of all the Jew's advantages, and Christianity besides,—but, though he has no parish, no preferment of any kind, still he is a clergyman. I would like very much to choose one of the three; but they are all disqualified. Formerly the case was worse; but it is bad enough now. We no longer profane the sacrament, by forcing it upon deists and infidels; but we exhibit the narrowness and sectarian character of our religious notions all the same. We shall reserve to another chapter the consideration of religious tests, and discuss, in this, property and personal qualifications. The first is defended on the grounds that it secures for the public service men whose means have obtained for them a higher class of education, who are less susceptible of interested motives, and who will make their order respected by connecting it with a higher grade of society. If these be true, then let property qualifications stand by all means; but let the allegations be first carefully investigated. I. It secures, they say, men whose means have procured for them a higher class of education. This is not the case; the best-educated men in England are those prepared for the higher grades of the legal and medical professions; and it would be exquisitely absurd to say that these are in any large proportion qualified *by property* for Parliament. The son of the Duke, the heir of the country gentleman, who succeeds to his two or three hundred a year, the poor curate, the briefless barrister, the struggling physician, the son of the wealthy tradesman, all obtain precisely the same amount of education, in general: so that the class of education obtained seems very little to depend on the wealth of the party receiving it. Besides, the question is not, is a man with a landed estate likely to give his son a better education than a man without one? but, if two persons are candidates to represent me in Parliament, and I find one better qualified by education, and talent, and virtue, so far as I can judge, than the other, why am I prevented from giving him my vote because he has not a certain amount of property?

II. It is said, that the comparatively wealthy man is less susceptible of interested motives. This is a more transparent fallacy than the other: the experience of all ages shows us that it is far more easy to bribe a rich man than a poor one; the rich man has, for the most part, a much keener sense of the value of money; he may be bribed secretly: if the poor man becomes rich, the fact is presently known; if the rich man becomes richer, none knows it. Again, there is a much more extensive scale of bribes for the one than for the other; honours and titles, which would add to the weight and dignity of the rich, are but burdensome encumbrances to the poor. We say nothing of the cynical misanthropy of the maxim.

III. It is alleged that the rich man does honour to his order by allying it to a higher grade in society; a very good reason why some rich men should be in Parliament: that "*the higher classes,*" as some love to call them, may be represented; but no reason whatever that they *alone* should be represented. This it is, in fact, that causes so much discontent, so many complaints of "*class legislation,*" of attention to "*class interests.*" A national senate should be for all, and it is difficult to see any valid reason why it should not also be *of* all.

It does not therefore appear that the property

qualification fulfils any of the purposes for which it is said to be instituted; and, as it is a restriction at once on honourable ambition, and on freedom of choice in electors, there seems but little reason why it should be retained. Of professional restrictions there is but one: officers in the army and navy, medical men, barristers, solicitors, all seek and all find entrance into the great council of the nation. No reply is made to the military or naval candidate; there are forty or fifty, or more, lords of your profession; be content with their representation of your class: the barrister is not excluded from the House of Commons by the presence of the law-lords in the Upper House; but the clergyman alone is thus prevented from occupying a place for which he may be better qualified than a large portion of those who are elected. Why is this? It is not simply a religious feeling (if indeed this have anything to do with the question) which prompts this restriction. Dissenting ministers of every class are eligible, and some have been elected; but it seems that our present enactment is an "*ex-post-facto*" law, passed to mortify the electors of Middlesex, and to prevent John Horne Tooke from sitting in the House of Commons! It may be very necessary that a clergyman should reside in his parish, and doubtless is so; but we find no objection raised to the rector of a vast metropolitan parish, with a princely income, possessing also an almost equally rich canonry in a distant city.

He may be a chairman or director of half a dozen insurance and cemetery companies; he may be treasurer of innumerable charities, corporations, and may rarely be seen in his parish at all; or he may join all these things together in one mass of corrupt plurality, and may defy alike church and public; *these things are done in our own time;* alas! that it should be so! But if a clergyman, without parochial cares, with neither canonries nor offices to distract his attention, aspire to represent any portion of a Christian people in the senate of a Christian legislature, he is met with a restriction which not only prohibits the attempt, but prevents his engaging in any kind of secular occupation, and vitiates all in which he takes a part. Surely this hardship is not met by the mere fact that a "small number of ecclesiastics are placed in the House of Lords." A law might easily be devised against non-residence, which would render it necessary for a clergyman, elected as a representative of the people, to resign his parochial charge; and by such an enactment a real grievance would be removed, and a right restored at once to electors and representatives.

CHAPTER XVII.

OF THE DURATION OF REPRESENTATIVE ASSEMBLIES, AND OF THE PAYMENT OF REPRESENTATIVES.

THE question, "how long ought a representative assembly to retain its functions?" will depend partly on the extent of the franchise, and partly on the view taken of the representative character. An assembly chosen by a small body of electors may retain office for a long period with much less inconvenience than that which represents a large constituency; and an assembly of mere delegates would obviously be bound to render an account of their trust more frequently than one of a more philosophically representative character. In adjusting this query and its reply to *our own* constitution, we have to consider the two preliminary questions: what is the *theory* of the franchise in England, and what is the *theory* of the representative character. These two points being settled, it will become comparatively easy to ascertain the proper duration of a British Parliament.

Now the *theory* of the franchise is, that in the House of Commons the whole nation is directly or indirectly represented: all the defence of bye-gone corruption rested upon this theory. Such a man has no vote, it is true; but his interests are not forgotten, his *class* is not unprotected. Such a borough contains not a single inhabitant, but its burgesses do not the less represent a valuable and easily appreciable interest. Such a great town sends no members; but the greater weight and importance in the House of the county members, in whose election it has a share, make up to it for the supposed inequality. Thus, before the Reform Act, the fiction of the constitution was, that the House of Commons represented *all* the commons of England; from the peasant working for six or seven shillings a week, to the untitled landowner whose rent-roll might show a hundred thousand a year.

Universal representation then was supposed to exist just as fully as though universal suffrage prevailed; and it is therefore on this admission that we are to found the doctrine as to the duration of Parliament.

Universal representation, if it do not imply universal intelligence, implies, at least, wide-spread education; a capacity on the part of the people for self-government, and recognizes that self-government as their right; but as this very education and capacity is only consistent with an advancing state, no representation can be an accurate one which does not serve to mark the progress of the people: and the more rapid the progress, the more frequently should the genuine voice of the people be heard. If I am in a very stationary condition of mind, I may elect a man to represent me for seven years, with tolerable certainty that at the end of that time I shall entertain similar views to those which I now hold; but if my political opinions are in a state of transition, if every day adds to my knowledge of political philosophy, enlarges my grasp of principle, and widens the circle of my requirements, the great probability is, that, in electing a representative for seven years, I shall be soon worse than *un*represented—I shall be *mis*represented. There can be scarcely any question that in our day the whole people are in a state of transition, as regards their political feelings and political information; and that if they are to be fairly represented, a septennial parliament is too long for the purpose. The choice seems to be between triennial and annual parliaments; we may almost be said, practically speaking, to have triennial parliaments at present, for it rarely happens that a parliament reaches its full term; still we have not parliaments renewable, by the course of the constitution, every three years; and we may therefore take the two periods as alike open to speculation. The advocates of the longer term, whether it may be seven or three years, object—

I. That when a member had made himself acquainted with public business, the forms of the House, and the exigencies of the nation, he would be called upon to resign his seat, just as he had become useful.

II. That the shortness of the duration of parliament would not make it worth while for men of experience and importance to undertake the duties, to neglect or resign their own private business, and to lay themselves open to the requirements of a numerous and exacting constituency.

III. That it is highly inexpedient for an election to take place during times of effervescence and excited public feeling; that, as such periods are not unfrequent, a long duration of parliament is the best protection against the evils which would result from an election taking place at such a juncture: and,

IV. That, in the face of constant elections, members would be apt rather to calculate the chances of their own re-election than the requirements of the state; that popularity rather than utility would be their aim; and that they would become very soon mere delegates, and not representatives.

These reasons resolve themselves into: the experience of members; the quality of members; the freedom from party spirit of members; and the independence of members.

The advocates of short parliaments, on the other hand, dispute all these positions; for they say—

I. That a man known to be a man of business, sincere and incorruptible, would be chosen annually or triennially, again and again, as such men now are septennially; that no really able senator is long without a seat in the House; and that if a man be deficient either in ability or integrity, the sooner he be displaced, the better; and thus, that the securing men of parliamentary experience is by no means rendered more difficult, even by the limiting the duration of parliament to a single year.

II. That the second objection would follow the fate of the first; for as the re-election of members year after year would be the rule rather than the exception, a candidate would look on his seat as held for a series of years, so long as he wished to retain it, and fairly represented his constituency. The English people, it is observed, are not fickle, nor prone to desert old and tried friends; so that the shortening the duration of Parliament would keep away from the candidature only the corrupt and incapable.

III. It is admitted that an election is an evil, when popular feeling runs high and parties are exasperated, but the very institution of annual election would tend to calm the violence of such feeling, by opening frequent opportunities of expressing the public will: that as popular ferments are quite likely to occur once in seven years, as once every year, or every three years, so, it is contended, that a Parliament chosen under the influence of such ferment would be far more likely to be mischievous if it had seven years to last, than if its errors could be corrected by a new election in the course of twelve months.

IV. The last objection has been, it is thought, answered by anticipation; and besides, the weight of personal character is no where so great as in England: the man who merely flattered transient prejudices would have comparatively little chance against him whose judgment was respected and whose integrity had been tried.

We come now to the *theory* of the representative character as we find it developed in the British constitution; and it will be amply sufficient to show the rigidness of the laws against bribery, the restrictions which hem in on every side the means of entering Parliament, the property and religious qualifications, and the comparatively small number of those to whom the franchise has been committed, to show that the member of Parliament never has been regarded as a mere *delegate*. He is strictly, and in the highest sense of the word, a *representative*. As such, it is desirable—nay, necessary—that he be a man of sound mind and honorable character; and hence the restrictions, wise or unwise, about which we have been speaking.

The balance of these arguments would incline us to the opinion that *if* the will of the nation were expressed in favour of annual Parliaments, there would be little, if any, danger in the experiment, and much in withholding from the people that which they have a right to demand.

Whether the representatives of the people should be paid for their services, or whether parliamentary labours should be purely honorary, is a question which stands upon a somewhat different footing, and the consequences of such an arrangement are differently represented, according to the political bias of those who make it the subject of discussion.

It is admitted on all hands, that, if a property qualification be no longer required from persons seeking to be representatives, many well-qualified persons may offer themselves who *cannot* give their services; and it may be that among those who are thus situated the most able and suitable candidate may be found. The question then becomes reduced to a small compass: is the nation to lose the benefit of his presence in the legislative body, for want of the power to render a suitable remuneration for his services?

This appears to be the sole necessity of the case. The arguments on the other side, though perhaps not more weighty, are at all events more numerous. We have men now in the House of Commons who are engaged actively in commercial pursuits: bankers, mill-owners, manufacturers, merchants, shop-keepers. We have men of every profession; none of these give up, few relax, their professional or commercial pursuits because the business of the nation at large is cast upon their shoulders. As, therefore, *the leisure* of men engaged in business has been found sufficient for public affairs, so far as the House of Commons is concerned, why should not such leisure be sufficient still? Moreover, it is not those who talk most in the House, who do the business of it. But again, if representatives were paid, there can be no doubt that there would be a vastly greater number of candidates, and that of these a considerable proportion would be seeking the honors of the senate, for the sake of gain. This in itself would be an evil; but a still greater one would accrue from the reluctance which many high and honorable men would feel to undertake the duties of representation. At present there is a reciprocity at once creditable and pleasing to both the elector and the elected: an exchange, on the one side, of patriotic labour; on the other, of confidence and respect. Let that labour be paid for in any other coin, and the representative becomes a delegate; the member, a servant, not in the high and noble sense in which the term *may* be applied, but liable to be called to an account for receiving money under false pretences, if his deliberate opinion should be, or become, different from that of his constituents.

It is quite true that a member thus paid might distribute in charities among his constituents the salary he received as their representative; and this has been thought a sufficient answer to the objection: but it must be observed—first, that if this rule became general, the payment of representatives would become merely an offensive fiction; and if it did not, those who adopted it would be at once reproaching the laws, and most unfairly bringing odium upon members not able to follow the same example.

I pass over the objection on the ground of public expense; for a small registration fee would at once defray this, and answer many useful purposes besides.

On the whole, the reasons against the payment of representatives would seem considerably to outweigh those in its favour. If universal suffrage, annual parliaments, and the abolition of all restrictions, save those absolutely necessary, and which have been already indicated, be not sufficient guarantees for the legislature attending to the interests of the people at large, it is difficult to see how the measure now under consideration can add to their efficacy. Yet, as the form of government best adapted for a free people is not so much that which is intrinsically the most excellent, as that most in accordance with their own views of necessity,—so it must be said, concerning the payment of representatives, that, should it ever become the decided will of the people, more evil would follow the refusing than the acceding to it.

BOOK II.

OF LAW AND JUSTICE.

CHAPTER I.

OF THE ADMINISTRATION OF JUSTICE.

The first maxim of a free state is, that the laws be made by one set of men, and administered by another; in other words, that the legislative and judicial characters be kept separate. When these offices are united in the same person or assembly, particular laws are made for particular cases, springing oftentimes from partial motives, and directed to private ends; whilst they are kept separate, general laws are made by one body of men, without foreseeing whom they may affect; and, when made, must be applied by the other, let them affect whom they will.

For the sake of illustration, let it be supposed, in this country, either that, Parliament being laid aside, the Courts of Westminster Hall made their own laws, or that the two Houses of Parliament, with the Sovereign at their head, tried and decided causes at their bar. It is evident, in the first place, that the decisions of such a judicature would be so many laws; and, in the second place, that, when the parties and the interests to be affected by the law were known, the inclinations of the law-makers would inevitably attach on one side or the other; and that, where there were neither any fixed rules to regulate their determinations, nor any superior power to control their proceedings, these inclinations would interfere with the integrity of public justice. The consequence of which must be, that the subjects of such a constitution would live either without any constant laws—that is, without any known pre-established rules of adjudication whatever, or under laws made for particular cases and particular persons, and partaking of the contradictions and iniquity of the motives to which they owed their origin.

Which dangers, by the division of the legislative and judicial functions, are effectually provided against. Parliament knows not the individuals upon whom its acts will operate; it has no cases or parties before it; no private designs to serve: consequently its resolutions will be suggested by the consideration of universal effects and tendencies, which always produces impartial, and commonly advantageous, regulations. When laws are made, courts of justice must abide by them; for the legislative being necessarily the supreme power of the state, the judicial, and every other power, is accountable to that: and it cannot be doubted but that the persons who possess the sovereign authority of government will be tenacious of the laws which they themselves prescribe, and sufficiently jealous of the assumption of dispensing any legislative power by any others.

This fundamental rule of civil jurisprudence is violated in the case of acts of attainder or confiscation, in bills of pains and penalties, and in all *ex-post-facto* laws whatever, in which Parliament exercises the double office of legislature and judge. And whoever either understands the value of the rule itself, or collects the history of those instances in which it has been invaded, will be induced, I believe, to acknowledge that it had been wiser and safer never to have departed from it. He will confess, at least, that nothing but the most manifest and immediate peril of the commonwealth will justify a repetition of these dangerous examples. If the laws in being do not punish an offender, let him go unpunished; let the legislature, admonished of the defect of the laws, provide against the commission of future crimes of the same sort. The escape of one delinquent can never produce so much harm to the community as may arise from the infraction of a rule upon which the purity of public justice and the existence of civil liberty essentially depend.

The next security for the impartial administration of justice, especially in decisions in which government is a party, is the independence of the judges. As protection against every illegal attack upon the rights of the subject by the servants of the crown is to be sought for from these tribunals, the judges of the land become not unfrequently the arbitrators between the king and the people; on which account, they ought to be independent of either; or, what is the same thing, equally dependent upon both; that is, if they be appointed by the one, they should be removable only by the other. This was the policy which dictated that memorable improvement in our constitution by which the judges, who, before the Revolution, held their offices during the pleasure of the king, can now only be deprived of them by an address from both Houses of Parliament, as the most regular, solemn, and authentic way by which the dissatisfaction of the people can be expressed.

There is one very peculiar anomaly in the English constitution with regard to this principle. It is that the chief judge, the Lord Chancellor, is necessarily a political partisan, and is changed with every ministry. He is, *ex-officio*, a member of the Cabinet, and Speaker in the House of Lords. This deviation from the rule observed in other cases seems to have no advantage to counterbalance its many mischievous consequences. The duties thrown on the shoulders of one man are too onerous to be satisfactorily fulfilled; the proceedings in the Court of Chancery are proverbially slow, and the interest of suitors, in the most important cases, is not unfrequently made dependent upon political changes with which neither suit nor suitor can have anything to do. It may, and not unfrequently does, happen, that just when a chancellor has made himself master of the details of some intricate cause, an adverse majority in the House of Commons on some commercial or financial question, a rupture, or apprehended rupture with some foreign power, may occasion a change of ministry, and the chancellor goes out of office; the judgment is not pronounced; a new judge is appointed, who has all the labour of investigating the case over again, and the least evil that can happen is unnecessary and often enormous delay. But, besides this, however well the choice may be made, there is an obvious impropriety in selecting a judge for any other than judicial qualifications; and no one who is in the slightest degree aware of the vast interests involved in chancery decisions, can doubt the necessity of a Lord Chancellor being able to bestow his whole time and learning on the business of his own court. This anomaly will, in all probability, soon cease to exist.

To make the independency of the judges complete, the public salaries of their office ought not only to be certain, both in amount and continuance, but so liberal as to secure their integrity from the temptation of secret bribes: which liberality will answer also the further purpose of preserving their jurisdiction from contempt, and their characters from suspicion; as well as of rendering the station worthy of the ambition of men of eminence in their profession.

A third precaution to be observed in the formation of courts of justice is, that the number of the judges be small. For, besides that the violence and tumult inseparable from large assemblies are inconsistent with the patience, method, and attention, requisite in judicial investigations; besides that all passions and prejudices act with augmented force upon a collected multitude; besides these objections, judges, when they are numerous, *divide* the shame of an unjust determination: they shelter themselves under one another's example; each man thinks his own character hid in the crowd; for which reason, the judges ought always to be so few, as that the conduct of each may be conspicuous to public observation; that each may be responsible in his separate and particular reputation for the decisions in which he concurs. The truth of the above remark has been exemplified in this country, in the effects of that wise regulation which transferred the trial of parliamentary elections from the House of Commons at large, to a select committee of that house, composed of thirteen members. This alteration, simply by reducing the number of judges, and, in consequence of that reduction, exposing the judicial conduct of each to public animadversion, has given to a judicature, which had long been swayed by interest and solicitation, the solemnity and virtue of the most upright tribunals. I should prefer an even to an odd number of judges, and four to almost any other number; for in this number, besides that it sufficiently consults the idea of separate responsibility, nothing can be decided but by a majority of three to one; and when we consider that every decision establishes a perpetual precedent, we shall allow that it ought to proceed from an authority not less than this. If the court be equally divided, nothing is done; things remain as they were; with some inconvenience indeed to the parties, but without the danger to the public of a hasty precedent.

A fourth requisite in the constitution of a court of justice, and equivalent to many checks upon the discretion of judges, is, that its proceedings be carried on in public, *apertis foribus;* not only before a promiscuous concourse of by-standers, but in the audience of the whole profession of the law. The opinion of the bar concerning what passes will be impartial, and will commonly guide that of the public. The most corrupt judge will fear to indulge his dishonest wishes in the presence of such an assembly; he must encounter, what few can support, the censure of his equals and companions, together with the indignation and reproaches of his country.

Something is also gained to the public by appointing two or three courts of concurrent jurisdiction, that it may remain in the option of the suitor to which he will resort. By this means a tribunal which may happen to be occupied by ignorant or suspected judges will be deserted for others that possess more of the confidence of the nation.

But, lastly, if several courts, co-ordinate to and independent of each other, subsist together in the country, it seems necessary that the appeals from all of them should meet and terminate in the same judicature; in order that one supreme tribunal, by whose final sentence all others are bound and concluded, may superintend and preside over the rest. This constitution is necessary for two purposes: to preserve an uniformity in the decisions of inferior courts, and to maintain to each the proper limits of its jurisdiction. Without a common superior, different courts might establish contradictory rules of adjudication, and the contradiction be final and without remedy; the same question might receive opposite determinations according as it was brought before one court or another, and the determination in each be ultimate and irreversible. A common appellant jurisdiction prevents or puts an end to this confusion. For when the judgments upon appeals are consistent (which may be expected, whilst it is the same court which is at last resorted to), the different courts from which the appeals are brought will be reduced to a like consistency with one another. Moreover, if questions arise between courts independent of each other, concerning the extent and boundaries of their respective jurisdiction, as each will be desirous of enlarging its own, an authority which both acknowledge can alone adjust the controversy. Such a power, therefore, must reside somewhere, lest the rights and repose of the country be distracted by the endless opposition and mutual encroachments of the courts of justice.

CHAPTER II.

OF MODES OF JUDICATURE.

There are two kinds of judicature: the one where the office of the judge is permanent in the same person, and consequently where the judge is appointed and known long before the trial; the other, where the judge is determined by lot at the time of the trial, and for that turn only. The one may be called a *fixed*, the other a *casual*, judicature. From the former may be expected those qualifications which are preferred and sought for in the choice of judges, and that knowledge and readiness which result from experience in the office. But then, as the judge is known before hand, he is accessible to the parties; there exists a possibility of secret management and undue practices; or, in contests between the crown and the subject, the judge appointed by the crown may be suspected of partiality to his patron, or of entertaining inclinations favorable to the authority from which he derives his own. The advantages attending the second kind of judicature, is indifferency; the defect, the want of that legal science which produces uniformity and justice in legal decisions. The construction of English courts of law, in which causes are tried by a jury, with the assistance of a judge, combines the two species with peculiar success. This admirable contrivance unites the wisdom of a fixed with the integrity of a casual judicature; and avoids, in a great measure, the inconveniences of both. The judge imparts to the jury the benefit of his erudition and experience; the jury, by their disinterestedness, check any corrupt partialities which previous application may have produced in the judge. If the determination were left to the judge, the party might suffer under the superior interest of his adversary; if it were left to an uninstructed jury, his rights would be in still greater danger, from the ignorance of those who were to decide upon them. The present wise admixture of chance and choice in the constitution of the court in which his cause is tried, guards him equally against the fear of injury from either of these causes.

In proportion to the acknowledged excellence of this mode of trial, every deviation from it ought to be watched with vigilance, and admitted by the legislature with caution and reluctance. Summary convictions before justices of the peace, especially for offences against the game laws; courts of conscience; extending the jurisdiction of courts of equity; urging too far the distinction between questions of law and matters of fact; are all so many infringements upon this great charter of public safety.

Nevertheless, the trial by jury is sometimes found inadequate to the administration of equal justice. This imperfection takes place chiefly in disputes in which some popular passion or prejudice intervenes; as where a particular order of men advance claims upon the rest of the community; which is the case of the clergy contending for tithes: or where an order of men are obnoxious by their profession, as are officers of the revenue, bailiffs, bailiffs' followers, and other low ministers of the law: or where one of the parties has an interest in common with the general interest of the jurors, and that of the other is opposed to it; as in contests between landlords and tenants, between lords of manors and the holders of estates under them: or, lastly, where the minds of men are inflamed by political dissensions or religious hatred. These prejudices act most powerfully upon the common people, of which order juries are made up. The force and danger of them are also increased by the very circumstance of taking juries out of the county in which the subject of dispute arises. In the neighbourhood of the parties, the cause is often prejudged; and these secret decisions of the mind proceed commonly more upon sentiments of favour or hatred,— upon some opinion concerning the sect, family, profession, character, connexions, or circumstances of the parties,—than upon any knowledge or discussion of the proper merits of the question. More exact justice would, in many instances, be rendered to the suitors, if the determination were left entirely to the judges; provided we could depend upon the same purity of conduct, when the power of these magistrates was enlarged, which they have long manifested in the exercise of a mixed and restrained authority. But this is an experiment too big with public danger to be hazarded. The effects, however, of some local prejudices might be safely obviated by a law empowering the court, in which the action is brought, to send the cause to trial in a distant county; the expenses attending the change of place always falling upon the party who applied for it.

There is a second division of courts of justice which presents a new alternative of difficulties. Either one, two, or a few sovereign courts may be erected in the metropolis, for the whole kingdom to resort to; or courts of local jurisdiction may be fixed in various provinces and districts of the empire. Great, though opposite, inconveniences attend each arrangement. If the court be remote and solemn, it becomes by these very qualities expensive and dilatory: the expense is unavoidably increased, when witnesses, parties, and agents must be brought to attend from distant parts of the country; and where the whole judicial business of a large nation is collected into a few superior tribunals, it will be found impossible, even if the prolixity of forms which retards the progress of causes were removed, to give a prompt hearing to every complaint, or an immediate answer to any. On the other hand, if, to remedy these evils, and to render the administration of justice cheap and speedy, domestic and summary tribunals be erected in each neighbourhood, the advantage of such courts will be accompanied with all the dangers of ignorance and partiality, and with the certain mischief of confusion and contrariety in their decisions. The law of England, by its circuit or itinerary courts, contains a provision for the distribution of private justice in a great measure relieved from both these objections. As the presiding magistrate comes into the country a stranger to its prejudices, rivalships, and connexions, he brings with him none of those attachments and regards which are so apt to pervert the cause of justice when the parties and the judges inhabit the same neighbourhood. Again, as this magistrate is usually one of the judges of the supreme tribunals of the kingdom, and has passed his life in the study and administration of the laws, he possesses, it may be presumed, those professional qualifications which befit the dignity and importance of his station. Lastly, as both he and the advocates who accompany him in his circuit are employed in the business of these superior courts (to which also their proceedings are amenable), they will naturally conduct themselves by the rules of adjudication which they have applied or learned there; and by this means maintain, what constitutes a principal perfection of civil government, one law of the land in every part and district of the empire.

Next to the constitution of courts of justice, we are naturally led to consider the maxims which ought to guide their proceedings; and, upon this subject, the chief inquiry will be, how far and for what reasons it is expedient to adhere to former determinations; or whether it be necessary for judges to attend to any other consideration than the apparent and particular equity of the case before them. Now, although to assert that precedents established by one set of judges ought to be incontrovertible by their successors in the same jurisdiction, or by those who exercise a higher, would be to attribute to the sentence of these judges all the authority we ascribe to the most solemn acts of the legislature: yet the general security of private rights and of civil life requires that such precedents, especially if they have been confirmed by repeated adjudications, should not be overthrown without a detection of manifest error, or without some imputation of dishonesty upon the court by whose judgment the question was first decided. And this deference to prior decisions is founded upon two reasons: first, that the discretion of judges may be bound down by positive rules; and, secondly, that the subject, upon every occasion in which his legal interest is concerned, may know before hand how to act, and what to expect. To set judges free from any obligation to conform themselves to the decisions of their predecessors, would be to lay open a latitude of judging with which no description of men can safely be entrusted; it would be to allow space for the exercise of those concealed partialities which, since they cannot by any human policy be excluded, ought to be confined by boundaries and land-marks. It is in vain to allege that the superintendency of Parliament is always at hand to control and punish abuses of judicial discretion. By what rules can Parliament proceed? How shall they pronounce a decision to be wrong, where there exists no acknowledged measure or standard of what is right; which, in a multitude of instances, would be the case, if prior determinations were no longer to be appealed to?

Diminishing the danger of partiality is one thing gained by adhering to precedents, but not the principal thing. The subject of every system of laws must expect that decision in his own case which he knows that others have derived in cases similar to his. If he expect not this, he can expect nothing. There exists no other rule or principle of reasoning, by which he can foretell, or even conjecture, the event of a judicial contest. To remove, therefore, the grounds of this expectation, by rejecting the force and authority of precedents, is to entail upon the subject the worst property of slavery; to have no assurance of his rights, or knowledge of his duty. The quiet also of the country, as well as the confidence and satisfaction of each man's mind, requires uniformity in judicial proceedings. Nothing quells a spirit of litigation like despair of success; therefore nothing so completely puts an end to law suits as a rigid adherence to known rules of adjudication. Whilst the event is uncertain, which it ever must be, whilst it is uncertain whether former determinations upon the same subject will be followed or not, law suits will be endless and innumerable; men will continually engage in them, either from the hope of prevailing in their claims, which the smallest chance is sufficient to encourage; or with the design of intimidating their adversary by the terrors of a dubious litigation. When justice is rendered to the parties, only half the business of a court of justice is done; the more important part of its office remains; to put an end, for the future, to every fear, and quarrel, and expense upon the same point, and so to regulate its proceedings, that not only a doubt once decided may be stirred no more, but that the whole train of law suits which issue from one uncertainty may die with the parent question. Now, this advantage can only be attained by considering each decision as a direction to succeeding judges. And it should be observed, that every departure from former determinations, especially if they have been often repeated or long submitted to, shakes the stability of all legal title. It is not fixing a point anew; it is leaving every thing unfixed. For by the same stretch of power by which the present race of judges take upon them to contradict the judgment of their predecessors, those who try the question next may set aside theirs.

From an adherence however to precedents, by which so much is gained to the public, two consequences arise which are often lamented; the hardship of particular determinations, and the intricacy of the law as a science. To the first of these complaints we must apply this reflection: "That uniformity is of more "importance than equity, in proportion as a general "uncertainty would be a greater evil than particular "injustice." The second is attended with no greater inconveniency than that of erecting the practice of the law into a separate profession, which this reason, we allow, makes necessary; for if we attribute so much authority to precedents, it is expedient that they be known, in every cause, *both to the advocates and to the judge;* this knowledge cannot be general, since it is the fruit oftentimes of laborious research, or demands a *memory stored with long-collected erudition.*

CHAPTER III.

OF THE NECESSITY FOR LEGAL ENACTMENTS.

To a mind resolving upon the subject of human jurisprudence, there frequently occurs this question: Why, since the maxims of natural justice are few and evident, do there arise so many doubts and controversies in their application? Or, in other words, how comes it to pass, that, although the principles of the law of Nature be simple, and for the most part sufficiently obvious, there should exist, nevertheless, in every system of municipal laws, and in the actual administration of relative justice, numerous uncertainties and acknowledged difficulty? Whence, it may be asked, so much room for litigation, and so many subsisting disputes, if the rules of human duty be neither obscure nor dubious? If a system of morality, containing both the precepts of revelation and the deductions of reason, may be comprised within the compass of one moderate volume, and the moralist be able, as he pretends, to describe the rights and obligations of mankind, in all the different relations they may hold to one another; what need of those codes of positive and particular institutions, of those tomes of statutes and reports, which require the employment of a long life even to peruse? And this question is immediately connected with the argument which has been discussed in the preceding chapter; for, unless there be found some greater uncertainty in the law of nature, or what may be called natural equity, when it comes to be applied to real cases and to actual adjudication, than what appears in the rules and principles of the science, as delivered in the writings of those who treat of the subject, it were better that the determination of every cause should be left to the conscience of the judge, unfettered by precedents and authorities; since the very purpose for which these are introduced is to give a certainty to judicial proceedings, which such proceedings would want without them.

Now, to account for the existence of so many sources of litigation, notwithstanding the clearness and perfection of natural justice, it should be observed, in the first place, that treatises of morality always suppose facts to be ascertained; and not only so; but the intention likewise of the parties to be known and laid bare. For example, when we pronounce that promises ought to be fulfilled in that sense in which the promiser apprehended at the time of making the promise, the other party received and understood it; the apprehension of one side, and the expectation of the other, must be discovered, before this rule can be reduced to practice, or applied to the determination of any actual dispute. Wherefore the discussion of facts which the moralist supposes to be settled, the discovery of intentions which he presumes to be known, still remain to exercise the inquiry of courts of justice. And as these facts and intentions are often to be inferred, or rather conjectured, from obscure indications, from suspicious testimony, or from a comparison of opposite and contending probabilities, they afford a never-failing supply of doubt and litigation. For which reason, the science of morality is to be considered rather as a direction to the parties who are conscious of their own thoughts, and motives, and designs, to which consciousness the teacher of morality constantly appeals, than as a guide to the judge, or to any third person, whose arbitration must proceed upon rules of evidence and maxims of credibility, with which the moralist has no concern. Secondly, there exist a multitude of cases in which the law of nature, that is, the law of public expediency, prescribes nothing, except that some certain rule be adhered to, and that the rule actually established be preserved; it either being indifferent what rule obtains, or, out of many rules, no one being so much more advantageous than the rest, as to recompense the inconveniency of an alteration. In all such cases, the law of Nature sends us to the law of the land. She directs that either some fixed rule be introduced by an act of the legislature, or that the rule which accident, or custom, or common consent hath already established, be steadily maintained. Thus, in the descent of lands, or the inheritance of personals from intestate proprietors, whether the kindred of the grandmother or of the great-grandmother shall be preferred in the succession; whether the degrees of consanguinity shall be computed through the common ancestor, or from him; whether the widow shall take a third or a moiety of her husband's fortune; whether sons shall be preferred to daughters, or the elder to the younger; whether the distinction of age shall be regarded amongst sisters, as well as between brothers; in these, and in a great variety of questions which the same subject supplies, the law of Nature determines nothing. The only answer she returns to our inquiries, is that some certain and general rule be laid down by public authority; be obeyed when laid down; and that the quiet of the country be not disturbed, nor the expectation of heirs frustrated, by capricious innovations.

This silence, or neutrality of the law of Nature, which we have exemplified in the case of intestacy, holds concerning a great part of the questions that relate to the right or acquisition of property. Recourse then must necessarily be had to statutes, or precedents, or usage, to fix what the law of Nature has left loose. The interpretation of these statutes, the search after precedents, the investigation of customs, compose therefore an unavoidable, and at the same time a large and intricate, portion of forensic business. Positive constitutions or judicial authorities are, in like manner, wanted to give precision to many things which are in their nature *indeterminate*. The age of legal discretion; at what time of life a person shall be deemed competent to the performance of any act which may bind his property; whether at twenty or twenty-one, or earlier, or later, or at some point of time between these years; can only be ascertained by a positive rule of the society to which the party belongs. The line has not been drawn by Nature; the human understanding advancing to maturity by insensible degrees, and its progress varying in different individuals. Yet it is necessary, for the sake of mutual security, that a precise age be fixed, and that what is fixed be known to all. It is on these occasions that the intervention of law supplies the inconstancy of Nature. Again, there are other things which are perfectly *arbitrary*, and capable of no certainty but what is given to them by positive regulation. It is fit that a limited time should be assigned to defendants to plead to the complaints alleged against them; and also that the default of pleading within a certain time should be taken for a confession of the charge: but to how many days or months that term should be extended, though necessary to be known with certainty, cannot be known at all by any information which the law of Nature affords. And the same remark seems applicable to almost all those rules of proceeding which constitute what is called the practice of the court: as they cannot be traced out by reasoning, they must be settled by authority.

Thirdly.—In contracts, whether express or implied, which involve a great number of conditions; as in those which are entered into between masters and servants, principles and agents; many also of merchandize, or works of art; in some likewise which relate to the negotiation of money or bills, or to the acceptance of credit or security; the original design and expectation of the parties was, that both sides should be guided by the course and custom of the country in transactions of the same sort. Consequently, when these contracts come to be disputed, natural justice can only refer to that custom. But as such customs are not always sufficiently uniform or notorious, but often to be collected from the production and comparison of instances and accounts repugnant to one another; and each custom being only that, after all, which, amongst a variety of usages, seems to predominate; we have *here* also ample room for doubt and contest.

Fourthly.—As the law of Nature, founded on the very construction of human society, which, formed to endure through a series of perishing generations, requires that the just engagements a man enters into should continue in force beyond his own life, it follows that the private rights of persons frequently depend upon what has been transacted, in times remote from the present, by their ancestors or predecessors, by those under whom they claim, or to whose obligations they have succeeded. Thus the questions which usually arise between lords of manors and their tenants, between the king and those who claim royal franchises, or between them and the persons affected by these franchises, depend upon the terms of the original grant. In like manner, every dispute concerning tithes, in which an exemption or composition is pleaded, depends upon the agreement which took place between the predecessor of the claimant and the ancient owner of the land. The appeal to these grants and agreements is dictated by natural equity, as well as by the municipal law: but concerning the existence, or the conditions, of such old covenants, doubts will perpetually occur, to which the law of Nature affords no solution. The loss or decay of records, the perishableness of living memory, the corruption and carelessness of tradition, all conspire to multiply uncertainties upon this head: what cannot be produced and proved, must be left to loose and fallible presumption. Under the same head may be included another topic of altercation—the tracing out of boundaries, which time, or neglect, or unity of possession, or mixture of occupation, has founded or obliterated. To which should be added, a difficulty which often presents itself in disputes concerning rights of *way*, both public and private, and of those easements which one man claims in another man's property; namely, that of distinguishing, after a lapse of years, the use of an indulgence from the exercise of a right.

Fifthly.—The quantity and extent of an injury, even when the cause and author of it are known, is often dubious and undefined. If the injury consist in the loss of some specific right, the value of the right measures the amount of the injury: but what a man may have suffered in his person from an assault, in his reputation by slander, or in the comfort of his life by the seduction of a wife or daughter, or what sum of money shall be deemed a reparation for damages such as these, cannot be ascertained by any rules which the law of Nature supplies. The law of Nature commands that reparation be made; and adds to her command, that, when the aggressor and the sufferer disagree, the damage be assessed by authorized and indifferent arbitrators. Here, then, recourse must be had to courts of law, not only with the permission, but in some measure by the direction, of natural justice.

Sixthly.—When controversies arise in the interpretation of written laws, they for the most part arise upon some contingency which the composer of the law did not foresee or think of. In the adjudication of such cases, this dilemma presents itself: if the laws be permitted to operate only upon the cases which were actually contemplated by the law-makers, they will always be found defective; if they be extended to every case to which the reasoning, and spirit, and expediency of the provision seem to belong, without any farther evidence of the intention of the legislature, we shall allow to the judges a liberty of applying the law, which will fall very little short of the power of making it. If a literal construction be adhered to, the law will often fail of its end; if a loose and vague exposition be admitted, the law might as well have never been enacted; for this licence will bring back into the subject all the discretion and uncertainty which it was the design of the legislature to take away. Courts of justice are, and always must be, embarrassed by these opposite difficulties; and, as it never can be known beforehand in what degree either consideration may prevail in the mind of the judge, there remains an unavoidable cause of doubt, and a place for contention.

Seventhly.—The deliberations of courts of justice upon every *new* question are encumbered with additional difficulties, in consequence of the authority which the judgment of the court possesses as a precedent to future judicatures; which authority appertains not only to the conclusions the court delivers, but to the principles and arguments upon which they are built. The view of this effect makes it necessary for a judge to look beyond the case before him; and, beside the attention he owes to the truth and justice of the cause between the parties, to reflect whether the principles, and maxims, and reasoning, which he adopts and authorizes, can be applied with safety to all cases which admit of a comparison with the present. The decision of the cause, were the effects of the decision to stop there, might be easy; but the consequence of establishing the principle which such a decision assumes, may be difficult, though of the utmost importance, to be foreseen and regulated.

Finally.—After all the certainty and rest that can be given to points of law, either by the interposition of the legislature, or the authority of precedents, one principal source of disputation, and into which indeed the greater part of legal controversies may be resolved, will remain still; namely, " the competition of oppo-" site analogies." When a point of law has been once adjudged, neither that question, nor any which completely and in all its circumstances corresponds with *that*, can be brought a second time into dispute: but questions arise which resemble this only indirectly and in part, in certain views and circumstances, and which may seem to bear an equal or a greater affinity to other adjudged cases; questions which can be brought within any fixed rule only by analogy, and which hold a relation by analogy to different rules. It is by the urging of the different analogies that the contention of the bar is carried on: and it is in the comparison, adjustment, and reconciliation of them with one another; in the discerning of such distinctions; and in the framing of such a determination as may either save the various rules alleged in the cause, or, if that be impossible, may give up the weaker analogy to the stronger; that the sagacity and wisdom of the court are seen and exercised. Amongst a thousand instances of this, we may cite one of general notoriety, in the contest that has lately been agitated concerning literary property. The personal industry which an author expends upon the composition of his work, bears so near a resemblance to that by which every other kind of property is earned, or deserved, or acquired; or rather there exists such a correspondence between what is created by the study of a man's mind and the production of his labour in any other way of applying it; that he seems entitled to the same exclusive, assignable, and perpetual right in both; and that right to the same protection of law. This was the analogy contended for on one side. On the other hand, a book, as to the author's right in it, appears similar to an invention of art; as a machine, an engine, a medicine: and since the law permits these to be copied, or imitated, except where an exclusive use or sale is reserved to the inventor by patent, the same liberty should be allowed in the publication and sale of books. This was the analogy maintained by the advocates of an open trade. And the competition of these opposite analogies constituted the difficulty of the case, as far as the same was argued, or adjudged, upon principles of common law. One example may serve to illustrate our meaning; but whoever takes up a volume of Reports, will find most of the arguments it contains capable of the same analysis; although the analogies, it must be confessed, are sometimes so entangled as not to be easily unravelled or even perceived.

Doubtful and obscure points of law are not, however, nearly so numerous as they are apprehended to be. Out of the multitude of causes which, in the course of each year, are brought to trial in the metropolis, or upon the circuits, there are few in which any point is reserved for the judgment of superior courts. Yet these few contain all the doubts with which the law is chargeable; for, as to the rest, the uncertainty, as hath been shown above, is not in the law, but in the means of human information.

CHAPTER IV.

OF CERTAIN ANOMALIES IN OUR JUDICIAL SYSTEM.

There are two peculiarities in the judicial constitution of this country which do not carry with them that evidence of their propriety which recommends almost every other part of the system. The first of these is the rule which requires that juries be *unanimous* in their verdicts. To expect that twelve men, taken by lot out of a promiscuous multitude, should agree in their opinion upon points confessedly dubious, and upon which oftentimes the wisest judgments might be held in suspense; or to suppose that any real *unanimity*, or change of opinion, in the dissenting jurors, could be procured by confining them until they all consented to the same verdict, bespeaks more of the conceit of a barbarous age, than of the policy which could dictate such an institution as that of juries. Nevertheless, the effects of this rule are not so detrimental as the rule itself is unreasonable. In criminal prosecutions, it operates considerably in favour of the prisoner; for, if a juror find it necessary to surrender to the obstinacy of others, he will much more readily resign his opinion on the side of mercy than of condemnation: in civil suits, it adds weight to the direction of the judge; for, when a conference with one another does not seem likely to produce, in the jury, the agreement that is necessary, they will naturally close their disputes by a common submission to the opinion delivered from the bench. However, there seems to be less of the concurrence of separate judgments in the same conclusion, consequently less assurance that the conclusion is founded in reasons of apparent truth and justice, than if the decision were left to a plurality, or to some certain majority of voices.

The second circumstance in our constitution, which, however it may succeed in practice, does not seem to have been suggested by an intelligible fitness in the nature of the thing, is the choice that is made of the House of Lords as a court of appeal from every civil court of judicature in the kingdom; and the last also and highest appeal to which the subject can resort. There appears to be nothing in the constitution of that assembly; in the education, habits, character, or professions, of the members who compose it; in the mode of their appointment, or the right by which they succeed to their places in it; that should qualify them for this arduous office; except, perhaps, that the elevation of their rank and fortune affords a security against the offer and influence of small bribes. Officers of the army and navy, courtiers, ecclesiastics; young men who have just attained the age of twenty-one, and who have passed their youth in the dissipation and pursuits which commonly accompany the possession or inheritance of great fortunes; country gentleman, occupied in the management of their estates, or in the care of their domestic concerns and family interests; the greater part of the assembly born to their station, that is, placed in it by chance; most of the rest advanced to the *peerage* for *services*, and *from motives* utterly *unconnected with legal erudition:* these men compose the tribunal to which the constitution intrusts the interpretation of her laws, and the ultimate decision of every dispute between her subjects. These are men assigned *to review* judgments of law, pronounced by *sages of the profession*, who have spent their lives in the study and practice of the jurisprudence of their country. Such is the order which our ancestors have established. The effect only proves the truth of this maxim: "That " when a single institution is extremely dissonant from " other parts of the system to which it belongs, it will " always find some way of reconciling itself to the " analogy which governs and pervades the rest." By constantly placing in the House of Lords some of the most eminent and experienced lawyers in the kingdom; by calling to their aid the advice of the judges, when any abstract question of law awaits their determination; by the almost implicit and undisputed deference which the *uninformed* part of the House find it necessary to pay to *the learning* of their colleagues, the appeal to the House of Lords becomes in fact an appeal to the collected wisdom of our supreme courts of justice; receiving indeed solemnity, but little perhaps of direction, from the presence of the assembly in which it is heard and determined*.

These, however, even if real, are minute imperfections. A politician, who should sit down to delineate a plan for the dispensation of public justice, guarded against all access to influence and corruption, and bringing together the separate advantages of knowledge and impartiality, would find, when he had done, that he had been transcribing the judicial constitution of England. And it may teach the most *discontented* amongst us to *acquiesce in the govern-*

---

* The arguments of Paley would be of weight, were it not for an anomaly mentioned in Chapter I of this book, with regard to the office of the Lord Chancellor as speaker of the House of Lords. In the case of an appeal from the Court of Chancery to the House of Lords, the Chancellor is in effect the judge of his own previous judgment; for the attendance of any other lords is compulsory only on two, and those by rota for a single day. If a case, therefore, take ten days in hearing, twenty lords will have heard each a tenth part of the case; and the two who assist the Chancellor in pronouncing judgment, will have, in all probability, nothing but the Chancellor's own summing-up.

ment of his country, to reflect that the pure, and wise, and equal administration of the laws, forms the first end and blessing of social union: and that this blessing is enjoyed by him in a perfection which he will seek in vain in any other nation of the world.

CHAPTER V.

OF CRIMES AND PUNISHMENTS.

THE proper end of human punishment is, not the satisfaction of justice, but the prevention of crimes. By the satisfaction of justice, I mean the retribution of so much pain for so much guilt; which is the dispensation we expect at the hand of God, and which we are accustomed to consider as the order of things that perfect justice dictates and requires. In what sense, or whether with truth in any sense, justice may be said to demand the punishment of offenders, I do not now inquire: but I assert, that this *demand* is not the motive or occasion of human punishment. What would it be to the magistrate that offences went altogether unpunished, if the impunity of the offender were followed by no danger or prejudice to the commonwealth? The fear lest the escape of the criminal should encourage him, or others by his example, to repeat the same crime, or to commit different crimes, is the sole consideration which authorizes the infliction of punishment by human laws. Now that, whatever it be, which is the cause and end of the punishment, ought undoubtedly to regulate the measure of its severity. But this cause appears to be founded, not in the guilt of the offender, but in the necessity of preventing the repetition of the offence: and from hence results the reason, that crimes are not by any government punished in proportion to their guilt, nor in all cases ought to be so, but in proportion to the difficulty and the necessity of preventing them. Thus, the stealing of goods privately out of a shop may not, in its moral quality, be more criminal than the stealing of them out of a house; yet, being equally necessary, and more difficult to be prevented, the law, in certain circumstances, denounces against it a severer punishment. The crime must be prevented by some means or other: and, consequently, whatever means appear necessary to this end, whether they be proportionable to the guilt of the criminal or not, are adopted rightly, because they are adopted upon the principle which alone justifies the infliction of punishment at all. From the same consideration it also follows, that punishment ought not to be employed, much less rendered severe, when the crime can be prevented by any other means. Punishment is *an evil* to which the magistrate resorts only from its being necessary to the prevention of a greater. This necessity does not exist, when the end may be obtained, that is, when the public may be defended from the effects of the crime, by any other expedients. The sanguinary laws which have been made against counterfeiting or diminishing the gold coin of the kingdom might be just (if capital punishment be ever so), until the method of detecting the fraud, by weighing the money, was introduced into general usage. Since that precaution was practised, these laws have slept; and an execution under them would be deemed at this day a measure of unjustifiable severity. The same principle accounts for a circumstance which has been often censured as an absurdity in the penal laws of this, and of most modern nations; namely, that breaches of trust are either not punished at all, or punished with less rigour than other frauds. Wherefore is it, some have asked, that a violation of confidence, which increases the guilt, should mitigate the penalty? This lenity, or rather forbearance, of the laws, is founded in the most reasonable distinction. A due circumspection in the choice of the persons whom they trust, caution in limiting the extent of that trust, or the requiring of sufficient security for the faithful discharge of it, will commonly guard men from injuries of this description; and the law will not interpose its sanctions to protect negligence and credulity, or to supply the place of domestic care and prudence. To be convinced that the law proceeds entirely upon this consideration, we have only to observe, that, where the confidence is unavoidable, where no practicable vigilance could watch the offender, as in the case of theft committed by a servant in the shop or dwelling-house of his master, or upon property to which he must necessarily have access, the sentence of the law is not less severe, and its execution commonly more certain and vigorous, than if no trust at all had intervened.

It is in pursuance of the same principle, which pervades indeed the whole system of penal jurisprudence, that the facility with which any species of crimes is perpetrated has been generally deemed a reason for aggravating the punishment. Thus, sheep-stealing, horse-stealing, the stealing of cloth from tenters or bleaching-grounds, did, by our laws, subject the offenders to sentence of death: not that these crimes are in their nature more heinous than many simple felonies which are punished by imprisonment or transportation; but because the property, being more exposed, required, as it was thought, the terror of capital punishment to protect it. This severity would have been allowed to be absurd and unjust, if the guilt of the offender were the immediate cause and measure of the punishment; but was a consistent and regular consequence of the supposition, that the right of punishment results from the necessity of preventing the crime; for, if this be the end proposed, the severity of the punishment must be increased in proportion to the expediency and the difficulty of attaining this end; that is, in a proportion compounded of the mischief of the crime, and of the ease with which it is executed. The difficulty of discovery is a circumstance to be included in the same consideration. It constitutes, indeed, with respect to the crime, the facility we speak of. By how much, therefore, the detection of an offender is more rare or uncertain, by so much the more severe must be the punishment when he is detected. Thus, the writing of incendiary letters, though in itself a pernicious and alarming injury, calls for a more condign and exemplary punishment, by the very obscurity with which the crime is committed.

From the justice of God we are taught to look for a gradation of punishment exactly proportioned to the guilt of the offender : when, therefore, in assigning the degrees of human punishment, we introduce considerations distinct from that guilt, and a proportion so varied by external circumstances, that equal crimes frequently undergo unequal punishments, or the less crime the greater; it is natural to demand the reason why a different measure of punishment should be expected from God, and observed by man; why that rule, which befits the absolute and perfect justice of the Deity, should *not* be the rule which ought to be pursued and imitated by human laws. The solution of this difficulty must be sought for in those peculiar attributes of the Divine Nature, which distinguish the dispensations of supreme wisdom from the proceedings of human judicature. A Being whose knowledge penetrates every concealment, from the operation of whose will no art or flight can escape, and in whose hands punishment is sure; such a Being may conduct the moral government of his creation in the best and wisest manner, by pronouncing a law, that every crime shall finally receive a punishment proportioned to the guilt which it contains, abstracted from any foreign consideration whatever; and may testify his veracity to the spectators of his judgments, by carrying this law into strict execution.

But when the care of the public safety is entrusted to men, whose authority over their fellow-creatures is limited by defects of power and knowledge; from whose utmost vigilance and sagacity the greatest offenders often lie hid; whose wisest provisions and speediest pursuit may be eluded by artifice or concealment; a different necessity, a new rule of proceeding, result from the very imperfection of their faculties. In their hands, the uncertainty of punishment must be compensated by the severity. The ease with which crimes are committed or concealed must be counteracted by additional penalties and increased terrors. The very end for which human government is established, requires that its regulations be adapted to the suppression of crimes. This end, whatever it may do in the plans of infinite wisdom, does not, in the designation of temporal penalties, always coincide with the proportionate punishment of guilt.

CHAPTER VI.

OF THE ARGUMENTS IN FAVOUR OF CAPITAL PUNISHMENTS.

AND here we enter upon the long and much-disputed question of capital punishments, a question which day by day assumes a greater importance, and which bids fair to be soon considered only on its own merits, and apart from the vulgar personalities in which too many writers on it have of late indulged.

We shall first consider the arguments of those who, like Paley, admit without question its expediency, as well as its lawfulness, and proceed to argue only as to when and how it shall be administered.

There are two methods of capitally administering penal justice.

The first method assigns capital punishments to few offences, and inflicts it invariably.

The second method assigns capital punishments to many kinds of offences, but inflicts it only upon a few examples of each kind. [Paley proceeds as follows :]

The latter of which two methods has been long adopted in this country, where, of those who receive sentence of death, scarcely one in ten is executed. And the preference of this to the former method seems to be founded in the consideration, that the selection of proper objects for capital punishment principally depends upon circumstances, which, however easy to perceive in each particular case after the crime is committed, it is impossible to enumerate or define beforehand, or to ascertain with that exactness which is requisite in legal descriptions. Hence, although it be necessary to fix by precise rules of law the boundary on one side, that is, the limit to which the punishment may be extended; and also that nothing less than the authority of the whole legislature be suffered to determine that boundary, and assign these rules; yet the mitigation of punishment, the exercise of lenity, may, without danger, be entrusted to the executive magistrate, whose discretion will operate upon those numerous unforeseen, mutable, and indefinite circumstances, both of the crime and the criminal, which constitute or qualify the malignity of each offence. Without the power of relaxation lodged in a living authority, either some offenders would escape capital punishment whom the public safety required to suffer, or some would undergo this punishment where it was neither deserved nor necessary. For if judgment of death were reserved for one or two species of crimes only (which would probably be the case if that judgment was intended to be executed without exception), crimes might occur of the most dangerous example, and accompanied with circumstances of heinous aggravation, which did not fall within any description of offences that the laws had made capital, and which consequently could not receive the punishment their own malignity and the public safety required. What is worse, it would be known beforehand that such crimes might be committed without danger to the offender's life. On the other hand, if, to reach these possible cases, the whole class of offences to which they belong be subjected to pains of death, and no power of remitting this severity remain any where, the execution of the laws will become more sanguinary than the public compassion would endure, or than is necessary to the general security.

The law of England is constructed upon a different and a better policy. By the number of statutes creating capital offences, it sweeps into the net every crime which, under any possible circumstances, may merit the punishment of death; but, when the execution of this sentence comes to be deliberated upon, a small proportion of each class are singled out, the general character or the peculiar aggravations of whose crimes render them fit examples of public justice. By this expedient, few actually suffer death, whilst the dread and danger of it hang over the crimes of many. The tenderness of the law cannot be taken advantage of. The life of the subject is spared, as far as the necessity of restraint and intimidation permits: yet no one will adventure upon the commission of any enormous crime, from a knowledge that the laws have not provided for its punishment. The wisdom and humanity of this design furnish a just excuse for the multiplicity of capital offences, which the laws of England are accused of creating beyond those of other countries. The charge of cruelty is answered by observing, that these laws were never meant to be carried into indiscriminate execution, that the legislature, when it establishes its last and highest sanctions, trusts to the benignity of the crown to relax their severity, as often as circumstances appear to palliate the offence, or even as often as those circumstances of aggravation are wanting, which rendered this rigorous interposition necessary. Upon this plan, it is enough to vindicate the lenity of the laws, that *some* instances are to be found in each class of capital crimes, which require the restraint of capital punishment, and that this restraint could be applied without subjecting the whole class to the same condemnation*.

---

* An instance of unjustifiable severity, unjustifiable even according to Paley's views, is given in the following passage, transferred from the text of his work. "There is, however, one species of crimes, the making of which capital can hardly, I think, be defended even upon the comprehensive principle just now stated; I mean that of privately stealing from the person. As every degree of force is excluded by the description

The prerogative of pardon is properly reserved to the chief magistrate. The power of suspending the laws is a privilege of too high a nature to be committed to many hands, or to those of any inferior officer in the state. The king, also, can best collect the advice by which his resolutions should be governed; and is at the same time removed at the greatest distance from the influence of private motives. But let this power be deposited where it will, the exercise of it ought to be regarded, not as the gift of a favour to be yielded to solicitation, granted to friendship, or, least of all, to be made subservient to the conciliating or gratifying of political attachments; but as a judicial act; as a deliberation to be conducted with the same character of impartiality, with the same exact and diligent attention to the proper merits, and reasons, and circumstances, of the case, as that which the judge upon the bench was expected to maintain and show in the trial of the prisoner's guilt. The questions, whether the prisoner be guilty? and whether,

---

of the crime, it will be difficult to assign an example, where either the amount or circumstances of the theft place it upon a level with those dangerous attempts to which the punishment of death should be confined. It will be still more difficult to show, that, without gross and culpable negligence on the part of the sufferer, such examples can ever become so frequent, as to make it necessary to constitute a class of capital offences, of very wide and large extent."

This law is happily repealed.

being guilty, he ought to be executed? are equally questions of public justice. The adjudication of the latter question is as much a function of magistracy as the trial of the former. The public welfare is interested in both. The conviction of an offender should depend upon nothing but the proof of his guilt; nor the execution of the sentence upon any thing beside the quality and circumstances of his crime. It is necessary to the good order of society, and to the reputation and authority of government, that this be known and believed to be the case in each part of the proceeding. Which reflections show, that the admission of extrinsic or oblique considerations, in dispensing with the power of pardon, is a crime, in the authors and advisers of such unmerited partiality, of the same nature with that of corruption in a judge.

CHAPTER VII.

OF AGGRAVATIONS AND MITIGATIONS*.

AGGRAVATIONS which ought to guide the magistrate in the selection of objects of condign punishment, are principally these three: repetition, cruelty, combination. The two first, it is manifest, add to every reason upon which the justice or the necessity of vigorous measures can be founded; and, with respect to the last circumstance, it may be observed, that when thieves and robbers are once collected into gangs, their violence becomes more formidable, the confederates more desperate, and the difficulty of defending the public against their depredations much greater, than in the case of solitary adventurers. Which several considerations compose a distinction that is properly adverted to in deciding upon the fate of convicted malefactors.

In crimes, however, which are perpetrated by a

---

* The remarks in this chapter are applicable to the infliction of any kind of punishment, and by no means confined to that of death.

multitude, or by a gang, it is proper to separate, in the punishment, the ringleader from his followers, the principal from his accomplices, and even the person who struck the blow, broke the lock, or first entered the house, from those who joined him in the felony; not so much on account of any distinction in the guilt of the offenders, as for the sake of casting an obstacle in the way of such confederacies, by rendering it difficult for the confederates to settle who shall begin the attack, or to find a man amongst their number willing to expose himself to greater danger than his associates. This is another instance in which the punishment which expediency directs does not pursue the exact proportion of the crime.

Injuries effected by terror and violence are those which it is the first and chief concern of legal government to repress; because their extent is unlimited; because no private precaution can protect the subject against them; because they endanger life and safety, as well as property; and, lastly, because they render the condition of society wretched, by a sense of personal insecurity. These reasons do not apply to frauds, which circumspection may prevent; which must wait for opportunity; which can proceed only to certain limits; and, by the apprehension of which, although the business of life be incommoded, life itself is not made miserable. The appearance of this distinction led some humane writers to express a wish that capital punishments might be confined to crimes of violence*.

In estimating the comparative malignancy of crimes of violence, regard is to be had, not only to the proper and intended mischief of the crime, but to the fright occasioned by the attack, to the general alarm excited by it in others, and to the consequences which may attend future attempts of the same kind. Thus, in affixing the punishment of burglary, or of breaking into dwelling-houses by night, we are to consider, not only the peril to which the most valuable property is exposed by this crime, and which may be called the direct mischief of it, but the danger also of murder in case of resistance, or for the sake of preventing discovery, and the universal dread with which the silent and defenceless hours of rest and sleep must be disturbed, were attempts of this sort to become frequent; and which dread alone, even without the mischief which is the object of it, is not only a public evil, but almost of all evils the most insupportable. These circumstances place a difference between the breaking into a dwelling-house by day, and by night; which difference obtains in the punishment of the offence by the law of Moses, and is probably to be found in the judicial codes of most countries from the earliest ages to the present.

---

* This desire has been long fulfilled. No executions take place save for murder; and it is confidently hoped that, before many years have passed, capital punishments will be altogether abolished.

CHAPTER VIII.

OF FRAUDULENT CRIMES.

Of frauds, or of injuries which are effected without force, the most noxious kinds are forgeries, counterfeiting or diminishing of the coin, and the stealing of letters in the course of their conveyance; in as much as these practices tend to deprive the public of accommodations, which not only improve the conveniences of social life, but are essential to the prosperity, and even the existence of commerce. Of these crimes it may be said, that although they seem to affect property alone, the mischief of their operation does not terminate there. For let it be supposed that the remissness or lenity of the laws should, in any country, suffer offences of this sort to grow into such a frequency as to render the use of money, the circulation of bills, or the public conveyance of letters, no longer safe or practicable; what would follow, but that every species of trade and of activity must decline under these discouragements; the sources of subsistence fail by which the inhabitants of the country are supported; the country itself, where the intercourse of civil life was so endangered and defective, be deserted; and that, beside the distress and poverty which the loss of employment would produce to the industrious and valuable part of the existing community, a rapid depopulation must take place, each generation becoming less numerous than the last; till solitude and barrenness overspread the land; until a desolation similar to what obtains in many countries of Asia, which were once the most civilized and frequented parts of the world, succeed in the place of crowded cities, of cultivated fields, of happy and well-peopled regions? When we carry forwards, therefore, our views to the more distant, but not less certain consequences of these crimes, we perceive that, though no living creature be destroyed by them, yet human life is diminished; that an offence, the particular consequence of which deprives only an individual of a small portion of his property, and which even in its general tendency seems only to obstruct the enjoyment of certain public conveniences, may, nevertheless, by its ultimate effects, conclude in the laying waste of human existence. This observation will enable those who regard the divine rule of "life for life, and blood for blood," as the only authorized and justifiable measure of capital punishment, to perceive, with respect to the effects and quality of the actions, a greater resemblance than they suppose to exist between certain atrocious frauds and those crimes which attack personal safety*.

---

* This remarkable passage has been strangely overlooked by the advocates of Capital Punishment; it shows clearly that

In the case of forgeries, there appears a substantial difference between the forging of bills of exchange, or of securities which are circulated, and of which the circulating and currency are found to serve and facilitate valuable purposes of commerce, and the forging of bonds, leases, mortgages, or of instruments which are not commonly transferred from one hand to another; because, in the former case, credit is necessarily given to the signature, and without that credit, the negotiation of such property could not be carried on, nor the public utility sought from it be attained; in the other case, all possibility of deceit might be precluded, by a direct communication between the parties, or by due care in the choice of their agents, with little interruption to business, and without destroying, or so much encumbering, the uses for which these instruments are calculated. This distinction I apprehend to be not only real, but precise enough to afford a line of division between forgeries which, as the law once stood, were almost universally capital, and punished with undistinguishing severity.

Perjury is another crime of the same class and magnitude. And when we consider what reliance is necessarily placed upon oaths; that all judicial decisions proceed upon testimony; that, consequently, there is not a right that a man possesses, of which

---

the very principle which condemns the murderer to death, dooms to the same fate the burglar, the forger, and the coiner.

false witnesses may not deprive him; that reputation, property, and life itself, lie open to the attempts of perjury; that it may often be committed without a possibility of contradiction or discovery; that the success and prevalency of this vice tend to introduce the most grievous and fatal injustice into the administration of human affairs, or such a distrust of testimony as must create universal embarrassment and confusion: when we reflect upon these mischiefs, we shall be brought, probably, to agree with the opinion of those who contend that perjury, in its punishment, especially that which is attempted in solemn evidence, and in the face of a court of justice, should be placed upon a level with the most flagitious frauds*.

The obtaining of money by secret threats, whether we regard the difficulty with which the crime is traced out, the odious imputations to which it may lead, or the profligate conspiracies that are sometimes formed to carry it into execution, deserves to be reckoned among the worst species of robbery.

---

* It will be evident that the stress of this argument lies against *false witness*, and would apply to the false affirmation of a member of the Society of Friends, as well as to a false oath strictly so called. It would lose nothing of its force, were judicial oaths altogether abolished.

CHAPTER IX.

ON THE PRESUMED NECESSITY OF FREQUENT EXECUTIONS.

THE frequency of capital executions in this country of old owed its presumed necessity to three causes: much liberty, great cities, and the want of a punishment, short of death, possessing a sufficient degree of terror. And, if the taking away of the life of malefactors were once more rare in other countries than in ours, the supposed reason will be found in some difference in these articles. The liberties of a free people, and still more the jealousy with which these liberties are watched, and by which they are preserved, permit not those precautions and restraints—that inspection, scrutiny, and control, which are exercised with success in arbitrary governments. For example, neither the spirit of the laws, nor of the people, will suffer the detention or confinement of suspected persons, without proofs of their guilt, which it is often impossible to obtain; nor will they allow that masters of families be obliged to record and render up a description of the strangers or inmates whom they entertain; nor that an account be demanded, at the pleasure of the magistrate, of each man's time, employment, and means of subsistence; nor securities to be required when these accounts appear unsatisfactory or dubious; nor men to be apprehended upon the mere suggestion of idleness or vagrancy; nor to be confined to certain districts; nor the inhabitants of each district to be made responsible for one another's behaviour; nor passports to be exacted from all persons entering or leaving the kingdom; least of all will they tolerate the appearance of an armed force, or of military law; or suffer the streets and public roads to be guarded and patrolled by soldiers; or, lastly, entrust the police with such discretionary powers as may make sure of the guilty, however they may involve the innocent. These expedients, although arbitrary and rigorous, are many of them effectual; and, in proportion as they render the commission or concealment of crimes more difficult, they subtract from the necessity of severe punishment.

Great cities multiply crimes, by presenting easier opportunities and more incentives to libertinism, which in low life is commonly the introductory stage to other enormities; by collecting thieves and robbers into the same neighbourhood, which enables them to form communications and confederacies that increase their art and courage; as well as strength and wickedness; but principally by the refuge they afford to villany, in the means of concealment, and of subsisting in secrecy, which crowded towns supply to men of every description. These temptations and facilities can only, say some, be counteracted by adding to the number of capital punishments. But a *third* cause, which increased the frequency of capital executions in England, was a presumed defect of the laws, in not being provided with any other punishment than that of death, sufficiently terrible to keep offenders in awe. Transportation, which is the sentence second in the order of severity, appeared to many to answer the purpose of example very imperfectly; not only because exile is in reality a slight punishment to those who have neither property, nor friends, nor reputation, nor regular means of subsistence at home, and because their situation was imagined to be made little worse by their crime than it was before they committed it; but, because the punishment, whatever it may be, is unobserved and unknown. A transported convict may suffer under his sentence, but his sufferings are removed from the view of his countrymen: his misery is unseen; his condition strikes no terror into the minds of those for whose warning and admonition it was intended. This chasm in the scale of punishment produces also two further imperfections in the administration of penal justice; the first is, that the same punishment is extended to crimes of very different character and malignancy; the second, that punishments separated by a great interval are assigned to crimes hardly distinguishable in their guilt and mischief.

CHAPTER X.

OF REFORMING PUNISHMENTS.

THE end of punishment is two-fold—*amendment* and *example*. In the first of these, the *reformation* of criminals, little has ever been effected, and little, I fear, is practicable. From every species of punishment that has hitherto been devised, from imprisonment and exile, from pain and infamy, malefactors return more hardened in their crimes, and more instructed*.

Of the *reforming* punishments which have not yet been tried, none promised so much success as that of *solitary* imprisonment, or the confinement of criminals in separate apartments. This improvement

---

* Paley observes, " If there be any thing that shakes the soul of a confirmed villain, it is the expectation of approaching death. The horrors of this situation may cause such a wrench on the mental organs, as to give them a holding turn; and I think it probable, that many of those who are executed, would, if they were delivered at the point of death, retain such a remembrance of their sensations as might preserve them, unless urged by extreme want, from relapsing into their former crimes. But this is an experiment that, from its nature, cannot be repeated often."

would, it was said, augment the terror of the punishment; would seclude the criminal from the society of his fellow prisoners, in which society the worse are sure to corrupt the better; would wean him from the knowledge of his companions, and from the love of that turbulent, precarious life in which his vices had engaged him; would raise up in him reflections on the folly of his choice, and dispose his mind to such bitter and continued penitence as might produce a lasting alteration in the principles of his conduct. Experience has shown, however, that it can be but sparingly employed, and that not unfrequently the intellect of the criminal gives way under the severity of the punishment. The experiment has been tried more largely in America than here.

As aversion to labour is the cause from which half of the vices of low life deduce their origin and continuance, punishments ought to be contrived with a view to the conquering of this disposition. Two opposite expedients have been recommended for this purpose: the one, solitary confinement, with hard labour; the other, solitary confinement, with nothing to do. Both expedients seek the same end—to reconcile the idle to a life of industry. The former hopes to effect this by making labour habitual; the latter, by making idleness irksome and insupportable: and the preference of one method to the other depends upon the question, whether a man is more likely to betake himself, of his own accord, to work, who has been accustomed to employment, or who has been distressed by the want of it. When gaols are once provided for the *separate* confinement of prisoners, which both proposals require, the choice between them may soon be determined by experience. If labour be exacted, I would leave the whole, or a portion, of the profit to the prisoner's use, and I would debar him from any other provision or supply; that his subsistence, however coarse or penurious, may be proportionate to his diligence, and that he may taste the advantage of industry, together with the toil. I would go further: I would measure the confinement, not by duration of time, but by quantity of work, in order both to excite industry, and to render it more voluntary. But the principal difficulty remains still; namely, how to dispose of criminals after their enlargement. By a rule of life, which is perhaps too invariably and indiscriminately adhered to, no one will receive a man or woman out of gaol, into any service or employment whatever. This is the common misfortune of public punishments, that they preclude the offender from all honest means of future support*. It seems incumbent upon the State to secure a maintenance to those who are willing to work

---

* Until this inconvenience be remedied, small offences had better go unpunished. I do not mean that the law should exempt them from punishment; but that private persons should be tender in prosecuting them.

for it; and yet it is absolutely necessary to divide criminals as far asunder from one another as possible. Whether male prisoners might not, after the term of their confinement had expired, be distributed in the country, detained within certain limits, and employed upon the public roads; and females be remitted to the overseers of country parishes, to be there furnished with dwellings, and with the materials and implements of occupation; whether by these, or by what other methods, it may be possible to effect the two purposes of *employment* and *dispersion,* well merits the attention of all who are anxious to perfect the internal regulation of their country. There are some punishments which are now generally abandoned, either as inexpedient in themselves, or because, from mismanagement, they have failed in their effect, and so fallen out of public favour*.

---

* Many of the suggestions in this chapter are beginning to attract public attention, and more especially the establishment of reformatory institutions for discharged criminals; one of the objects of which is, that they may obtain permanent employment when their probationary period is past.

CHAPTER XI.

OF INEXPEDIENT PUNISHMENTS.

TORTURE is applied either to obtain confessions of guilt, or to exasperate or prolong the pains of death. No bodily punishment, however excruciating or long-continued, receives the name of torture, unless it be designed to kill the criminal by a more lingering death; or to extort from him the discovery of some secret which is supposed to be concealed in his breast. *The question by torture* appears to be equivocal in its effects; for, since extremity of pain, and not any consciousness of remorse in the mind, produces those effects, an innocent man may sink under the torment as soon as the guilty. The latter has as much to fear from yielding as the former. The instant and almost irresistible desire of relief may draw from one sufferer false accusations of himself or others, as it may sometimes extract the truth out of another. This ambiguity renders the use of torture, as a means of procuring information in criminal proceedings, liable to the risk of grievous and irreparable injustice. For which reason, though recommended by ancient and general example, it has been properly exploded from the mild and cautious system of penal jurisprudence established in this country.

Barbarous spectacles of human agony are justly found fault with, as tending to harden and degrade the public feelings, and to destroy that sympathy with which the sufferings of our fellow creatures ought always to be seen; or, if no effect of this kind follow from them, they counteract in some measure their own design, by sinking men's abhorrence of the criminal. But if a mode of execution could be devised which would augment the horror of the punishment, without offending or impairing the public sensibility by cruel or unseemly exhibitions of death, it might add something to the efficacy of the example; and, by being reserved for a few atrocious crimes, might also enlarge the scale of punishment—an addition to which seems wanting. Somewhat of the sort we have been describing, was the proposal, once suggested, of casting murderers into a den of wild beasts, where they would perish in a manner dreadful to the imagination, yet concealed from the view*.

Infamous punishments are mismanaged in this country, with respect both to the crimes and the criminals. In the first place, they ought to be confined to offences which are held in indisputable and

---

* Like this also, but less barbarous, was the proposal made in the year 1849 of substituting secret for public executions.

universal detestation. To condemn to the pillory the author or editor of a libel against the state, who has rendered himself the favorite of a party, if not of the people, by the very act for which he stands there, is to gratify the offender, and to expose the laws to mockery and insult. In the second place, the delinquents who receive this sentence are for the most part such as have long ceased either to value reputation, or to fear shame; of whose happiness, and of whose enjoyments, character makes no part. That the low ministers of libertinism, the keepers of disorderly houses, are threatened in vain with a punishment that affects a sense which they have not; that applies solely to the imagination, to the virtue and the pride of human nature. The pillory, or any other infamous distinction, might be employed rightly, and with effect, in the punishment of some offences of higher life; as of frauds and peculations in office; of collusions and connivances, by which the public treasury is defrauded; of breaches of trust; of perjury and subornation of perjury; of the clandestine and forbidden sale of places; of flaggrant abuses of authority, or neglect of duty; and, lastly, of corruption in the exercise of confidential or judicial offices. In all which, the more elevated was the station of the criminal, the more signal and conspicuous would be the triumph of justice.

The *certainty* of punishment is of more consequence than the severity. Criminals do not so much flatter themselves with the lenity of the sentence, as with the hope of escaping. They are not so apt to compare what they gain by the crime with what they may suffer from the punishment, as to encourage themselves with the chance of concealment or flight. For which reason, a vigilant magistracy, an accurate police, a proper distribution of force and intelligence, together with due rewards for the discovery and apprehension of malefactors, and an undeviating impartiality in carrying the laws into execution, contribute more to the restraint and suppression of crimes than any violent exacerbations of punishment. And, for the same reasons, of all contrivances directed to this end, those perhaps are most effectual which facilitate the conviction of criminals. The offence of counterfeiting the coin could not be checked by all the terrors and the utmost severity of the law, whilst the act of coining was necessary to be established by specific proof. The statute which made the possession of the implements of coining criminal—that is, which constituted that possession complete evidence of the offender's guilt—was the first thing that gave force and efficiency to the denunciations of law upon this subject. The statute of James the First, relative to the murder of bastard children, which ordains that the concealment of the birth should be deemed incontestible proof of the charge, though a harsh law, was, in like manner with the former, well calculated to put a stop to the crime.

It is upon the principle of this observation, that I apprehend much harm to have been done to the community by the overstrained scrupulousness or weak timidity of juries, which demands often such proof of a prisoner's guilt as the nature and secrecy of his crime scarce possibly admit of; and which holds it the part of a *safe* conscience not to condemn any man, whilst there exists the minutest possibility of his innocence. Any story they may happen to have heard or read, whether real or feigned, in which courts of justice have been misled by presumptions of guilt, is enough, in their minds, to found an acquittal upon, where positive proof is wanting. I do not mean that juries should indulge conjectures, should magnify suspicions into proofs, or even that they should weigh probabilities in *gold scales;* but when the preponderance of evidence is so manifest as to persuade every private understanding of the prisoner's guilt; when it furnishes that degree of credibility upon which men decide and act in all other doubts, and which experience hath shown that they may decide and act upon with sufficient safety: to reject such proof, from an insinuation of uncertainty that belongs to all human affairs, and from a general dread lest the charge of innocent blood should lie at their doors, is a conduct which, however natural to a mind studious of its own quiet, is authorized by no considerations of rectitude or utility*. It counteracts the care and damps

---

* It is obvious that this difficulty is at once overcome by the substitution of secondary for capital punishments.

the activity of government; it holds out public encouragement to villany, by confessing the impossibility of bringing villains to justice; and that species of encouragement which, as hath been just now observed, the minds of such men are most apt to entertain and dwell upon.

There are two popular maxims, which seem to have a considerable influence in producing the injudicious acquittals of which we complain. One is, "That cir-"cumstantial evidence falls short of positive proof." This assertion, in the unqualified sense in which it is applied, is not true. A concurrence of well-authenticated circumstances composes a stronger ground of assurance than positive testimony, unconfirmed by circumstances, usually affords. Circumstances cannot lie. The conclusion also which results from them, though deduced by only probable inference, is commonly more to be relied upon than the veracity of an unsupported solitary witness. The danger of being deceived is less, the actual instances of deception are fewer, in the one case than the other. What is called positive proof in criminal matters, as where a man swears to the person of the prisoner, and that he actually saw him commit the crime with which he is charged, may be founded in the mistake or perjury of a single witness. Such mistakes and such perjuries are not without many examples. Whereas, to impose upon a court of justice a chain of *circumstantial* evidence in support of a fabricated accusation, requires such a number of false witnesses as seldom meet together; a union also of skill and wickedness which is still more rare; and, after all, this species of proof lies much more open to discussion, and is more likely, if false, to be contradicted, or to betray itself by some unforeseen inconsistency, than that direct proof, which, being confined within the knowledge of a single person, which appealing to, or standing connected with, no external or collateral circumstances, is incapable, by its very simplicity, of being confronted with opposite probabilities.

The other maxim which deserves a similar examination is this: "That it is better that ten guilty "persons escape, than that one innocent man should "suffer." If by saying it is *better*, be meant that it is more for the public advantage, the proposition, I think, cannot be maintained. The security of civil life, which is essential to the value and the enjoyment of every blessing it contains, and the interruption of which is followed by universal misery and confusion, is protected chiefly by the dread of punishment. The misfortune of an individual (for such may the sufferings, or even the death, of an innocent person be called, when they are occasioned by no evil intention) cannot be placed in competition with this object. I do not contend that the life or safety of the meanest subject ought in any case to be knowingly sacrificed; no principle of judicature, no end of punishment, can ever require *that*. But when certain rules of adjudication must be pursued, when certain degrees of credibility must be accepted, in order to reach the crimes with which the public are infested, courts of justice should not be deterred from the application of these rules by *every* suspicion of danger, or by mere possibility of confounding the innocent with the guilty. They ought rather to reflect, that he who falls by a mistaken sentence may be considered as falling for his country: whilst he suffers under the operation of those rules, by the general effect and tendency of which the welare of the community is maintained and upheld.

CHAPTER XII.

OF CAPITAL PUNISHMENTS MORALLY AND POLITICALLY CONSIDERED.

It is contended, as we have seen, in favour of capital punishments, that they are necessary on moral and political grounds, and that they have the sanction of a divine command; and though our chief object is to disprove the latter assertion, so far, at least, as regards men living under a Christian dispensation, yet we must briefly touch on the moral and political, as well as the theological question, partly because this treatise may fall into many hands to whom the train of thought which it presents would otherwise be incomplete, and partly because the two questions are so involved and interlaced the one with the other, that it is impossible to regard them from entirely separate points of view.

What, then, are the moral and political reasons for death as a punishment? We dismiss at once the idea of reformation, as absurd, and that of vengeance as unchristian; and we have—I. The safety of society, by the deterring others from similar crimes; II. The putting it out of the criminal's power to offend again.

To the first of these assertions it may be replied, that capital punishment *never did* effectually deter men from crime, and statistical researches will prove that, in cases were it has been abolished, the kind of crime affected by it has decreased. We do not suppose that men stand in greater fear of transportation or imprisonment than of death; but parties offended will more readily prosecute, and witnesses will more freely give evidence, and juries will more unhesitatingly convict, when the life of a fellow-creature is not placed in jeopardy.

There is not a punishment inflicted by law, how slight soever it may be, that is not far more prejudicial to the party punished, than the proceeds of the crime can be beneficial. No criminal balances between the pleasure or advantage obtained by his offence, and the injury done to his person or prospects by the sentence of a court. His only inducement to violate the law is the expectation of absolute impunity; and if, in addition to the chance of not being found out, be added the improbability of prosecution, or full evidence, or conviction, on account of the great severity of the law, it is evident that an additional prospect is given to the success of crime.

This is a general proposition, but it is not the less forcible when applied to the punishment of death in particular; and if it be replied, that death is no longer inflicted except in cases of murder, and that therefore the manifest injustice is avoided of subjecting to the same terrific penalty offences of widely different degrees of criminality, we answer, that it is impossible to bring forward two cases of *murder* in which the same exact amount of atrocity is exhibited; and that juries have been obliged to give verdicts of manslaughter, simply because a more correct decision would endanger the life of the criminal.

And as allusion has been made to juries, who does not see the little regard paid by them to the *literal terms* of their oath? If the law had not, by its excessive severity, given a somewhat conventional meaning to that solemn obligation, would a jury have found, in times past, that a ten-pound note was under the value of forty shillings? or, in our own day, acquitted criminals so notorious as some who have escaped? And if the moral feelings of juries in general had not been manifestly weakened, would such verdicts have been returned as those which have been returned in many late lamentable cases?

In thus speaking, it is not intended to infer that jurors are more deficient in integrity than other men; but only that, in adopting the office of a juror, they adopt a code of morality by which they would not be guided in other cases; and this arises from their willingly losing sight of the principle on which they are empanelled, and regarding the sentence which their verdict will produce rather than the evidence on which that verdict is to be given. It can scarcely admit of a doubt, that this erroneous view of a juror's duties has arisen from the severity of the law. Men are not sufficient casuists to see that, in judging according to evidence, they have accomplished their duty; they confound the sentence of the law with the verdict of the jury, and look on themselves as having consigned a fellow-creature to death. And in proportion as they feel the importance of Christian duties, and the consequences in another world of their neglect, in the same ratio will they be unwilling to be in any way instrumental to the destruction of an unprepared man.

It may be perceived, by statistic evidence carefully and impartially prepared, that, as deterring others from the commission of crime, the punishment of death has signally failed. Nay, the very execution of the tremendous sentence has been attended by the commission of a host of minor offences; and young criminals have made their first essays in crime before the dead body of their more hardened brother was removed from their eyes. Besides this, there is a martyrology of the gibbet. The last words and demeanour of eminent criminals have been carefully recorded, and related as soldiers relate those of a Wolfe, or churchmen those of a Ridley.

As to any restraint upon the criminal himself, it is evident that society may be protected in many ways against further attempts on his part. Indeed, the happy rarity of executions is enough to convince us that but little fear is entertained on that account; while the number of murders which have lately filled our newspapers afford a melancholy proof that, as a preventive, capital punishment cannot be relied on. We shall not occupy more time in regarding the moral and political aspect of the question, but shall proceed to a chief object of this portion of our work; viz. the investigation of the sanction which the punishment of death is supposed to derive from Holy Scripture. And here, on the very threshold of the argument, we wish to avoid the imputation of disputing the *abstract lawfulness* of death-punishment. The Church, in her 37th article, has spoken plainly on this point, and we see no reason whatever to differ from her. But it is one thing to declare that capital punishments are abstractedly lawful; and a widely different thing to maintain *that they may not lawfully be repealed.* Many institutions which have been lawful in their day, are now lawfully obsolete. Many a law is necessary in one age, but barbarous in another; and while we do not tax governors with keeping up an institution absolutely unlawful in punishing offences with death, we do venture to assert that they MAY LAWFULLY *abrogate the penalty,* and that its abrogation would be *an incalculable blessing to the age.*

CHAPTER XIII.

OF CAPITAL PUNISHMENT AS SUPPOSED TO BE SUPPORTED BY SCRIPTURE.

It has been already premised that we address ourselves to Christians, to those who accept the anthority of Scripture *in toto,* and who are willing to accept *any* conclusions to which it can be fairly shown to lead them; and not to those who cite it as binding upon others, without allowing it to be binding upon themselves. Thus premising, we shall find that the chief support which capital punishments receive will be found—

I. In the sixth verse of the ninth chapter of Genesis, where occur *in our version* the words, "Whoso sheddeth man's blood, by man shall his blood be shed."

II. In the frequent repetition of similar sanctions under the Mosaic dispensation.

III. In the absence of any express prohibition on the part of our Lord and his Apostles.

But before we proceed to support capital punishment by reason of the sanction supposed to be given to them in the ninth chapter of Genesis, we must prove two things:

I. That the spiritual condition of man under the Gospel is *precisely* the same with respect to his *responsibilities*, as it was under the Patriarchal and Mosaic dispensations; for if the parallel fail here, the argument falls to the ground; and,

II. That the passage referred to *really does* enjoin the punishment of death in cases of bloodshed.

We think that we shall be able to prove that neither of these things can be proved. The case is, however, one by no means clear from difficulty; for,

If it be said that, knowing the terrible consequences of death to the unprepared sinner, we have no right to diminish his chances of salvation by shortening his life; it will be replied, that the soul of man is of no more value than it was under the law of Moses, and that if *he* commanded by inspiration the punishment of death, our objection amounts to an imputation against the mercy of God, and implies a desire on our part to rectify a defect on His. Thus the ground appears to be cut away from beneath our feet; for who would not hesitate at embracing a theory which seems to reflect on the Divine goodness, and to elevate the wisdom of man above that of God.

And yet, when we regard the condition of a murderer, habituated for many years to the commission of crime (and we have a right for our argument to take an extreme case), when we regard, then, the mental and moral state of such a man, the hardened heart, the seared conscience, the degraded tastes, we shall see but little chance of his speedy conversion. Every day of such a life as that which he has led has tended to alienate him still more from his Maker, and to make repentance still more difficult; his moral perceptions are daily more blunted, and the agitation which the approach of a violent death *must* produce can hardly be a favourable preparation for eternity. Indeed, we find, on inquiry, that the faculties of such men become affected with a moral paralysis. They may conduct themselves with outward decorum; but too often the mind has become incapable of serious attention, and wanders apathetically through the mazes of the past.

All Christians acknowledge the extreme danger in which such a man is placed; and we have no reason to suppose that God will pardon any man's offences simply on the ground that he was cut off in the midst of them. "The soul that sinneth, it shall die;" and if the Divine mercy is necessarily to be extended to every man who is prevented by a violent death from a timely repentance, then, not the gibbet alone, the garote, or the guillotine; but murder, drowning, the sword of an enemy in battle, apoplexy, or any accidental death, must be a sufficient passport to eternal happiness.

And as this part of our argument is one of great consequence, we shall, even at the risk of being tedious, place it in as strong a light as we can. It is an awful thought that man should be accessory to the damnation of his fellow-man, and *that* in the way of a just punishment, and it is impossible to say that the temporal death inflicted by the law shall not be followed by the second death denounced by the wrath of God against sin. If a murderer has sent his victim unprepared to stand before his Maker, and by this crime has been instrumental to the ruin of a soul, the mischief is not remedied by the ruin of another; nor does it altogether suffice to say that the guilt of the murderer, and not our sentence, has been the cause of his destruction; for, had he lived, he might have lived to repent.

Again, it is altogether unsatisfactory to say that time is given for repentance; inasmuch as we have no means of ascertaining what period is sufficient, or how the respite actually allowed may have been employed. The last days of some notorious malefactors—Shepherd, for instance—were employed far otherwise than in any preparation for eternity; and a case occurred not long since of a criminal who died with a lie in his mouth. What hope can the Christian have of such characters?

But there seems to have tacitly grown up in many minds the notion, that, as man has taken away from such persons the opportunity of repentance—that is to say, the amount of opportunity enjoyed by men in general—they are taken out of the ordinary category of sinners, and that they will therefore be judged by a different rule. Not that such a theory is ever formally enunciated; but it is permitted more or less to appear. We are reminded of the "*uncovenanted mercies* of God;" we are told of the allowance which he will make for different circumstances and different capacities; and thus men endeavour to persuade themselves that no more harm is done by the block or the gibbet than the removal of an evil doer from among men.

But if we imagine that this extraordinary mercy *is* to be shown, it is of course in consequence of the sudden cutting off of the criminal. Let us then suppose that a man who has led a wicked life, and who might at any time have repented of his sins, is drowned at sea, do we augur well for his salvation by reason of this catastrophe? And yet, according to the views alluded to, if the man who has perhaps two, three, or four weeks to prepare for death, is to be judged by a more lenient rule than other men, much more should the same mercy be extended to him who has but an hour or two; besides, a fever, an attack of cholera, or indigestion, will be far more rapid in its effects than the process of law, even when sentence of death is pronounced, and a criminal left for execution.

From all this it results that capital punishment tends awfully to the spiritual destruction of those submitted to it; and as it is certain that, under the Mosaic dispensation at least, it *was* commanded, we must be prepared either to show that its consequences were *then* less terrific, or to sit down with all the doubt and perplexity which such reflections as those which we have been led to make, must occasion us. We shall have reason and revelation arrayed one against the other, and the Divine sanction justifying a course dangerous to the souls of men. Nor can we escape from the dilemma by saying that our reason is not competent to judge of the case; for it is not unaided reason, but reason supported by a thousand passages of the revealed Word of God! We have too many texts which set forth the fearful consequences of death to the ungodly; the difficulties in the way of repentance; the rarity of sudden conversions; and the danger of self-deception; not to feel how awfully perilous is the situation of a malefactor condemned to death.

Let us, then, consider whether, under earlier dispensations, the responsibilities of mankind were lighter, and their spiritual condition in any other respects different from our own.

Infidels have triumphantly asserted that the Old Testament Scriptures contain no allusions to a future state, and do not teach the immortality of the soul; and though it would be too much to admit this assertion in all its extent, we are compelled, with Warburton, to allow that the law of God, as given to Moses, was a law proposing only temporal rewards in cases of obedience, and temporal punishments in cases of transgression. If the mass of the chosen people had any idea of future rewards and punishments, it would appear that it was by tradition, and not by express revelation.

The punishments of that law were arranged according to a scale, commencing with pecuniary fines of a small extent, and reaching through certain temporary separations from the congregation to the penalty of death by stoning, or, in some cases, even by fire. But one idea runs through every enactment of the Mosaic code, whether it be penalty, or whether it be sacrifice; viz. that of PROPITIATION; and thus the punishment of death inflicted upon the offender assumes as direct an aspect of expiatory sacrifice as the offering of a bull or of a goat for sin. We are led to this conclusion from observing that the provisions of the law by which death is denounced against certain offences are found among others which expressly state this principle: if a man kill the ox or the ass of his neighbour, he shall make it good*; if he deprive his neighbour of an eye, he shall suffer the loss of an eye himself; if an ox gore a man, the ox shall be put to death, and his flesh shall not be eaten†; but if the animal was known to be dangerous, then the life of the owner, as well as the life of the beast, were to be sacrificed. Indeed, blood was in a pecu-

---

* Levit. xxiv, 18 et seq. † Exodus, xxi. 28 et seq.

liar manner regarded as sacred—the blood of beasts as well as the blood of man: and there is one passage so remarkable on this topic, that, were there no others, it would be sufficient to make us pause before we accepted the Mosaic value of blood as binding upon us. It occurs in the third and fourth verses of the seventeenth chapter of Leviticus, and provides that any person slaying a sacrifice to the Lord from among his own cattle in the fields, instead of bringing it to the door of the tabernacle, shall be put to death. "He hath shed blood, and that man shall be cut off from among his people."

Whence, then, this high value set upon blood? It is clear that it regarded not the *actual*, but the *typical* value. Every part of the Mosaic law was calculated to bring before the mind of the Israelite a constant system of expiation, and the fact that "without shedding of blood, there is no remission of sins." But if God requires the life of *man* as an expiation according to the scale by which in like manner he required the life of *an ox*, it is clear that the expiation was as satisfactory in the one case as in the other, and the temporal punishment received as a satisfaction for the crime. But this theory demands that there should be an onward looking to some more perfect atonement, of which all these expiatory sacrifices, whether human or animal, were but the types and shadows; and hence, as Christians, we believe that it was by faith in a *coming Saviour* that the Israelite obtained salvation.

If we are right in regarding these enactments as providing a *typical* but *expiatory* sacrifice, it is clear that they were then looked on in a light in which it is impossible *now* to contemplate them. Now that " there remaineth no more sacrifice for sin*," that types and shadows have passed away, and that we look back on an atonement already accomplished— on one full, perfect, and sufficient sacrifice; " oblation, and satisfaction for the sins of the whole world†"—it must be clear that capital punishments follow the rule of the daily sacrifice, and are no longer required. The spiritual condition of the man whose life is taken *as an expiation for his offences,* under a typical dispensation, is manifestly widely different from that of a man whose life is taken from him without any idea of expiation, and whose acceptance with God is to be sought on totally different grounds.

But a still further light is thrown on the subject by the great variety of offences punished with death: cursing a father or mother, striking them, blaspheming the name of the Lord, the eating of blood, adultery, incest, rape, murder, and a host of other transgressions, were all punished with death. These enactments prove to us that we must regard the philosophy of the Mosaic code as a whole, and with reference to

---

* Heb. x, 26.

† Communion Service.   Consecration Prayer.

its typical and expiatory character, and not as a system of legislature capable of application to Christian times.

Then again the permission of polygamy, concubinage, and many other practices prohibited under Christianity, evidences a different standard of morals. Indeed, this is expressly allowed in the New Testament; for our Lord himself remarks—"Moses, for the hardness of your hearts, suffered you to put away your wives*." And St. Paul applies the same rule *generally*, when he declares to the Athenians that " the times of this ignorance God winked at†." We find polygamy and concubinage, and what we, as Christians, should call a lax system of morals on cognate subjects, prevailing among the patriarchs long before Moses. We have instances in Abraham, Lot, Jacob, Judah: in two of these cases at least, without offence to God; and in the others, without any intimation to that effect. We do not allude, be it observed, to the incest of Lot; but his offering his daughters to the men of Sodom. As we have all these præ-mosaic instances of a different standard of morals to that introduced by our Lord, and as we know that typical sacrifices were coeval with Abel, if not earlier,—so we may safely declare, that mankind were regulated by a different moral code before the

---

* Matthew, xix, 8.   † Acts, xvii, 30.

coming of Christ, and subjected to inferior responsibilities, proportionate to their inferior light; and more especially that the man put to death for transgression under the Mosaic law, stood in a very different and far more favorable relation to God, than a man similarly put to death under the Gospel dispensation.

CHAPTER XIV.

OF THE NOACHIC PRECEPT AS APPLIED TO CAPITAL PUNISHMENT.

We shall now examine the passage in Genesis to which allusion has already been made: "Whoso sheddeth man's blood, by man shall his blood be shed:" and it is contended that this cannot be repealed by Christianity, in as much as it was no part of the Mosaic ceremonial law; but that, being of prior obligation, it was necessarily universal. Faber, in his admirable work on "The Three Dispensations," has pointed out the universality of the patriarchal, the restrictive character of the Judaic, and the renewed universality of the Gospel scheme. Thus we admit the Sabbath to be binding upon us, not merely because we find it in the Decalogue, but because it was of patriarchal, and indeed of Paradisaic, obligation.

But even here we must make a difference between those observances which are typical of Christ, and those which are not; and we shall find many patriarchal laws which follow the rule of the Mosaic ceremonial, and cease because their great ANTITYPE has been revealed. Sacrifices were of partriarchal obligation; circumcision of patriarchal obligation; yet the first have been forbidden, and the latter remitted by the express authority of the Gospel, and manifestly because that which they foreshadowed had been fully revealed. Hence it will not be sufficient to show that any ordinance was by divine appointment observed by the patriarchs; *we must also show that it was not typical of Christ, and therefore not repealed by his incarnation.* On this ground sacrifices *are* prohibited, because they did adumbrate his perfect expiation, which is now accomplished. On this ground the Sabbath is *not* repealed, because it typified, and does typify, the rest that remaineth for the people of God.

We are not, therefore, entitled to continue the use of capital punishments simply on the ground that it was of divine authority during the patriarchal ages, unless we are prepared to show that the moral and spiritual condition of man is unchanged, and unless also we are prepared to adopt animal sacrifices and circumcision, as resting upon the same ground.

But it is yet to be shown that the passage (Gen. ix, 6) does give any command for the shedding of man's blood. We will first take the authorized version:

"Whoso sheddest man's blood, by man shall his blood be shed." This contains no necessary command; it may be a prophetic warning, it may be a denunciation; but scarcely a sufficient warrant for execution, even as it stands: it is not "let him be put to death;" it is not "thou shalt stone him with stones that he die;" it is not "he shall be cut off from among his people;" it is not "let him die the death;" it is not, in short, a phrase implying any judicial sentence at all. The more natural and obvious meaning would be, "I will not allow crime to be unpunished;" "whoso committeth violence, I will cause to fall by violence;" "with the froward man, I will show myself froward;" "and so sacred will I hold blood, that even at the hand of beasts will I require the blood of man which they have shed." Furthermore, we do not treat Scriptural denunciations in the same rigid manner ordinarily: when the voice of inspiration declares that "bloody and deceitful men shall not live out half their days*," we do not suppose that any command is given to put them to death when we suppose that their days are half spent. We do not put to death the warrior because it is said, "they that take the sword shall perish by the sword." We know that the sacred pages speak of the punishment of sin in the hands of God; and we take all these and similar denunciations but as intimations of the certainty of that justice which must sooner or later overtake the guilty. Once more—there are *three* Noachic precepts, if precepts they be: one we altogether disregard, viz. that which requires the shedding of a beast's blood, if it have caused the death of

---

* Psalm lv, 23.

a human being; one we allow to fall into disuetude, viz. that which prohibits the eating of blood; and the third only is now contended for. But in the next place,

It is doubtful whether our version does give the exact sense of the passage, or whether the original will *bear* the translation which we have given it. The great Calmet translated the verse thus:

"Quiconque aura répandu le sang humain SERA
"PUNI par l'effusion de son propre sang."

In this version, the words in capitals are his own interpolation.

John Frederick Ostervald, on the other hand, renders it,

"Qui aura répandu le sang de l'homme dans
"l'homme, son sang sera répandu."

This is as nearly literal as can be.

The Vulgate has,

"Quicumque effuderit humanum sanguinem, fu-
"detur sanguis illius."

The Septuagint has,

"Ο ἐχέων αἷμα ἀνθώπου, ἀντὶ τοῦ αιματος αὐτοῦ ἐκχυθή-
σεται."

The Spanish version of Scio gives us:

"Todo el que derramare sangre humana, sera
"derramada su sangre."

To these we may add Wycliffe, who renders the passage,

"𝔚𝔥𝔬𝔰𝔬𝔢𝔳𝔢𝔯 𝔰𝔥𝔢𝔡𝔡𝔢𝔱𝔥 𝔬𝔲𝔱 𝔪𝔞𝔫𝔫𝔰'𝔰 𝔟𝔩𝔬𝔬𝔡𝔢, 𝔥𝔶𝔰 𝔟𝔩𝔬𝔬𝔡𝔢 𝔰𝔥𝔞𝔩𝔩 𝔟𝔢 𝔰𝔥𝔢𝔡𝔡𝔢*."

Thus there are five important versions, to which might be added many of less note, which altogether reject the words "*by man,*" in the second member of the sentence. On the other hand, Cranmer, Tonstall, and Ridley, Coverdale, Matthew, Beza, and the Bishops, interpolate the words "by man."

In this agree Luther and Giovanni Diodati. The Chaldee has a curious gloss; it may be translated,

"Whoso sheddeth man's blood before men, that
"is, before witnesses, shall by the sentence of the
"judge be exposed to the same pain†."

The Rabbis generally understood it,

"Whoso sheddeth man's blood by means of false
"witnesses, shall suffer the same penalty which has
"been unjustly inflicted by his means."

The varieties thus given will suffice to show that the passage is not one on which we should depend for the continuance of so terrible an institution as that of capital punishments.

But an examination of the original, in connexion with the above-given versions, will, perhaps, enable us to form a clearer opinion; the difficulty obviously lies in those words which the English translators in general have rendered "*by man,*" which Ostervald translates "in man," and which the LXX, the Vulgate, Wy-

---

* MS. Sion College.   † Calmet, vol. i, p. 82.

cliffe, and Scio, omit altogether. Let us then see how stands the original.

שֹׁפֵךְ דַּם הָאָדָם בָּאָדָם דָּמוֹ יִשָּׁפֵךְ כִּי
בְּצֶלֶם אֱלֹהִים עָשָׂה אֶת־הָאָדָם׃

The difficulty therefore lies in the words בָּאָדָם, "*in man,*" "*through man,*" "*with man,*" how it should be rendered, and to which member of the sentence it belongs; whether, in fact, with Cranmer and Luther, we are to divide the verse,

"Whoso sheddeth man's blood,
By man shall his blood be shed;"

or, adopting the word expressed by Ostervald, read

"Whoso sheddeth the blood of man that is in him,
His blood shall be shed."

Of all the versions given above, the most important is doubtless that of the Seventy; and this, while it affords *some* countenance to capital punishments, does so by giving the whole passage an expiatory meaning; so that Calmet rightly paraphrases the LXX:

"Celui qui répandra le sang humain, sera mis au "mort pour expier ce sang."

Calmet himself advocates the punishment of death on the authority of this passage, and Luther and Diodati take the same view.

But, setting authority aside, and applying ourselves only to the meaning of the words, what sense can we suppose in the translation of Ostervald, the most exact of all?

"Whoso sheddeth the blood of man that is in man,
His blood shall be shed."

If, with Wycliffe, Jerome, and Scio, we suppose the words "that is in man" are but a pleonasm, we may leave them out, as we treat other pleonasms: "He opened his mouth and said," and similar phrases. It does appear that this is the right view; the phrase seems to resemble such as the following:

"The fruit of a tree bearing seed whose seed is in itself."

"Who knoweth the things of a man, save the spirit of a man *that is in him?*"

And then we shall be led to conclude that the *best* translation is that by the author of the Vulgate:

"Whosoever sheddeth human blood, his blood shall be shed."

And the passage will rank with this:

"All they that take the sword shall perish by the sword*."

We have devoted so much time to the examination of this passage, because it is allowed to be the strongest; it is a declaration of God himself speaking immediately, and not by prophet and patriarch; in a dream or in a vision; it is præ-mosaic, and consequently cannot be treated as a part of the Jewish ceremonial code.

I think we have shown that this most formidable

---

* Matthew, xxvi, 52.

text is too doubtful in its meaning, susceptible of too many interpretations, to be taken as the chief support of capital punishment. We have seen how difficult it is to ascertain whether the blood of the murderer is to be shed "*by man*," or not; whether the text contains a command or merely a threat; and we have remarked that the best authorities, the LXX among the ancients, and Calmet among the moderns, who *do* accept it as speaking of the punishment of death, take care to show that they regard the death of the murderer *as an expiatory sacrifice*. There results, then, from this investigation two *probabilities:*

One, that there is no command remaining to us of older date than Moses, to condemn the murderer to death. Secondly, that if such command do exist, and the ninth chapter of Genesis present it, it can no longer be applicable in our days; inasmuch as the death of a murderer among us cannot be an expiatory sacrifice.

Of these probabilities I am satisfied with the first. Nor does it in the slightest degree matter to my argument, if it could be shown that the punishment of death was really practised among the patriarchs; because, as we have already shown, their practice can be no sufficient pattern for us, by reason of the different moral code under which they lived.

CHAPTER XV.

OF THE PRACTICE OF THE PRE-MOSAIC WORLD WITH RESPECT TO CAPITAL PUNISHMENTS.

WE pass by a natural transition from the theory to the practice of the præ-mosaic world, *we have* NO SINGLE INSTANCE *on record of capital punishment being inflicted previous to the time of Moses.* Murders we have, and other crimes, in lamentable abundance; but NOT ONE EXECUTION; we find particularly three homicides, two of which at least were murders: 1, The death of Abel; 2, The slaughter of a young man by Lamech; 3, The massacre of the Shechemites by Simeon and Levi. The two former were not only præ-mosaic, but also antediluvian. The history of the first murderer is very striking. As soon as his crime had been committed, he was called by his Maker to receive judgment; and here one would suppose, that if it had been intended to link together, by a perpetual connection, murder and death by law, Cain would have been immediately put to death; but we find not only the fratricide spared, but *not a single word* spoken concerning death as a legal punishment. Nay, when Cain himself expressed his fears lest he should fall a victim rather to vengeance than to justice, God made an especial covenant with him *that he should not be slain.* The term, "The Lord set a mark upon Cain," and which Rabbi Joseph, one of the Doctors of the Talmud, wisely supposes to have been a long horn growing out of his forehead, signifies rather "The Lord appointed a sign or token unto Cain."

Many hasty readers have supposed that it must have been a needless fear on the part of Cain that he might be killed, when we only hear of three persons beside him in the world. But if we recollect that this event took place in the hundred and twenty-ninth year of the world, the lowest probable calculation will give us a population of upwards of twelve hundred persons. (For further information on this topic, see Dodd and Clarke *in loco.*) Here we obtain a very remarkable element in our reasoning; the rising population of the young world had before their eyes the spectacle of a murderer, nay, a fratricide; they beheld him banished from the presence of God; condemned to be a fugitive and a vagabond on the earth; they heard the ground doubly cursed for him; and they yet knew that God had guaranteed the life of this vagabond, this fratricide, by a special covenant!

Let us turn to the case of Lamech. In about the year of the world 500, and consequently 370 years after the murder of Abel, we find another homicide. Lamech, the fifth in descent from Cain, is introduced

THE PRACTICE OF THE PRE-MOSAIC WORLD. 249

as speaking, in the earliest metrical verse extant, of his having slain a man; into the particulars of this event we have no means of inquiring. St. Jerome, following some Jewish traditions, says that Lamech had accidentally slain his unhappy ancestor, the first murderer. If the great Latin father be right, the passage is calculated to cast an awful light upon that which we have already discussed. Prior to it in chronology, it might be alluded to in the covenant which Jehovah made with Noah. There might be, and probably were, persons in the family of that patriarch to whom such allusion might be peculiarly needful. But whoever was the person to whose death Lamech was, whether accidentally or not, accessory—and, we confess, we do not see how Cain could be called a "young man"—certain it is, from the context, that Adah and Zillah, Lamech's wives, were in alarm for the consequences of his act. Referring to the previous case of Cain, he desires them to banish their fears, and addresses them thus:

> "Adah and Zillah, hear my voice,
> Ye wives of Lamech, hearken to my speech,
> I have slain a man for wounding me,
> A young man for bruising me;
> If Cain be avenged seven-fold,
> Surely Lamech seventy and seven."

In the uncertainty of the circumstances, not knowing whether Lamech slew a young man in self-defence, or destroyed him afterwards in revenge, our arguments cannot be so strong from this case as from that of Cain; but there are clues given to us here which may help us to at least a probable account of these circumstances.

Lamech would hardly have supposed his life in danger, for having, accidentally or in self-defence, slain a young man. His family were active, powerful, and popular. The case of Cain was well known, and esteemed, as we see, a kind of precedent. If we imagine, on the other hand, that Lamech, in revenge for an attack made upon him, had slain the aggressor, we can then well understand the apprehensions of Adah and Zillah, and Lamech's verses would bear some such interpretation as this: Do not be alarmed for my safety. If Cain, who had no cause of complaint against Abel, has not been put to death for murdering his brother; but, on the contrary, to slay *him* is a crime which must be avenged seven-fold; surely to kill me, who *had* cause of complaint against the person whom I have killed, is a crime which must be avenged seventy and seven-fold. At all events, it seems generally understood that, whether a murderer or not, Lamech had shed the blood of man; and he did not, so far as we hear, suffer any judicial penalty for it.

The next case is a postdiluvian one, the massacre —viz. of the men of Shechem by Simeon and Levi, the sons of Jacob. Here there can be no doubt whatever of the character of the offences; it was a murder as treacherous and as brutal as any recorded in the pages of history. It is true that the family of Jacob had been insulted; but the insult had been the doing of one man, and *all the men* of the city were slain for it. Now, though Jacob probably had little influence over his turbulent sons, yet had there been any universal command enjoining the punishment of death, he must have caused them to undergo the penalty of their crime; for Jacob was not only the head of his family, but a prince, and a great man. Yet we hear not a word of any judicial sentence passed on those fierce and cruel men.

The patriarchal age, therefore, gives us no light, save in the instance of Cain; and in the negative evidence afforded by the cases of Lamech and the sons of Jacob. There is no proof that the punishment of death was ever inflicted by the hands of the law, and it is more than probable that such penalty was neither commanded nor contemplated.

In a case of such vast moment, too, we have a right to expect the clearest and most unmistakable evidence, a direct command spoken by the mouth of Deity, and incapable of being interpreted in any other manner; and even this would require strengthening by proof, that those to whom it was addressed so understood and so acted upon it; at least, we should require the absence of proof to the contrary. How, then, stands the case? It is admitted that patriarchal law and practice are more important by far to us than

Mosaic, both because of their greater antiquity and their greater universality; and when we regard that dispensation with a view to its theory and practice on this topic, we find it doubtful, to say the least, whether any command existed, and more than doubtful whether any general adoption of the practice prevailed. At least, we may repeat what we have said before, that there is NO ONE instance on record of death-punishment.

CHAPTER XVI.

OF THE MOSAIC LAW OF CAPITAL PUNISHMENTS.

ENTERING upon the era of Moses, we shall find our theme will assume a new aspect. The punishment of death is pronounced by the Divine authority against a long list of offences—the fact cannot be denied—the sentence cannot be otherwise explained—the practice cannot be disputed. The questions, then, which we have to solve are two:

1. Are the circumstances of Christians sufficiently parallel to those of the Jews of old, for us to be warranted in adopting the same philosophy?

2. Is the Mosaic law binding upon us in those parts where capital punishments are pronounced?

The first of these questions we have already considered, with regard to the consequences of death to the party slain; and we must here observe, that the *position of the* JUDGE is also different. We must not allow it to escape from our remembrance, that the constitution for which the Mosaic code was established was not a monarchy, nor a republic, nor any kind of mere human government, but a PURE THEOCRACY. God himself ruled among HIS people; HIS visible presence rested on His mercy seat. He was King—He was Leader—He was Judge. He appointed his own ministers. In some cases, He instituted a trial by ordeal, engaging *Himself* to declare the guilt or innocence of the parties accused: the waters of jealousy will furnish an instance*. He appointed the Urim and Thumim, by which He might at all times be consulted. He inspired His priests and His prophets, and thus not only supplied by His Spirit the spiritual and eternal sanctions which are not to be found in the written law of Moses, but, by constituting Himself the final Judge of appeal, He made it impossible that the innocent should perish, or the guilty escape.

This very important fact is entirely lost sight of by those who argue in favor of capital punishments because they formed a part of the Jewish code. And as it is not lawful to argue against any thing from its abuse, so it is illogical to deny the validity of a principle by reason of a corrupt practice. We know that the pure THEOCRACY of the Jews did not continue, that the oracles of Urim and Thumim became silent, that in degenerate days the Spirit of God no longer inspired the judges of Israel. But the lofty theory of the law remained the same, and its principles were no more changed by the degeneracy of the people, than those of our church are changed by the fact that nine-tenths

---

* Numb. v, 12 et seq.

of our population are self-excommunicated. The law was made for a congregation of believers, presided over by their Maker; and when that congregation became idolatrous, when they substituted a king for their immediate and Divine Ruler, then many portions of the law of Moses became as little applicable to the Jews as they would have been to the Greeks.

We are compelled, in our day, to judge according to evidence; and that evidence, as we well know, may be false; it may be given in malice or revenge, or with a view to screen the guilty; but, unless there be counter-evidence, it must be received. Again—*circumstantial* evidence may mislead us; and there are instances on record of persons who have been put to death on such proof, who have been subsequently discovered to have been innocent. Yet this is an unavoidable defect in all human courts: we must either judge thus, or leave crime unpunished; and the consequences in this latter case would be far more appalling. So that, in addition to the expiatory character of the malefactor's death, a character no longer admissible, the law of Moses contemplated A PERFECT CERTAINTY, and not a *high probability* merely, of guilt. Thus at every step we diverge still further from the supposed parallel between the system of capital punishment under Moses, and the system of capital punishment in Christian states.

Again—*if we seek to uphold our practice by the sanction of the Levitical law, we are proving too* much. What right can we possibly have to select one, two, three, or four offences, and say, these we will punish with death, because God thus commanded Moses, and remit, on our own authority, the same punishment in other cases? What title, for instance, have we to leave the adulterer and adultress unpunished—to fine the blasphemer five shillings—to recognize as a lawful act the eating of blood—and to put the murderer to death—when the written law denounces the same penalty against all? The practice of our courts is to pronounce, or rather to record, sentence of death against persons convicted of treason, arson, and certain other offences (altogether forming eight classes); but these persons are never now executed; their sentences are commuted for various terms of imprisonment or transportation, and the murderer only is expected, according to a phrase once correct, but no longer applicable, " to *expiate* his offences on the gallows." When, however, we thus reason, the Levitical sanction is given up, and we are referred back to the covenant with Noah.

But, further, in considering what parts of the Mosaic code are still obligatory, we shall be much aided in our researches by the *possibility* of observance. It is agreed that the whole of the ceremonial system is repealed—that the sacrificial institution, with its dependencies, has been rendered unlawful—that circumcision is remitted, and the exclusive character of the dispensation has passed away: there remains, therefore, only the moral code, and that moral code at once divides itself into two parts—1st. That spoken by the mouth or God himself; and 2nd. That which was conveyed to his people through Moses. The first is *complete*, and is capable of universal application; every moral obligation, as well as every spiritual duty, may be elicited from it; the peculiarities of no age, and the circumstances of no climate or race, render it inappropriate; and hence, whatever decision we arrive at about the law delivered by the lips of Moses, we feel ourselves reverently bound to receive that delivered by the mouth of God.

It may be taken as an axiom, that whatever has been *immediately* revealed by the Great Supreme is in some sense more important than that which is *mediately* revealed; and, in accordance with this canon, the Jews themselves have ever looked upon the rest of the law as a divinely inspired comment upon the Decalogue, as applying the provisions of that code to the chosen people, and as constituting the *exclusive* portion of the Mosaic covenant. That they were right in so deeming it, may be shown from the general consent of nations, who have allowed devotion to God and reverence to parents to be duties of universal obligation, and, by an equally universal agreement, have condemned blasphemy, false worship, murder, theft, adultery, false witness, and covetousness: thus they have, without collusion, come to the same determination as the Jews; while these latter have ever considered their law—that is, the commands of God, delivered to them through Moses—as a peculiar inheritance, with which other nations have nothing to do. If, therefore, the Jewish theory of their own institutions be the correct one, it will follow that all of the Old Covenant that is binding upon Christians is comprised in the Decalogue.

But the Decalogue is a list of duties to be performed, and of crimes to be avoided; it has no provisions for the enforcement, by human means, of its enactments. Some of them, such as the fifth and tenth commandments, are incapable of such enforcement; for who can define with accuracy what shall be a legal amount of honor to parents? and who can see into a man's heart, whether he be covetous or not? Hence it is that the Decalogue, which is the highest degree of legal generalization, says nothing about punishment by the hand of the law for any offence whatever; and, if we be right in taking the Jewish theory as to the exclusive parts of their constitution, and in accepting "the law written on two tables by the finger of God" as that which *alone* is binding upon us, we shall conclude that the Levitical dispensation gives us no sanction whatever for the continuance of capital punishments.

CHAPTER XVII.

OF THE SUPPOSED CHRISTIAN SANCTION OF CAPITAL PUNISHMENTS.

The last ground on which the penalty of death has been advocated is a negative one, and may be stated thus:

Christ our Lord declared that he came "not to destroy the law, but to fulfil it*;" and therefore every portion of that law which was not strictly ceremonial, or typical, or expressly repealed by him, must be still in force. Now, capital punishment is not typical, nor ceremonial, nor did He indirectly or directly repeal it; therefore it must be still in force. This statement, which we have taken great care not to *understate*, contains a fallacy in every portion of it. For, first, the declaration of our Lord, "I came not to destroy, but to fulfil," is misunderstood as though he had said "I came not to repeal, but to confirm;" whereas the true meaning of the Saviour is, I came not to annul the sanctions of the law, and to defraud it of its claims, but to fulfil what you and your ancestors, and

---

* Matt. v, 17.

those who shall succeed you, neither have been nor ever will be able to perform; I came to fulfil in your stead the works of the law, that the deficiencies of those, who with a true and lively faith believe on me, may not be reckoned against them. Our Lord thus propounded a great theological truth. The Scribes and Pharisees fancied that he came to annul the law of Moses. He shows them that he does it the greatest honour. HE, in his character of man, as the great spiritual representative of our race—the second Adam, executes all the conditions of that law; and as a covenant, all of whose conditions are fully and faithfully executed, is not destroyed but fulfilled, so he did not destroy the law but fulfilled it. But though the moral law is still binding on us as a rule of life, we are no longer placed under it *as a covenant;* we are under a covenant of grace; and FAITH, not WORKS, is to be the instrumental cause of our acceptance with God.

We are driven into this "pure theology" by the fallacy which it refutes, and thus is induced a second necessity of protesting against the doctrine of faith *without* works. Works are necessary as evidences of our faith; for where no works are produced, there faith is dead, and consequently unacceptable before God. To return to our subject: Christ's fulfilment of the conditions, and suffering the penalties of the law, abrogates those conditions, and remits those penalties, so far as we are concerned; and thus the very passage, which, misunderstood and *politically* regarded, makes against our argument, does, when rightly viewed and *theologically* considered, greatly support it.

With regard to the assertion that capital punishment is not ceremonial, we willingly admit it. Neither the axe, nor the guillotine, nor the gibbet, can easily be ranked among *ceremonies;* but when we are told that it is not typical, we come to another fallacy; we know that it is not *now* typical, and hence we object to it; but previous to the incarnation of our Lord, the death of a malefactor was looked upon as an *expiatory sacrifice*, and was consequently as decidedly typical as the offering up of a bull, or the letting free of a scape-goat. So far, then, as it is allowed that all *typical* portions of the Old Testament dispensation were, *ipso facto*, repealed by the revelation of the New; so far as it is admitted that on the appearance of the antitype the type loses its significancy, so far must it be conceded that the very incarnation of the Saviour, without rendering a single word necessary, did repeal, *ipso facto*, the punishment of death.

But is it true that neither directly nor indirectly did our Lord intimate such repeal? Has he left the matter altogether as it was? We think not. We do not, indeed, find that, *totidem verbis*, the penalty of death is pronounced unlawful; but we have a new system with which the former one was inconsistent; and it will not be difficult to show that it formed no part of our Lord's intention to develope, during his human life, every consequence of his divine mission.

In the first place, till his own sacrifice was accomplished, the Mosaic law continued in full force, and he could not, therefore, in his human person repeal it. It was not till the awful words, "*It is finished,*" were pronounced, that the edifice of types and shadows, like a building whose purpose was accomplished, and whose days were completed, fell into ruins. So long, therefore, as the preaching of the Lord was heard, so long was the law of Moses the only authorized channel of salvation; and this, too, will account for what, on any other principle, would be perfectly incomprehensible; viz. the far greater development of theological truth in the writings of the Apostles than in the recorded teaching of the Lord. He spake while he was fulfilling the law, and thus changing the covenant with man, but while the covenant of works was still in force. They wrote when the covenant had passed away, and they were instructed by His Spirit in the "things pertaining to the kingdom."

We have thus seen that our Lord could not, consistently with the scheme of his office as Redeemer and substitute, repeal the law; it was binding upon HIM as a man, till he had accomplished it. But if we suppose that he gave no instructions as to the sublimer philosophy and loftier morality of the "truth as it is in Jesus," we shall be greatly mistaken. It was not to be expected that he would go through every precept of the Levitical code, and repeal or confirm, as the case might require. But if he gave any clue to the principles on which he intended to base his morality, it will be amply sufficient—AND THIS HE DID. In the first place, he entirely repealed the *lex talionis* which had pervaded the Jewish mind*. He instituted a system of ethics, in which the curb was placed far more decidedly and universally on the heart, instead of the outward actions; and at the same time that he thus led men to understand that God expected more of them than hitherto they had apprehended, he gave them less right to be rigid one with another.

On one occasion only, the punishment of death was brought before him as a matter for his decision. A woman was taken in adultery, "in the very act†." Those who brought her before Christ stated the circumstances, and observed, that Moses had enacted against such the penalty of death by stoning, but referring the case at the same time to him for judgment. The persons who thus questioned him were captiously disposed; and we have already seen reasons why Christ could not, during his own life, repeal that law which he had come to fulfil. He evinced an unwillingness to decide—"stooping down, he wrote with his fingers upon the ground, as though he heard them not." But they were determined to be heard; and, after a second time thus exhibiting a disposition to evade their importunity, he rose up and replied in the memorable words: "He that is without sin amongst

---

* Matt. v. † John, viii, 3 et seq.

you, let him first cast a stone at her." On hearing this, they, "being convicted by their own conscience, went out, one by one, beginning at the eldest, even to the last." The answer of the Lord is in all respects remarkable. I, For its wisdom. The Scribes and Pharisees, had he replied Yes or No, had an accusation ready against him. Had he said, "Let her life be spared, he would have been accused as hostile to the law of Moses. Had he answered, let the law take its course, he would have been accused to the Roman governor as arrogating to the Jewish law the right of life and death, which the Romans had taken away. But it is, II, Remarkable for its insight into the human heart. He knew how guilty, even of that very sin, were those who brought the woman before him; and from the context, we may assume that he saw the penitence of the woman herself. When the woman was left alone before the Saviour, he said unto her, "Woman, where are those thine accusers? Hath no man condemned thee?" She saith unto him, "No man, Lord." And Jesus said unto her, "Neither do I condemn thee—go and sin no more*." It is singularly to our purpose, that this narrative has been perversely cited as proof that Christ did not condemn adultery; and the way in which Paley vindicates the

---

* We do not enter here into the genuineness of the narrative, thinking it enough that it is supported by Chrysostem, Jerome, Ambrose, Augustine, and many other Fathers.

morality of the Gospel is strongly against the infliction of capital punishment. "Hath no man condemned thee?" That is, hath no man adjudged thee to death? "No man, Lord." *In their private judgment* all had condemned her, but judicially no one had done so; and her reply, as well as our Lord's acceptance of it, prove that it was of a judicial condemnation both spake. "Neither do I condemn thee!" that is again, Neither do I judge thee to death.

Now, we may reasonably presume, that, had our Lord intended the punishment of death to be in any future age denounced against adultery, he would have qualified this sentence. It would have been easy for him to have informed her of the due punishment of her offence; to have declared that the law was just and right, and would ever be so; and, finally, to have pardoned her, in consideration of her penitence. It would have been easy to have given then (the only recorded opportunity) his sanction to the continuance of the penal code; but he did none of these things; he simply asserted that he did not judicially declare her worthy of death; and thus, whatever becomes of the rest of the penal system, it is quite clear that adultery is no longer a capital crime. Now, if a great moral offence, as this is, be thus specially exempted from the pain of death, and be thus specially exempted, not because it was selected purposely, but because it was accidentally brought before the notice of the Lord, may it not be assumed that all offences of less enormity are exempted by the effect of this provision? And what offences are there of greater criminality, if we except murder? At all events, the class of crimes to be punished with death must be reduced to a very small number.

But if any portion of the penal system of Moses be repealed by our Lord, it must be perfectly arbitrary on our part to decide, concerning the rest, that we will consider some in force and some not; and though we may have good reason for rejecting capital punishments in cases of any crime short of murder, are we justified by such negative evidence as we have in retaining it even in these? Is the course of our reasoning and the tenor of our action the same in other instances? Take the case of slavery, an institution regulated by the law of Moses, and recognized by the writings of the Apostles. What do we say when this topic is brought before us? We at once reply, without hesitation, that Christ did not rectify all the evils that were in the world at once; that he left the consequences of his religion to develope themselves; that the Apostles were not the founders of the Roman polity; and that, in declaring all men equal before God, they implied an equality of civil rights among men. Further, we say that negative evidence is not sufficient to sustain a system so charged with evils as that of slavery; and that, in default of positive testimony in its favour, it must be abolished. Thus spake the voice of Christian England, and was heard.

An argument has been frequently adduced in favour of death as a punishment from the words of St. Paul (Rom. xiii, 4), "for he beareth not the sword in vain;" and it is contended that as the sword is an instrument of destruction, so it can only, in the hands of the civil magistrate, denote the power of putting offenders to death. To this we would reply, first, that it by no means follows that because the sword is an instrument of destruction, therefore, to speak *of the sword of justice*, must imply the power of inflicting capital punishment.

The sword is the emblem of sovereignty, and signifies *the right of making war*, which is peculiarly the prerogative of the sovereign authority. The fasces, the axe, the letter Tau, were symbolical of judicial death; but not the sword, which was never, save in exceptional cases, the instrument of punishment. St. Paul himself furnished one of these exceptional cases, for he was beheaded with a sword. But at the time at which the passage before us was written, the common mode of death-punishment was crucifixion, with which the sword had not the slightest connexion.

If we take the sword of justice to signify the sovereign authority, delegated to inferior magistrates from the chief, for the purpose of repressing crime and preserving peace, we shall see how apt is the apostolic caution. If we wished to warn those who were already well disposed against any conduct which could bring them under legal censure, we should not say—"If you do wrong, be afraid; for the magistrate has power to put you to death;" but we might, and very likely should say, "so long as you keep clear from evil-doing, you have no occasion to fear the power of the magistrate; but if you transgress the law, then you may be apprehensive, for his authority is delegated from the sovereign, and is not to be had in contempt."

What, again, can the sword signify in cases of slight offences, petty thefts, brawls, disturbances, drunkenness, all which this same *sword* has to repress?

To take a modern instance, the *pointless sword* borne before our own sovereign signifies not death, but mercy.

But even were we disposed to allow our opponents all they claim from this passage, does it establish a perpetual propriety and necessity of death as a judicial punishment? St. Paul enjoins obedience to the civil governors, and submission to the laws—such as they were in his day—and we find slavery and capital punishment among them. We are not surely to argue for the perpetuity of these things as a matter of duty.

A figure of speech, moreover, is a very sandy foundation for a logical superstructure; and till we can find something far more positive than this "bearing of the sword" in his writings, we must be pardoned if we decline to reckon the great Apostle of the Gentiles among the advocates of judicial death.

Thus we have briefly passed in review the grounds of what has hitherto been considered a melancholy necessity. We have considered the sanction of the patriarchal, the Mosaic, and the Christian dispensations, and have slightly touched on the moral and political question. But, before we recapitulate, there is one circumstance which ought not to be passed over in silence: it is, that sections of the Christian communion, however widely differing one from another, are capable of agreement on this point, regarding it as a theological question; and it not unfrequently happens that the very ground stated as an objection by one party shall be the very reverse of the ground given by another. Thus the Roman Catholic, whose belief concerning the sacrament of penance and the right of absolution tends to persuade him, if not of the perfect and absolute security, at least of the comparative safety of the sinner dying, albeit by the hands of justice, in that faith, cannot without alarm see the same sentence carried into effect on those destitute of such advantages: while the Protestant, disbelieving the efficacy of spiritual efforts thus referred to, is in equal alarm for the safety of those who perish for their crimes with their minds blinded and their consciences deceived. The one beholds a sinner "sent to his rest unshrived and unblest;" the other, a hardened malefactor, dying in delusive hope. Those who still maintain that man is to be saved by his works, see the desperate condition of a man whose works are evil, and who has no opportunity afforded him of amendment. Those who know that " without holiness, no man can see the Lord," and who know the difficulties in the way of the necessary change, cannot but shudder at the probable results of death as a legal penalty.

We shall now recapitulate. We began this investigation by a brief inquiry into the moral and political necessity of capital punishments. We had reason to conclude, that, as a preventive, they have utterly failed; that they tend to harden the hearts of the multitude, and to depreciate, among them, the value of human life; that they have established an " aristocracy" of evil; and that they have brutalized the public taste.

We went on to show that the spiritual condition of the person thus put to death must be perilous in the highest degree. That, in many, if not most, cases, the chance of his conversion is an exceedingly remote one; and that we have not the slightest reason to believe that God will set aside his ordinary judgment on account of human enactments.

Thus far we referred to the nature of the case, independently of any divine command, or any divine sanction, expressed or implied. But as it is stated that God gave a command to Noah to put the murderer to death, we examined the passage supposed to contain such injunction; and were led to believe that the very fact itself—i. e. the existence of such a command—was exceedingly doubtful. We found that there were many ways in which the text had been interpreted, and that many of the most important versions entirely left out that clause which committed to the hand of man the office of avenging the blood of the slain.

In addition to this, we were led to regard the death of the murderer, whenever it did take place (and this too is more than doubtful, under the patriarchal system), as an expiatory sacrifice, and consequently differing in character from the same kind of punishment in our own days. When, from the patriarchal, we proceeded to review the capital punishments of the Levitical dispensation, we found not only this difference, but a provision whereby the innocent could *never* suffer, and the guilty could *never* escape. We noticed the long list of offences punished with death, and perceived that in nearly all these cases the law had, rightly or wrongly, been repealed in Christian states. Hence it was plain that no practical adherence to the penal code of Moses prevailed: and we have also shown that such adherence was not expected on the part of the Jews, who considered *all* their law, save the Decalogue, as their national and peculiar inheritance. We noticed also the evidence that the Decalogue *alone* is binding on us as Christians, and showed that no system of punishments could find a place in so strict a generalization. Thus it appeared that neither the law as given to Noah, nor the premosaic practice, nor the Levitical code, afforded the supposed sanction: the first two from want of sufficient evidence; the last from want of any parallel between the Jewish condition and our own.

When we turned to the Christian era, we found many parts of the Levitical system, *ipso facto*, repealed; we found our Lord's declaration that " he came not to destroy, but to fulfil," capable of a theological meaning *only*, and one which is as much against the punishment of death, as its first and apparent meaning is in favor of it. We saw too, that, in the only case where he was called on to adjudicate as to the infliction or non-infliction of death, he decided against it: and thus we may fairly assume that the genius of Christianity is opposed to capital punishments. Even if our case had been less strongly supported, if the *positive* evidence by which it is sustained had been weaker by far, still that on the other side is so doubtful, and so much of it negative in its character, that we may well question the *lawfulness* of *death* by the hands of the executioner.

Lastly, it is but to weigh the difference between one punishment and another. Our adversaries sometimes tell us that we have no right to advocate the abolition of capital punishment, till we are in a position to suggest some secondary one which may with sufficient advantage take its place; but this is a most transparent fallacy. Surely we may do away with that which we find to be evil, without being bound to substitute a positive good. If I saw a man taking medicine which I knew would cause his death, I should at once tell him to forbear, and, if I could do so, pluck the poison from his hand; and I should think it a marvellously weak objection on his part, were he to say, I am ill, and unless you can give me medicine calculated to effect a cure, you have no right to take away that which I am using. I feel at once that it is competent for me to reply—I know that what you are taking will poison you, but I am not prepared to prescribe for your disease. Go to a physician. Just in like manner we feel that death punishment is a quack nostrum—a political poison—and even if *none* of those who advocate its abolition were able to suggest a secondary penalty to stand in its stead, their advocacy would not be the less valid on that account.

None but an infallible judge should inflict an irrevocable punishment. There are many modes which would obviate the necessity of the gibbet, and would yet furnish a penalty dreaded as much, if not more, by the malefactor. If such should be tried, and (as a preventive of crime) should fail, they will then but be in the same category in which capital punishment now stands, and there would be removed from the national responsibilities the sending so many unprepared souls to appear before God. If, on the other hand, they should be found more successful, there will be a double gain. Under all circumstances, the experiment may safely be tried. The wisdom of our law-givers can hardly fail to devise appropriate and effective means for securing the public peace and preserving the public virtue.

CHAPTER XVIII.

OF LAWS CONCERNING MARRIAGE, DIVORCE, ETC.

IN cases of crime perpetrated by fraud or violence, a Christian code draws a minute distinction between such as are to be punished by the strong arm of the law, and such as may be left to the decision of a civil tribunal; and this is not unfrequently left to the choice of the injured party, who may proceed by way of indictment or by way of civil action, according as he conceives the ends of justice will be best answered by one or the other. But this choice is only given within certain limits, for it leaves one of the parties to decide the important question, whether the act shall be treated as a crime; that is, an offence against society; or merely a wrong, that is, an offence against an individual.

There is, therefore, a large class of sinful acts which can only be treated by the civil, and another equally large class which fall exclusively under the cognizance of the criminal, law. Those offences, which arise out of the constitution of the sexes, present sometimes great difficulty to the legislature. For those which are in their very nature acts of violence, such as rape, the criminal law affords a ready and appropriate punishment. In abduction, which is sometimes effected by force and sometimes by fraud, the same mode of proceeding can be adopted. But what can the Christian law-giver do with such as are neither crimes of fraud or violence; or if the former have a share in them, it is too small to characterize them? What can be done in cases of seduction and adultery? Our own law considers them as wrongs rather than crimes, and leaves the parties supposed to be chiefly aggrieved the power of obtaining redress by means of a civil action. The question before us is, whether this be the most Christian enactment on the subject, whether acts that have consequences so frightful ought not to be viewed rather as crimes than as mere wrongs? and the discussion of this question opens a wide field for debate; for there are few which offer greater scope for differences of opinion. We have already laid down two principles.

First, That Christian legislature has no right to punish sins, *as sins:* this is God's work.

Secondly, That a Christian legislature has no right to punish *at all*, except so far as such punishment is calculated to reform the offender, to repress the offence, or to do both.

Now, both adultery and seduction are crimes as well as sins; they strike at the very root of Christian society—they lower the tone of character—they destroy worldly prospects—they break up the peace of families; these are their direct and immediate effects:

indirectly, they debase the feeling of society; they have a peculiar tendency to reproduce themselves; they feed the channels of prostitution—in itself an evil of the greatest magnitude, whether the health or the morals of the people be considered. For these reasons, I apprehend that a Christian legislature has clearly *a right* to remove these offences from the civil to the criminal branch of jurisdiction, if by so doing they could the more easily or the more effectually be repressed. There is perhaps no sin, in many cases not even murder itself, accompanied by an amount of moral delinquency so great as seduction; yet our law only punishes it by the infliction of a fine, greater or smaller in amount according to the judgment of a jury; and even this is only levied by the quaintest and oddest fiction in the world. It is supposed that every young woman is the servant of her parents; that the consequence of her sin—pregnancy, child-birth, and the subsequent care necessary for her infant—deprive her parents of her household labour; and for this an action lies against the seducer. Nothing is said of the ruin of the unhappy girl's prospects in life, of the injury done to her character and powers of usefulness; nothing of the shame, misery, and remorse, ending sometimes in madness and suicide; nothing of the agony of the family thus dishonored; nothing indeed of aught that requires consideration. A crime of the deepest dye is committed, injury the most widely spread and of the most enduring character is inflicted, and the victim is passed over without notice, while the law says to the broken-hearted parent: There is a certain number of pounds sterling; take it; be comforted, and hold your peace. As redress, then, it is nothing, or worse than nothing: as a punishment, it is still more open to objection: the rich man, he who has leisure and opportunity to pursue this atrocious wickedness, as he would hunting or fishing, or any other sport,—he escapes with absolute impunity; for a fine in the shape of damages is to him no punishment. The poorer offender is rarely brought to judgment at all! If he will maintain his illegitimate offspring, it is all that is expected from him; and this he must do, were that offspring born in wedlock. Hence it would seem that the law might almost as well be absolutely dormant. On the other hand, let seduction be an indictable offence, and a vast amount of evil will at once ensue. Let it be considered that there are two parties to the sin; that the temptation to it may arise on either side; that, in the majority of cases, it is absolutely impossible to ascertain the relative amount of guilt; that promises to marry may be pleaded in another court, and are rarely, if ever, treated with leniency when unfulfilled; and it will become evident that the present state of the law is by no means so bad as it seems. Instances may arise in which imprisonment and hard labour, or even transportation, would be no more than fitting punishment; but the law *must* deal with *classes of offences*, and not with particular cases as they arise. Frequently the burden would be laid on the wrong back; frequently prosecutions merely malicious would be instituted for the sake of extorting money. Frequently the previous character and conduct of the so-called victim would be virtually overlooked; for where exposure is the great evil dreaded, the amount of punishment inflicted is but a secondary consideration: the least injured, because the least virtuous, would be the first and loudest to threaten; and the most atrocious offender would not uncommonly receive the smallest amount of severity. Yet it may be said, with justice, that some personal and not pecuniary infliction would alone be a fit retribution to the wealthy seducer, and would affect, through him, the whole class of society to which he belongs. Many men, who will not be deterred by the prospect of damages, would shrink from imprisonment with hard labour; and an offence visited by such a penalty would soon come to be looked upon as disgraceful as it really is: six weeks at the treadmill would soon bring down the social reputation of the most graceful and elegant roué to its proper level. After weighing all the chief arguments on both sides, we come again to the consideration, that it is a sin in which two parties share; it is the joint act of the complainant and the person from whom redress is sought; that it is obviously unfair to punish, as a wrong, an act to which the wronged party knowingly consents; and that Providence punishes many crimes which human laws cannot reach. Thus it would appear that our own law acts, on the whole, wisely in leaving a civil tribunal, in such cases, to apportion justice. It is, however, quite certain that the form in which such actions are brought is worse than ridiculous; they should be direct, and specify the real nature of the injuries inflicted; and juries should, as they have it in their power, award, in more than usually bad cases, damages to such an amount as to be a real and severe punishment.

Marriage is looked upon by our law under the two-fold aspect of a civil and religious contract. In consequence of this view, any breach of the civil contract may be redressed by a civil process: with the religious contract no earthly power has any thing to do. This topic has already been discussed in a preceding paragraph, and it will be unnecessary to recur to it again. The question then reduces itself to a very simple one: whether adultery should be considered as a *crime* or a *wrong*. Our law has decided in favour of the latter view; and as all the arguments applicable to the case of seduction apply with double force to the present, it would appear that the decision is a wise one. It is true that a new sufferer is introduced, and that the mischief is, in many instances, much greater; but, on the other hand, the female offender has far greater advantages in the way of experience, position, and protection, and cannot plead that which in cases of seduction is the greatest palliation; viz. promise of marriage.

Again, if there be a new sufferer, there is a new remedy; the injured husband may sue for and obtain a divorce, in which case a punishment every way adequate to the guilt falls on the unhappy woman, while the husband obtains every satisfaction which human ingenuity can devise.

The question of divorce is surrounded by difficulties rather apparent than real; the Christian can see but one rule; CHRIST himself has spoken plainly on the subject, and while He distinctly allows divorce in cases of adultery, He as distinctly prohibits it in any other; but the divorce of which He speaks is not a mere separation, but a dissolution of the marriage contract, and a consequent permission to marry again. It may be doubted whether this permission is granted to *both* parties, or whether unfaithfulness on *either* side is a *Christian* cause for divorce: our law has practically decided both questions in the negative. This divorce is called "à vinculo matrimonii," because it sets both parties free from their marriage obligations; but there is another kind of divorce, called "à mensa et thoro," which, while it separates the parties, does not enable either to contract any new marriage. I apprehend it can scarcely be a question with Christians, whether our Lord's rule may be enlarged; and although many politicians have contended that it may, or rather have argued as though it had no existence at all, there is one consideration which will bring back all right-minded economists to a cheerful acquiescence in it. To exemplify this, we shall take an extreme case; let it be supposed (and unhappily it need not be a mere supposition) that a man finds his wife utterly unsuited to him in temper, habits, and pursuits, negligent of all her duties, careless of her children, destitute of all affection either for him or them, betraying his interests, insulting his friends, thwarting his purposes, and yet free from all suspicion of adultery; the question is, whether he should have the power of divorcing her and marrying again. In such a case, the evils which would fall on the wife would be richly deserved; but how many instances would occur in which divorces would be sought on morally inadequate grounds, and where and by whom should the line of distinction be drawn? The position of the woman would be of incalculable disadvantage; supposing her to be destitute of property, how is she to be supported? The time of her vigour and beauty may be past; there may be no hope for her of a second marriage; and though the children may be provided for by their father, yet the advantages of the divorce rest with the husband almost wholly, the disadvantages almost wholly with the divorced wife.

If it be said, that no divorce would take place under such circumstances, save with the consent of both parties, I reply, that there are many ways in which the consent of the woman might be obtained, short of actual violence, and yet by no means leaving her to her own unbiassed judgment; nor, indeed, should the law of a Christian country *permit* her to abdicate a position which the Founder of our holy religion has absolutely secured to her. From these considerations, it would appear that, in those countries where divorce *à vinculo matrimonii* is permitted for other causes than adultery, the rule of our Lord is relaxed, and the national code placed in an unenviable opposition to that of Christ.

But there is another point to which the Christian politician has to direct his attention, before he dismisses from his mind the subject of divorce *à vinculo matrimonii*. In *one* case our Lord as decidedly permits this, as he forbids it in others; the operation of our law makes this permission almost a dead letter; even in the most aggravated and scandalous instances, divorce is only attainable by the rich; for, first, legal proof of the adultery must be obtained, and this is seldom done, save by means of an action at law; this proof must then be pleaded in the ecclesiastical courts, by a still more expensive process; and, lastly, after a hearing before the House of Lords, an act must pass the Imperial Legislature, enabling the applicant to marry again; this last step in the transaction costing as much as the other two. Now this is an anomaly of the most intolerable character; in *almost* every instance it frees the offending wife from the possibility of being divorced, and, in not a few, it enables her to violate her marriage vows with all but perfect impunity. There can be but little doubt that much immorality prevails in consequence of this legislative imperfection. If, in all well-proved cases of adultery, divorce were speedily and cheaply attainable, and if the support of the female offender were thrown on her paramour (her bare support, nothing more, and this only till she married again), it can hardly be doubted that the crime itself would greatly and rapidly decrease.

There is another kind of divorce, that *à mensa et thoro*, a merely legalized separation, which permits the parties to re-unite themselves, should they think fit, and which does not allow either to contract any other matrimonial engagement during their joint lives; this kind of divorce should be more easily attainable; indeed, either party ought to have the right to demand it independently of the other; and it should be accompanied by an equitable adjustment of property, a fair arrangement with regard to the support and education of children, and an adequate maintenance for the separated wife. For this kind of divorce, it ought to be sufficient to lay before a competent tribunal proofs of cruelty, gross neglect, or hopeless incompatibility of temper; and its effect should be, during the time it operated, to release both parties from all obligations to each other, save those pecuniary ones specified in the deed of divorce.

And here, perhaps, will be a fitting place to notice some of the theories lately put forth with regard to prohibited marriages. That persons standing towards each other in certain degrees of blood-relationship should be prevented from intermarrying, is clear, from the physical as well as moral mischiefs which attend such unions, and the great evils which result from their bare permission. But the difficulty is, in forbidding incestuous marriages, to decide what are incestuous and what are lawful.

If we consider ourselves bound by the Levitical law, we shall be sure not to err by taking too much latitude; for, though there may be more than doubt whether in this respect that code is universally binding, we are certainly not bound by any thing more stringent. By that law*, all intermarriages are prohibited between persons in the direct ascending and descending line, together with their respective wives and husbands. Grand-parents, parents, children, grand-children, whether by blood or marriage—a father's wife standing in the same position as a mother, and a daughter's husband as a son. Marriages are in like manner prohibited between brothers and sisters, and half brothers and sisters; but their respective wives and husbands are not all included in the prohibition; thus it is not forbidden for a man to marry his deceased wife's sister, while that of a woman with her deceased husband's brother would seem to have been in some cases permitted, and in others commanded. Again, marriage with an uncle or aunt by blood was

---

* Leviticus, chapters xviii and xx.

forbidden; but it was not unlawful for a man to marry the daughter of his deceased wife's sister, although he was not permitted to marry his uncle's wife.

And here appears to end the Mosaic scale of prohibitions, and the scale of the canon law adds those mentioned above as not forbidden by Moses. Of these, there is only one which needs especial remark; viz. that between a man and his deceased wife's sister. In such unions there are many advantages; they were permitted and continually contracted among the Jews; they were tacitly allowed for ages by the law of this country, as being voidable, but not void; they are to this day, in spite of the revival of the Romish canon law against them, of constant occurrence amongst ourselves, and the only reason against them is, that the Pope's code prohibits them, though the Pope continually grants dispensations to contract them. The enactment, then, by which they are at this moment forbidden, is a violation of Christian and national rights, an indefensible submission to the superstitious laws of the Papacy, and the needless creation of an offence*: the long permission had no evil

---

* The present Lord Chief Justice of the Court of Queen's Bench, Lord Campbell, was not ashamed to say, in his place in Parliament, with regard to the efforts made to repeal this most objectionable law, " that he disapproved *the kind of agitation* " adopted by its opponents, the delivering of public lectures, the " printing of speeches, and the circulation of pamphlets!!"

consequence, the short prohibition has already produced the most lamentable results.

We will close this chapter with a few words on the rights, and what has been called the "enfranchisement," of women. It will be evident to the student of the Old and New Testament, that neither Moses nor our Lord placed the sexes upon a footing of perfect equality; they have their separate spheres, and are supreme in each respectively; but the government, the actual rule and management, whether of the family or the state, devolves, by divine authority, upon man; the vast majority of women not only cheerfully acquiesce in this dispensation, but hail it as a blessing and a boon to themselves; they are released from a kind of duty for which they have rarely a desire, and still more rarely qualifications, and are enabled to devote themselves to those high and holy duties, the fulfilment of which constitutes their true mission. This is not a mere arbitrary enactment on the part of Providence, still less a contrivance of man to keep his help-mate in subjection: there can be no rights without correlative duties; so long as human nature remains what it is, we shall have wars and contentions; those who would make all offices held by men open to women, should be prepared to assert that the fatigues and dangers of war and seamanship, of mining and manufacture, of the forge and the dockyard, are within the compass of female powers; that, in spite of pregnancy, childbirth, and the cares of a family, a woman may be depended upon at all times to act as a senator, or to practise as a surgeon, a physician, an attorney, or a barrister, and must dispute with the Apostle the propriety of her occupying the pulpit also. It is quite possible that some of our present laws respecting property may be susceptible of a change for the better with regard to female possessions; but the so-called *enfranchisement* of women must be needless as well as absurd, in a land where a Queen reigns, and so many women have rendered themselves illustrious in the paths of science and literature.

CHAPTER XIX.

OF THE LAW OF PRIMOGENITURE.

The law of primogeniture takes its rise from the necessity or supposed necessity of keeping up the state, dignity, and importance of particular families; we say *particular* families, because it affects many for whose benefit it was not formed. It is a provision for keeping up an aristocracy *in aid* of that natural desire which most men feel for the perpetuity of their name and position. It provides that titles shall descend, when hereditary, to the eldest son, and that *real property* or land shall, unless otherwise devised, descend also to him undivided. The effects of this enactment are manifold. So far as an hereditary aristocracy is desirable—and we, in this country, are generally of opinion that it is so—the law of primogeniture has a good effect in preventing our hereditary legislators from falling into unseemly poverty; it keeps together, beneficially, many small and moderate properties, and tends to obviate the too great division of land. The power of entailing estates has the same tendency, and *so far* has a beneficial operation. The chief evil seems to be, that it makes one member of a family comparatively idle, and the rest comparatively needy; and as this effect is produced in a class of hereditary legislators who have necessarily great control over the public funds, it offers the temptation—a temptation, also, to which little or no resistance is offered—to quarter the unprovided members of such families on the country; thus the army, the navy, the church, and diplomacy, are crowded with the younger sons or relatives of noble families, to the exclusion of far superior merit and talent among men placed in positions of less influence. It has often been contended that this is not the case, and army and navy lists and other such documents triumphantly referred to; but the test is a false one; it is not intended that the *number* of persons from noble families thus provided for is overwhelmingly great, but that they have for themselves and their adherents the *chief* disposable places. A man of humble origin and fortune may, at what, *to him*, is a great expense, become a curate, or an ensign, or he may at much less cost become a clerk in a government office; but against the *majority* of such, the higher grades of his profession are hermetically sealed. Towards the avoidance of this evil, the abolition of the law of primogeniture would be a step, though far less important than some writers seem to suppose. So long as every man has the power of disposing of his property by will, and it is clearly to a very small extent that the state has a right to interfere with this power, so long will due provision be made for the *keeping up of families,* whether there be any law of primogeniture or not. The practice of entailing estates may and should be discouraged and limited; but there is an extent to which " it is lawful for every man to do what he will with his own," and within these bounds every act of state interference is an act of tyranny. In France, not only has the law of primogeniture been abolished, but the power of devising estates by will has been much crippled: the consequence of this has been the great and rapid subdivision of the soil, and the prospect of the land being parcelled out among a race of mere peasant proprietors. The mere abolition of the law of primogeniture would not have this effect; and if it were accompanied by restrictions on the power of entail, and the removal of those enactments which make a difference between land and other descriptions of property, some of the evils which have been mentioned might possibly be alleviated; and, at all events, the law would be simplified, and a true principle carried out a few steps further.

CHAPTER XX.

OF GAME LAWS.

IN the course of the present work, much has been said on the evil effects of redundant legislation; but the most mischievous instance which the statute book of this country affords, is to be found in the operation of the game laws. According to these enactments, certain wild animals are made private property, and the right to pursue or destroy them vested in those called Lords of Manors. I may purchase from government a general qualification to kill game, and obtain permission, by purchase or otherwise, from those to whom the manorial right belongs, to pursue that game on their lands. If one of these be wanting, I am liable to imprisonment for knocking down a hare with a stick on the highway, for carrying a gun, or being followed by a particular breed of dog; if the other be wanting, I must confine my *sport* to the highway and a few other places. Now, as this game is in many places very strictly preserved, in order that *sport* may abound for the wealthy, the farmer is not allowed to kill that which would at the same time supply his own table and prevent the devastation of his lands. His crops are injured, his revenues diminished, because he may not kill what *he* calls, and with good reason, "vermin." The basis of our inquiry must be the *right* which any state has to constitute these "*feræ naturæ*" property, and to prohibit the farmer from killing, if he think fit, every animal of the kind on his farm. Bramble berries on a common are allowed to be public property; and sparrows, if I can catch them with bird-lime, I may capture in any number that I please. Rats and mice, weazels and stoats, may be destroyed with impunity. Now, as the community of property in these things rests on the ground that no man has been at an expense to rear or feed them, and no man has taken any care to provide them with a habitation, so it would appear that in all similar cases a similar rule should prevail. Hares, grouse, and partridges, have no greater claim to protection than larks or sparrows; indeed, the only protection which they do receive, is a preservation for a time, in order to be slaughtered *en masse*. Now, common rights are among those which by their very nature cannot be alienated. A man may be prevented by force from availing himself of them, or he may be punished for so doing, and this may be by course of law; but the right still remains*. No state, therefore, is entitled to interfere with their

---

* Such common rights may be restrained as a punishment for offences: imprisonment interferes with many of them.

exercise; and any such act of interference is in itself an act of tyranny, save only when it serves as a punishment for offences.

But there are many other considerations to be examined. Whatever may be said of "*sporting*" as a Christian amusement, man has clearly a right to kill for food the animals indicated by the game laws. Nor should the legislature interfere, if he choose to make that killing a source of pastime. A landlord has clearly a right to say to his tenant—I will have no game destroyed on this farm, save at such times, in such manners, and by such persons, as I permit; for the tenant will pay a rent accordingly: but he has no right to extend this prohibition to the highway or the common. All that *ought* to be effected by the game laws can be just as well done by the simple law of trespass. I have no more right to walk into my neighbour's field than into his garden; if there be a right of way, I am bound to keep the path; and my having killed a hare or a partridge is no legal justification of my intrusion. With respect to pheasants and other game which require care and entail expense, the case is just the same; the laws of larceny and trespass are quite sufficient. It is evidently as just to punish a man for walking into his neighbour's preserve and knocking down a pheasant, as for walking into his neighbour's farm and carrying off a barn-door fowl: the care and expense entailed makes the pheasant as much private property as the domestic

fowl, and the law is bound to regard it accordingly. But that the game laws are needless, is a very small part of the objection against them; they are the fruitful source of demoralization among the peasantry. A labouring man sees a hare on a common; his own sense of right tells him that the hare is as much his property as that of any other man; he knows that the creature consumes as much as would furnish the fourth part of the support of a sheep; he knows that the farmer would in his heart thank him for destroying it; he knows that his family are fed on the coarsest fare, and have not for years tasted a meal so nourishing, so wholesome, and so palatable, as the hare would afford them. On the other hand, he feels that he is doing no wrong to any man; he approaches slowly, lifts his stick, knocks down the hare, and is seized by a man who leaps from behind the hedge, as an offender against the game laws! He is cast into prison, condemned to herd with the vilest of mankind; his scruples are laughed at; he is shown much easier and more luxurious modes of life than the course of simple industry; his notions of right and wrong are hopelessly confused by the manifest injustice of which he has been made the victim; he sees, as he supposes, and with too much reason, that there is one law for the rich, and another for the poor; he exclaims—
" The world is not my friend, nor the world's law:"
he finds his employment gone, his prospects ruined, his character blasted, his family in the workhouse;

and all for an act which by every law of God and nature he had a full right to do. The leaven ferments in his heart, and he leaves the prison a poacher, if not worse. There has thus arisen, in the minds of the poor, a well-founded opinion that their interests, physical, moral, social, and spiritual, are deliberately set aside, in order to facilitate a very questionable diversion for the wealthy—a diversion which, in addition, entails great damage to the agriculturist, and which, moreover, would be quite as well enjoyed without any of these mischiefs. Deer and pheasants are by their nature private property. Moor-game would never be seriously diminished even if the game laws were repealed. The law of trespass would sufficiently protect the rest: and there seems to be no valid reason why so crying an iniquity should not be at once removed from our statute book.

CHAPTER XXI.

OF CERTAIN INSTANCES OF PROBABLY REDUNDANT LEGISLATION.

THERE is a class of offences which admit only of allusion, and concerning which the Apostle says, "they ought not so much as to be named." For these crimes our law provides very severe punishments; and from time to time the public ear is pained and the public mind polluted by the narratives of evil deeds of this nature. It appears to me that this is an instance in which the old Roman maxim, "*facinora puniri, flagitia abscondi,*" may with great benefit be practised. I would desire to see all enactments against this class of crimes removed. I apprehend that no mischief whatever would result from this step. The offenders do not intrude their evil example upon society; they seek the dark places of the earth for their detestable enormities; and are for the most part far more afraid of the public disgust and contempt than of any punishment prescribed by the law. On the other hand, I cannot help thinking that the present state of the law favours the multiplication of these crimes; the loathsome details narrated in our crowded courts of justice fall on ears unprepared by religion or refinement to repel their poisonous effect; a prurient curiosity is excited, and it is well known to the bar that one or two cases *tried* produce a sure harvest of similar misdemeanours during the ensuing period. There are some sins which are as it were epidemic; certain kinds of suicide do not happen in isolated instances; poisoning appears to follow the same rule; they have but to be described, in order to be imitated; these, however, are "*facinora*" rather than "*flagitia.*"

If it be recollected how many there are, habituated to every kind of licentious indulgence, satiated with ordinary vice, and restrained by no principle either of morality or religion, it will be evident that our present practice is but setting the spark to the train already laid. It has been said, and I think truly, that the offences of which we speak are the consequence of a diseased and indeed insane state of mind; if this be so, there is an additional inducement for changing the laws which affect them; but there is yet another reason, more weighty than all the rest; these very enactments produce a class of crime even more abominable than that which they are framed to suppress; there are, it is well known, persons who make a degraded living by practising on the fears of the timid, and who exact money by threatening to accuse them of these hideous offences; there is more weight in this argument than is at first evident. It is said the persons who thus support themselves are not few, and are singularly successful in their nefarious pursuit. It is, however, very rarely that their threats are put in practice; from which it may be concluded that in the great majority of cases they are bought off. The public is very apt to conclude that accusations so frightful are not made without some ground of truth; and thus the unhappy individual who is the subject of such, however honourably acquitted, labours still under an imputation which is sometimes never removed. To avoid this fearful stigma, the threatened person freely pays money, and thus feeds the source of the blackest stream of iniquity. This shows us that, whether the person accused be innocent or guilty, it is exposure to the public contempt which he most fears (for in most cases, it must be evident to him that the case will break down); and hence he would be no more likely to offend against public decency, were the laws referred to repealed, than he is at present. We should avoid a most demoralizing spectacle in our courts of law; we should almost extinguish the force of a most pestilent example; and utterly annihilate a most abominable traffic. It will be needless to follow up so disagreeable a subject further; had it not been for the great and manifold evils which, as it appears to me, the present state of the law entails, I would gladly have avoided it altogether.

BOOK III.

POLITICAL ECONOMY.

CHAPTER I.

OF POPULATION.

It will be obvious that the sketch of Political Economy given in this volume must be a very brief one, scarcely more than serving as an introduction to the works of Smith, Stuart, Mill, Alison, Malthus, Ricardo, Bentham, Porter, and others.

The final view, says Paley, of all rational politics is, to produce the greatest quantity of happiness in a given tract of country*. The riches, strength, and glory of nations; the topics which history celebrates, and which alone almost engage the praises and possess the admiration of mankind, have no value farther

---

* There is a slight fallacy here; Paley should have said " among a given number of people," for a very small consideration would show that the extent of terrority has nothing to do with the question.

than as they contribute to this end. When they interfere with it, they are evils, and not the less real for the splendour which surrounds them.

Secondly.—Although we speak of communities as of sentient beings; although we ascribe to them happiness and misery, desires, interests, and passions; nothing really exists or feels but individuals. Arguing from these principles, Paley lays it down as a law of Political Economy, that the greater the population, the greater the amount of happiness; and that, therefore, all governments are bound, so far as in them lies, to encourage an increase of population. It is true he means this to be done by the institution of marriage; and requires also that the government, especially in times of scarcity, should watch over the public morals with an express view to the formation of matrimonial connections. His reasonings on this subject we have thrown into the form of a note; for few will be inclined, in the present improved condition of political science, to accept them precisely as Paley has enunciated them in his work*.

---

* The happiness of a people is made up of the happiness of single persons; and the quantity of happiness can only be augmented by increasing the number of the percipients, or the pleasure of their perceptions.

Thirdly.—Notwithstanding that diversity of condition, especially different degrees of plenty, freedom, and security, greatly vary the quantity of happiness enjoyed by the same number of individuals; and notwithstanding that extreme cases may be

It is by no means a self-evident proposition, that a country with a large population, enjoying a moderate degree of happiness, is in a better condition than one found of human beings so galled by the rigours of slavery, that the increase of numbers is only the amplification of misery; yet, within certain limits, and within those limits to which civil life is diversified under the temperate governments that obtain in Europe, it may be affirmed, I think, with certainty, that the quantity of happiness produced in any given district, *so far* depends upon the number of inhabitants, that, in comparing adjoining periods in the same country, the collective happiness will be nearly in the exact proportion of the numbers, that is, twice the number of inhabitants will produce double the quantity of happiness; in distant periods and different countries, under great changes or great dissimilitude of civil condition, although the proportion of enjoyment may fall much short of that of the numbers, yet still any considerable excess of numbers will usually carry with it a preponderance of happiness; that, at least, it may and ought to be assumed in all political deliberations, that a larger portion of happiness is enjoyed amongst *ten* persons, possessing the means of healthy subsistence, than can be produced by *five* persons, under every advantage of power, affluence, and luxury.

From these principles it follows, that the quantity of happiness in a given district, although it is possible it may be increased, the number of the inhabitants remaining the same, is chiefly and most naturally affected by alteration of the numbers; that, consequently, the decay of population is the greatest evil that a state can suffer; and the improvement of it the object which ought, in all countries, to be aimed at, in preference to every other political purpose whatsoever.

The importance of population, and the superiority of *it* to

the population of which is less by half, but which affords to each of its citizens double the amount of enjoyment. Let the matter be mathematically ex-

---

every other national advantage, are points necessary to be inculcated and to be understood; inasmuch as false estimates, or fantastic notions of national grandeur, are perpetually drawing the attention of statesmen and legislators from the care of this, which is, at all times, the true and absolute interest of a country; for which reason, we have stated these points with unusual formality. We will confess, however, that a competition can seldom arise between the advancement of population and any measure of sober utility; because, in the ordinary progress of human affairs, whatever, in any way, contributes to make a people happier, tends to render them more numerous.

In the fecundity of the human, as of every other species of animals, nature has provided for an indefinite multiplication. Mankind have increased to their present number from a single pair; the offspring of early marriages, in the ordinary course of procreation, do more than replace their parents; in countries, and under circumstances very favourable to subsistence, the population has been doubled in the space of twenty years; the havoc occasioned by war, earthquakes, famine, or pestilence, is usually repaired in a short time. These indications sufficiently demonstrate the tendency of nature, in the human species, to a continual increase of its numbers. It becomes therefore a question that may reasonably be propounded, what are the causes which confine or check the natural progress of this multiplication? And the answer which first presents itself to the thoughts of the inquirer is, that the population of a country must stop when the country can contain no more, that is, when the inhabitants are already so numerous as to exhaust all the provision which the soil can be made to produce. This, how-

pressed, and it will appear thus, that it is better to divide an amount of happiness represented by x among 100 participants than among 50; a proposition which scarcely any amount of argument will render credible.

---

ever, though an inseparable bar, will seldom be found to be *that* which actually checks the progress of population in any country of the world; because the number of the people have seldom, in any country, arrived at this limit, or even approached to it. The fertility of the ground in temperate regions is capable of being improved by cultivation to an extent which is unknown; much, however, beyond the state of improvement in any country in Europe. In our own, which holds almost the first place in the knowledge and encouragement of agriculture, let it only be supposed that every field in England, of the same original quality with those in the neighbourhood of the metropolis, and consequently capable of the same fertility, were, by a like management, made to yield an equal produce; and it may be asserted, I believe with truth, that the quantity of human provision raised in the island would be increased five-fold. The two principles, therefore, upon which population seems primarily to depend, the fecundity of the species, and the capacity of the soil, would in most, perhaps in all countries, enable it to proceed much further than it has yet advanced. The number of marriageable women, who in each country remain unmarried, afford a computation how much the agency of nature in the diffusion of human life is cramped and contracted; and the quantity of waste, neglected or mismanaged surface,—together with a comparison like the preceding, of the crops raised from the soil in the neighbourhood of populous cities, and under a perfect state of cultivation, with those which lands of equal or superior quality yield in different situations,—will show in what proportion the

But in addition to this objection, another arises, still more immediately fatal to this theory. The matter is one over which government has little power, and still

---

indigenous productions of the earth are capable of being further augmented.

The fundamental proposition upon the subject of *population*, which must guide every endeavour to improve it, and from which every conclusion concerning it may be deduced, is this:

" Wherever the commerce between the sexes is regulated by
" marriage, and a provision for that mode of subsistence, to
" which each class of the community is accustomed, can be pro-
" cured with ease and certainty; there the number of people,
" and the rapidity, as well as the extent of the increase, will be
" proportioned to the degree in which these causes exist."

This proposition we will draw out into the several principles which it contains.

I. First—the proposition asserts the "necessity of con-
" fining the intercourse of the sexes to the marriage union." It is only in the marriage union that this intercourse is sufficiently prolific. Beside which, family establishments alone are fitted to perpetuate a succession of generations. The offspring of a vague and promiscuous concubinage are not only few, and liable to perish by neglect, but are seldom prepared for, or introduced into, situations suited to the raising of families of their own. Hence the advantages of marriages. Now, nature, in the constitution of the sexes, has provided a stimulus which will infallibly secure the frequency of marriages, with all their beneficial effects upon the state of population, provided the male part of the species be prohibited from irregular gratifications. This impulse, which is sufficient to surmount almost every impediment to marriage, will operate in proportion to the difficulty, expense, danger, or infamy, the sense of guilt, or the fear of punishment, which attend licen-

less right. By just laws, by a cheap and easy means of executing them, so as to render an appeal practicable at all times as well to the poor as to the rich; by removing all unnecessary restrictions, especially those on commerce; by a fair and equal system of taxation; and by a wise and liberal economy in the use of the public funds; government may indirectly but powerfully inculcate habits of industry, energy, and foresight among the governed; and where these exist, the growth of population will not be more than equal to its requirements; the coming age will not be in a worse condition, to say the very least, than the present, still less than the past.

But there are *two* theories concerning population: one, that of Paley, which regards it in *all actual* cases as a good, and therefore to be encouraged; another, that of Malthus and his disciples, which regards it *under certain circumstances* as an evil, and requiring a check. And though it may be sufficient for the political economist to show that government has *directly* neither right nor power in the matter, yet the student who regards politics as a Christian science,

---

tious indulgences. Wherefore, in countries in which subsistence is become scarce, it behoves the state to watch over the public morals with increased solicitude; for nothing but the instinct of nature, under the restraint of chastity, will induce men to undertake the labour, or consent to the sacrifice of personal liberty and indulgence, which the support of a family in such circumstances requires.

will be anxious to know whether there be any divine law on the subject, and if so, what it is. Now the divine law may be read as well in the constitution of nature as in the pages of revelation; and both these make marriage an indefeasible right, belonging to both sexes and under all circumstances. It would seem too, that so long as the earth can support her inhabitants, this *right* is a *duty* also; and unquestionably the period is too far off for us to calculate when the productions of the whole globe shall not be sufficient to support *in comfort* all its inhabitants, even were they to increase according to the most rapid rates with which experience has made us acquainted.

God, then, having established this law and made this provision, any system which, '*as a rule*, disallows or even discountenances marriage, is essentially unchristian. The too great crowding together of mankind in vast cities, the artificial modes of life adopted by the rich, the perpetual rivalry in show and luxury among all classes, the restrictions which exist on commerce, and especially on articles of food, are evils which do not affect us through any divine laws; they are but the product of human error, and are capable of being removed; and if they were removed, our population would be far from being excessive.

In the mean time, such is the actual relation existing in this country between provision and its distribution, such the want of a proper balance between the supply and demand of labour, that very many thousands are compelled to live in misery; and if they marry, their children are ill-fed, ill-clothed, ill-housed, ill-educated, and ill-provided with the means of subsistence when they arrive at the age of labour.

Marriage, *then*, adds to the number of sufferers; for it should be noted that the human race is generally most prolific under the unfavorable circumstances of bad and scanty provision for *all* its wants. The children of parents so situated are diseased, stunted, and feeble; they never attain the average stature or power of body, nor the average *healthy* power of mind; yet what they want in individual development, they make up in numbers.

Now, if this be a true theory—and the late condition of Ireland, the poor of our overgrown cities, parts of China, and many other places, furnish the evidence that it is so—it will follow that the way to check the excess of population is, not to discountenance marriage, but to raise the condition of the labouring class. As a proof, we may take the existing state of our own country: few will deny that the poor *on the whole* are better off than they were twenty years ago, and every day tends to ameliorate their condition; yet the population, if it has not doubled, has at least greatly increased.

Agriculture seems to be yet in its infancy; large tracts of land, even in the most civilized countries, are still uncultivated: new materials are continually brought into use; new branches of manufacture are constantly starting up; so that for many centuries the prospects of the poor have not been so good as they are now.

Of emigration, as a means of carrying off a redundant population, we shall speak presently: we return to the state of our own poor, as connected with their overwhelming numbers.

The great requisite is a moral training; we want a sense of responsibility in the poor themselves. If it be unchristian to say—do not marry, because the population is already too great,—it is not unchristian to say—do not marry prematurely—do not marry too young—do not marry with the view of being supported by the parish. Any measures which check such marriages as these, must, *cæteris paribus*, be beneficial.

After all, one of the great advantages of emigration, and all its kindred plans for improving the condition of the poor, and lessening their too great congregation in the same spots, is, that it will remove restraints on marriage, and restore mankind to the exercise of their inherent rights.

CHAPTER II.

OF MODES OF LIFE AS BEARING ON THE QUESTION OF POPULATION.

THE second requisite which our proposition states as necessary to the success of population, or, in other words, to the natural and prosperous development of the human race, is, " The ease and certainty with " which a provision can be procured for that mode of " subsistence to which each class of the community " is accustomed." It is not enough that man's *natural* wants be supplied; that a provision adequate to the actual exigencies of human life be attainable: habitual superfluities become real wants; opinion and fashion convert articles of ornament and luxury into necessaries of life. And it must not be expected from men in general, at least in the present relaxed state of morals and discipline, that they will enter into marriages which degrade their condition, reduce their mode of living, deprive them of the accommodations to which they have been accustomed, or even of those ornaments or appendages of rank and station which they have been taught to regard as belonging to their birth, or class, or profession, or place in society. The same consideration—namely, a view to their *accustomed* mode of life, which is so apparent in the superior orders of the people—has no less influence upon those ranks which compose the mass of the community. The kind and quality of food and liquor, and species of habitation, furniture, and clothing, to which the common people of each country are habituated, must be attainable with ease and certainty, before marriages will be sufficiently early and general to carry the progress of the population to the just extent. It is in vain to allege, that a more simple diet, ruder habitations, or coarser apparel, would be sufficient for the purposes of life and health, or even physical ease and pleasure. Men will not marry with this encouragement. For instance, when the common people of a country are accustomed to eat a large proportion of animal food, to drink wine, spirits, or beer, to wear shoes and stockings, to dwell in stone houses,—they will not marry to live in clay cottages, upon roots and milk, with no other clothing than skins, or what is necessary to defend the trunk of the body from the effects of cold; although these last may be all that the sustentation of life and health requires, or that even contribute much to animal comfort and enjoyment.

The ease, then, and certainty with which the means can be procured, not barely of subsistence, but of that mode of subsisting which custom hath in each country established, form the point upon which the state and progress of population chiefly depend. Now, there are three causes which evidently regulate this point: the mode itself of subsisting which prevails in the country; the quantity of provision suited to that mode of subsistence which is either raised in the country, or imported into it; and, lastly, the distribution of that provision.

These three causes merit distinct considerations.

I. The mode of living which actually obtains in a country. In China, where the inhabitants frequent the sea-shore, or the banks of large rivers, and subsist in a great measure upon fish, the population is described to be excessive. This peculiarity arises, not probably from any civil advantages, any care or policy, any particular constitution or superior wisdom of government, but simply from hence—the species of food to which custom hath reconciled the desires and inclinations of the inhabitants, is that which, of all others, is procured in the greatest abundance, with the most ease, and stands in need of the least preparation*. The natives of Indostan being confined by the laws of their religion to the use of vegetable food, and requiring little except rice, which the country produces

---

* Rice, as in India, forms one of the chief articles of food in China; it is raised with little trouble, and is extremely cheap. The common use of fish may be one cause of the great population; a fish diet is frequently found to conduce to that effect, and fishing villages are generally remarkably populous.

in plentiful crops—and food, in warm climates, composing the only want of life—these countries are populous under all the injuries of despotic, and the agitations of unsettled, government. If any revolution, or what would be called perhaps refinement of manners, should generate in these people a taste for the flesh of animals, similar to what prevails amongst the Arabian hordes—should introduce flocks and herds into grounds which are now covered with corn—should teach them to account a certain portion of this species of food amongst the necessaries of life,—the population, from this single change, would suffer, in a few years, a great diminution; and this diminution would follow in spite of every effort of the laws, or even of any improvement that might take place in civil condition. In Ireland, the simplicity of living alone long maintained a considerable degree of population, under great defects of policy, industry, and commerce. Under this head, and from a view of these considerations, may be understood the true evil and proper danger of *luxury*.

Luxury, so far as it supplies employment and promotes industry, assists population. But then there is another consequence attending it, which counteracts and often overbalances these advantages. When, by introducing more superfluities into general reception, luxury has rendered the usual accommodations of life more expensive, artificial, and elaborate, the difficulty of maintaining a family, conformable with the established mode of living, becomes greater, and what each man has to spare from his personal consumption proportionably less: the effect of which is, that marriages grow less frequent, agreeable to the maxim above laid down, and which must be remembered as the foundation of all our reasoning upon the subject, that men will not marry to *sink* their place or condition in society, or to forego those indulgences which their own habits, or what they observe amongst their equals, have rendered necessary to their satisfaction. This principle is applicable to every article of diet and dress, to houses, furniture, attendance; and this effect will be felt in every class of the community. For instance, the custom of wearing broad-cloth and fine linen repays the shepherd and flax-grower, feeds the manufacturer, enriches the merchant, gives not only support but existence to multitudes of families. Hitherto, therefore, the effects are beneficial; and, were these the only effects, such elegancies, or, if you please to call them so, such luxuries, could not be too universal. But here follows the mischief: when once fashion hath annexed the use of these articles of dress to any certain class—the middling ranks, for example—of the community, each individual of that rank finds them to be *necessaries* of life; that is, finds himself obliged to comply with the example of his equals, and to maintain that appearance which the custom of society requires. This obligation creates such a demand upon his income, and, withal, adds so much to the costs and burden of a family, as to put it out of his power to marry, with the prospect of continuing his habits, or of maintaining his place and situation in the world. We see, in this description, the cause which induces men to waste their lives in a barren celibacy; and this cause, which impairs the very source of population, is justly placed to the account of luxury.

It appears, then, that luxury, considered with a view to population, acts by two opposite effects; and it seems probable that there exists a point in the scale to which luxury may ascend, or to which the wants of mankind may be multiplied with advantage to the community, and beyond which the prejudicial consequences begin to preponderate. The determination of this point, though it assume the form of an arithmetical problem, depends upon circumstances too numerous, intricate, and undefined, to admit of a precise solution. However, from what has been observed concerning the tendency of luxury to diminish marriages, in which tendency the evil of it resides, the following general conclusions may be established.

1st. That, of different kinds of luxury, those are the most innocent which affords employment to the greatest number of artists and manufacturers: or those, in other words, in which the price of the work bears the greatest proportion to that of the raw material. Thus, luxury in dress or furniture is universally preferable to luxury in eating; because the articles which constitute the one are more the productions of human art and industry than those which supply the other.

2ndly. That it is the *diffusion* rather than the *degree* of luxury which is to be dreaded as a national evil. The mischief of luxury consists, as we have seen, in the obstruction which it forms to marriage. Now, it is only a small part of the people that the higher ranks in any country compose; for which reason, the facility or the difficulty of supporting the expense of *their* station, and the consequent increase or diminution of marriages amongst *them*, will influence the state of population but little. So long as the prevalency of luxury is confined to a few of elevated rank, much of the benefit is felt, and little of the inconveniency. But when the imitation of the same manners descends, as it always will do, into the mass of the people; when it advances the requisites of living beyond what it adds to men's abilities to purchase them; then it is that luxury checks the formation of families, in a degree that ought to alarm the public fears.

3rdly. That the condition most favourable to population is that of a laborious, frugal people, ministering to the demands of an opulent, luxurious nation; because this situation, whilst it leaves them every advantage of luxury, exempts them from the evils which naturally accompany its admission into any country.

CHAPTER III.

OF PROVISION, AND ITS INFLUENCE ON POPULATION.

II. NEXT to the mode of living, we are to consider " the quantity of provision suited to that mode, " which is either raised in the country, or imported " into it;" for this is the order in which we assigned the causes of population, and undertook to treat of them. Now, if we measure the quantity of provision by the number of human bodies it will support in due health and vigour, this quantity—the extent and quality of the soil from which it is raised being given— will depend greatly upon the *kind*. For instance, a piece of ground capable of supplying animal food sufficient for the subsistence of ten persons, would sustain at least the double of that number with grain, roots, and milk. The first resource of savage life is in the flesh of wild animals; hence the numbers amongst savage nations, compared with the tract of country which they occupy, are universally small; because this species of provision is, of all others, supplied in the slenderest proportion. The next step was the invention of pasturage, or the rearing of flocks and herds of tame animals. This alteration added to the stock of provisions much. But the last and principal improvement was to follow: namely, tillage, or the artificial production of corn, esculent plants, and roots. This discovery, whilst it changed the quality of human food, augmented the quantity in a vast proportion. So far as the state of population is governed and limited by the quantity of provisions, perhaps there is no single cause that affects it so powerfully as the kind and quality of food which change or usage hath introduced into a country. In England, notwithstanding the produce of the soil has been of late considerably increased, by the enclosure of wastes and the adoption in many places of a more successful husbandry, yet we do not observe a corresponding addition to the number of inhabitants*: the reason of which appears to me to be the more general consumption of animal food amongst us. Many ranks of people, whose ordinary diet was, in the last century, prepared almost entirely from milk, roots, and vegetables, now require every day a considerable portion of the flesh of animals. Hence a great part of the richest lands of the country are converted to pasturage. Much also of the bread corn, which went directly to the nourishment of human bodies, now only contributes to it by fattening the flesh of sheep and oxen. The mass and volume of provisions are hereby diminished; and what is gained in the melioration of the soil, is lost in the quality of produce. This consideration teaches us that tillage,

---

* This observation now no longer applies (1854).

as an object of national care and encouragement, is universally preferable to pasturage; because the kind of provision which it yields, goes much further in the sustentation of human life. Tillage is also recommended by this additional advantage—that it affords employment to a much more numerous peasantry. Indeed, pasturage, when almost exclusively pursued, seems to be the act of a nation either imperfectly civilized, as are many of the tribes which cultivate it in the internal parts of Africa, or of a nation, like Spain*, declining from its summit of luxury and inactivity.

The kind and quality of provision, together with the extent and capacity of the soil from which it is raised, being the same, the quantity procured will principally depend upon two circumstances: the *ability* of the occupier, and the *encouragement* which he receives. The greatest misfortune of a country is an indigent tenantry. Whatever be the native advantages of the soil, or even the skill and industry of the occupier, the want of a sufficient capital confines every plan, as well as cripples and weakens every operation of husbandry. This evil is felt where agriculture is accounted a servile or mean employment; where farms are extremely subdivided and badly furnished with habitations; where leases are unknown, or are of short or precarious duration.

---

* Spain is now no longer more than partially liable to this reproach.

With respect to the *encouragement* of husbandry, in this, as in every other employment, the true reward of industry is in the price and sale of the produce. The exclusive right to the produce is the only incitement which acts constantly and universally; the only spring which keeps human labour in motion. All therefore that the laws can do, is to secure this right to the occupier of the ground; that is, to constitute such a system of tenure, that the full and entire advantage of every improvement go to the benefit of the improver; that every man work for himself and not for another; and that no one share in the profit who does not assist in the production. By the *occupier*, I here mean, not so much the person who performs the work, as him who procures the labour and directs the management; and I consider the whole profit as *received* by the occupier, when the occupier is benefited by the whole value of what is produced, which is the case with the tenant who pays a fixed rent for the use of land, no less than with the proprietor who holds it as his own. The one has the same interest in the produce, and in the advantage of every improvement, as the other. Likewise the proprietor, though he grant out his estate to farm, may be considered as the *occupier*, in so much as he regulates the occupation by the choice, superintendence, and encouragement of his tenants, by the disposition of his lands, by erecting buildings, providing accommodations, by prescribing conditions, or supplying implements and materials of improvement; and is entitled, according as he does this, by the rule of public expediency above-mentioned, to receive, in the advance of his rent, a share of the benefit which arises from the increased produce of his estate. The violation of this fundamental maxim of agrarian policy constitutes the chief objection to the holding of lands by the state, by the king, by corporate bodies, by private persons in right of their offices or benefices. The inconveniency to the public arises not so much from the unalienable quality of lands thus holden in perpetuity, as from hence—that proprietors of this description seldom contribute much either of attention or expense to the cultivation of their estates, yet claim, by the rent, a share in the profit of every improvement that is made upon them. This complaint can only be obviated by " long leases at a fixed rent," which convey a large portion of the interest to those who actually conduct the cultivation. The same objection is applicable to the holding of lands by foreign proprietors, and, in some degree, to estates of too great extent being placed in the same hands.

CHAPTER IV.

OF THE DISTRIBUTION OF PROVISION.

III. Besides the *production* of provision, there remains to be considered the DISTRIBUTION. It is in vain that provisions abound in the country, unless I be able to obtain a share of them. This reflection belongs to every individual*. Now, there is but one principle of distribution that can become universal; namely, the principle of "exchange;" or, in other words, that every man have something to give in return for what he wants. Bounty, however it may come in aid of another principle, however it may occasionally qualify the rigour or supply the imperfection of an established rule of distribution, can never itself

---

* Paley, bearing in mind his theory of population, observes here: The plenty of provision produced, the quantity of the public stock, affords subsistence to individuals, and encouragement to the formation of families, only in proportion as it is *distributed;* that is, in proportion as these individuals are allowed to draw from it a supply for their own wants. The *distribution,* therefore, becomes of equal consequence to population with the *production.*

become that rule or principle; because men will not work to give the produce of their labour away. Moreover, the only equivalents that can be offered in exchange for provision are *power, capital,* and *labour*. All property or capital is *power*. What we call property in land is the power to use it, and to exclude others from the use. Money is the representative of *power*, because it is convertible into power; the value of it consists in its faculty of procuring *power* over things and persons. But *power* which results from civil conventions (and of this kind is what we call a man's fortune and estate) is necessarily confined to a few, and is withal soon exhausted; whereas the capacity of *labour* is every man's natural possession, and composes a constant and renewing fund. The hire, therefore, or produce of personal industry is that which the bulk of every community must bring to market, in exchange for the means of subsistence; in other words, employment must in every country be the medium of distribution and the source of supply to individuals. But when we consider the *production* and *distribution* of provision as distinct from and independent of each other, when, supposing the same quantity to be produced, we inquire in what way, or according to what rule, it may be *distributed,* we are led to a conception of the subject not at all agreeable to truth and reality; for, in truth and reality, though provision must be produced before it be distributed, yet the production depends, in a great measure, upon the distribution. The quantity of provision raised out of the ground—and the same rule, of course, holds good with regard to every other article necessary for life or comfort—whether the produce of the soil or not, so far as the raising of it requires human art or labour, will evidently be regulated by the demand; the demand, or, in other words, the price and sale, being that which alone rewards the care, or excites the diligence, of the husbandman. But the sale of provision depends upon the number, not of those who want, but of those who have something to offer in return for what they want; not of those who would consume, but of those who can buy; that is, upon the number of those who have the fruits of some other kind of industry to tender in exchange for what they stand in need of from the production of the soil*. Of that

---

* Following up the theory of population, Paley adds here: We see, therefore, the connexion between population and *employment*. Employment affects population "directly," as it affords the only medium of distribution by which individuals can obtain from the common stock a supply for the wants of their families; it affects population "indirectly," as it augments the stock itself of provision, in the only way by which the production of it can be effectually encouraged—by furnishing purchasers. No man can purchase without an equivalent; and that equivalent, by the generality of the people, must in every country be derived from employment. And upon this basis is founded the public benefit of *trade;* that is to say, its subserviency to population, in which its only real utility consists.

industry, and of those arts and branches of trade which are employed in the production, conveyance, and preparation of any principal species of human food, as of the business of the husbandman, the butcher, baker, brewer, corn-merchant, &c. we acknowledge the necessity; likewise of those manufactures which furnish us with warm clothing, convenient habitations, domestic utensils, as of the weaver, tailor, smith, carpenter, &c. we perceive (especially* in climates like ours, removed at a distance from the sun) the utility†, by their rendering human life more healthy, vigorous, and comfortable‡. The absolute

---

* "However" (Paley).

† "Conducive to population" (Paley).

‡ Paley is in error, when he states that not one half of the occupations which compose the trade of Europe fall within either of these descriptions. "Perhaps two thirds of the manufacturers of England are employed upon articles of confessed luxury, ornament, or splendour; in the superfluous embellishment of some articles which are useful in their kind; or upon others which have no conceivable use or value, but what is founded in caprice or fashion. What can be less necessary, or less connected with the sustentation of human life, than the whole produce of the silk, lace, and plate manufactory? Yet what multitudes labour in the different branches of these arts! What can be imagined more capricious than the fondness for tobacco and snuff? Yet how many various occupations, and how many thousands in each, are set at work in administering to this frivolous gratification! Concerning trades of this kind (and this kind comprehends more than half of the trades that

necessity of foreign commerce cannot be proved in the same way, at least among ourselves. Paley may be right, when he says, "I believe it may be affirmed of Great Britain what Bishop Berkeley said of a neighbouring island, that, if it were encompassed with a wall of brass fifty cubits high, the country might maintain the same number of inhabitants that find subsistence in it at present; and that every necessary, and even every real comfort and accommodation of human life, might be supplied in as great abundance as they now are. Here, therefore, as before, we may fairly ask, by what operation it is that foreign commerce, which brings into the country no one article of human subsistence, promotes the happiness* of human life?"

---

are exercised), it may fairly be asked, "How, since they add "nothing to the stock of provision, do they tend to increase the "number of the people?" We are taught to say of trade, "that it maintains multitudes;" but by what means does it *maintain* them, when it produces nothing upon which the support of human life depends? In like manner, with respect to foreign commerce, of that merchandise which brings the necessaries of life into a country, which imports, for example, corn, or cattle, or cloth, or fuel, we allow the tendency to advance population, because it increases the stock of provision by which the people are subsisted."

* Multiplication (Paley). It must not be forgotten that Paley's theory is, that the multiplication of the species is the multiplication of happiness.

The answer of this inquiry will be contained in the discussion of another: viz. Since the soil will maintain many more than it can employ, what must be done, supposing the country to be full, with the remainder of the inhabitants? They who, by the rules of partition (and some such must be established in every country) are entitled to the land; and they who, by their labour from the soil, acquire a right in the produce; will not part with their property for nothing; or rather, they will no longer raise from the soil what they can neither use themselves, nor exchange for what they want. Or, lastly, if these were willing[*] to distribute what they could spare of the provision which the ground yielded, to others who had no share or concern in the property or cultivation of it, yet still the most enormous mischiefs would ensue from great numbers remaining unemployed. The idleness of one half of the community would overwhelm the whole with confusion and disorder. One only way presents itself of removing the difficulty which this question states, and which is simply this: that they, whose work is not wanted, nor can be employed in the raising of provision out of the ground, convert their hands and ingenuity to the fabrication of articles which may gratify and requite those who are so employed; or

---

[*] This argument is a good one, but it is an argument for the sake of argument; the case being one which could not occur; such "willingness" is far beyond human nature.

who, by the division of lands in the country, are entitled to the exclusive possession of certain parts of them. By this contrivance, all things proceed well. The occupier of the ground raises from it the utmost that he can produce, because he is repaid for what he can spare by something else which he wants, or with which he is pleased; the artist or manufacturer, though he have neither any property in the soil, nor any concern in its cultivation, is regularly supplied with the produce; because he gives, in exchange for what he stands in need of, something upon which the receiver places an equal value; and the community is kept quiet, while both sides are engaged in their respective occupations.

It appears, then, that the business of one half of mankind is to set the other half at work; that is, to provide articles which, by tempting the desires, may stimulate the industry and call forth the activity of those, upon the exertion of whose industry, and the application of whose faculties, the production of human provision depends. A certain portion only of human labour is, or can be, *productive* of food; the rest is *instrumental*; both equally necessary, though the one have no other object than to excite the other. It appears, also, that it signifies nothing, as to the main purpose of trade, how superfluous the articles which it furnishes are; whether the want of them be real or imaginary, whether it be founded in nature or in opinion, in fashion, habit, or emulation; it is enough that they be actually desired and sought after. Flourishing cities are raised and supported by trading in tobacco; populous towns subsist by the manufactory of ribands. A watch may be a very unnecessary appendage to the dress of a peasant, yet, if the peasant will till the ground in order to obtain a watch, the true design of trade is answered; and the watchmaker, while he polishes the case, or files the wheels of his machine, is contributing to the production of corn as effectually, though not so directly, as if he handled the spade or held the plough. The use of tobacco has been mentioned already, not only as an acknowledged superfluity, but as affording a remarkable example of the caprice of human appetite; yet, if the fisherman will ply his nets, or the mariner fetch rice from foreign countries, in order to procure to himself this indulgence, the market is supplied with two important articles of provision, by the instrumentality of a merchandize which has no other apparent use than the gratification of a vitiated palate.

But it may come to pass that the husbandman, land-owner, or whoever he be that is entitled to the produce of the soil, will no longer exchange it for what the manufacturer has to offer. He is already supplied to the extent of his desires. For instance, he wants no more cloth; he will no longer, therefore, give the weaver corn in return for the produce of his looms: but he would readily give it for tea, or for wine. When the weaver finds this to be the case, he has nothing to do but to send his cloth abroad, in exchange for tea or wine, which he may barter for that provision which the offer of his cloth will no longer procure. The circulation is thus revived; and the benefit of the discovery is, that whereas the number of weavers who could find subsistence from their employment, was before limited by the consumption of cloth in the country, that number is now augmented in proportion to the demand for tea and wine. This is the principle of *foreign* commerce. In the magnitude and complexity of the machine, the principle of motion is sometimes lost or unobserved; but it is always simple and the same, to whatever extent it may be diversified and enlarged in its operation.

The effect of trade upon agriculture, the process of which we have been endeavouring to describe, is visible in the neighbourhood of trading towns, and in those districts which carry on a communication with the markets of trading towns. The husbandmen are busy and skilful; the peasantry laborious; the land is managed to the best advantage, and double the quantity of corn or herbage (articles which are ultimately converted into human provision) raised from it, of what the same soil yields in remoter and more neglected parts of the country. Wherever a thriving manufactory finds means to establish itself, a new vegetation springs up around it. I believe it is true that agriculture never arrives at any considerable, much less at its highest, degree of perfection, where it is not connected with trade, that is, where the demand for the produce is not increased by the consumption of trading cities*.

From this it follows, by no very circuitous mode of reasoning, that the comparative utility of different branches of national commerce is measured by the number which each branch *employs*. Upon which principle a scale may easily be constructed which shall assign to the several kinds and divisions of foreign trade their respective degrees of public importance. In this scale, the *first* place belongs to the exchange of wrought goods for raw materials, as of broad-cloth for raw silk, cutlery for wool, clocks or watches for iron, flax, or furs; because this traffic provides a market for the labour that has already been expended, at the same time that it supplies materials

---

* Paley adds: "Let it be remembered, then, that agriculture is the immediate source of human provision; that trade conduces to the production of provision only as it promotes agriculture; that the whole system of commerce, vast and various as it is, hath no other public importance than its subserviency to this end." There is a strange fallacy here: the importance of commerce consists in its increasing the comforts and conveniences of life; in its promoting the inter-communion of nations; in its antagonism to war; in the opportunities which it affords for the propagation of truth; in the encouragement which it gives to art and science; and in the generally enlarged and enlightened tone which it imparts to public feeling.

for new industry. Population always flourishes where this species of commerce obtains to any considerable degree. It is the cause, or the certain indication of employment. As it takes off the manufactures of the country, it promotes employment; as it brings in raw materials, it supposes the existence of manufactories in the country, and a demand for the article when manufactured. The *second* place is due to that commerce which barters one species of wrought goods for another; as stuffs for calicoes, fustians for cambrics, leather for paper, or wrought goods for articles which require no farther preparation, as for wine, oil, tea, sugar, &c. This also assists employment; because, when the country is stocked with one kind of manufacture, it renews the demand by converting it into another; but it is inferior to the former, as it promotes this end by one side only of the bargain—by what it carries out*. The *last*, the lowest and most disadvantageous species of commerce, is the exportation of raw materials in return for wrought goods: as, when wool is sent abroad to purchase velvets; hides or peltry, to procure shoes, hats, or linen cloth. This trade would be among us, for the most part, unfavourable†; because it would leave no room or demand for

---

* It must be remembered that this last argument applies not to countries which produce immense quantities of raw material, and where labour is more profitably employed in raising than in manufacturing this material.

† To population (Paley).

employment, either in what it takes out of the country or what it brings into it. Its operation on both sides is noxious. By its exports, it diminishes the very subject upon which the industry of the inhabitants ought to be exercised; by its imports, it lessens the encouragement of that industry in the same proportion that it supplies the consumption of the country with the produce of foreign labour. Hence, we see in this country little of any of such trade; it naturally flourishes where it is beneficial, and not where, as among ourselves, it would be prejudicial. Of different branches of *manufactory*, those are in their nature the most beneficial in which the price of the wrought article exceeds, in the highest proportion, that of the raw material; for this excess measures the quantity of employment, or, in other words, the number of manufacturers which each branch sustains*.

---

* Paley, in the words which follow, falls into an error in supposing that the *natural* circumstances of all countries are alike, and argues from our condition to theirs. If his doctrine were universally acted upon, we should have from foreign lands neither tea, wine, oil, coffee, fruits, cotton, timber; in fact, commerce would soon cease to exist. But, in the following paragraph, he returns or rather adverts to a truer theory. "The produce of the ground is never the most advantageous article of foreign commerce. Under a perfect state of public economy, the soil of the country should be applied solely to the raising of provisions for the inhabitants, and its trade be supplied by their industry. A nation will never reach its proper extent of population, so long as its principal commerce consists in the

It must be here, however, noticed that we have all along considered the inhabitants of a country as maintained by the produce of the country; and that what we have said is applicable, with strictness, to this supposition alone. The reasoning, nevertheless, may easily be adapted to a different case: for when provision is not produced, but *imported*, what has been affirmed concerning provision will be, in a great measure, true of that article, whether it be money, produce, or labour, which is exchanged for provision. Thus, when the Dutch raise madder, and exchange it for corn; or when the people of America plant tobacco, and send it to Europe for cloth; the cultivation of madder and tobacco becomes as necessary to the subsistence of the inhabitants, and by consequence will affect the state of population in these countries as sensibly, as the actual production of food, or the manufactory of raiment. In like manner, when the same inhabitants of Holland earn money by the carriage of the produce of one country to another, and with that money purchase the provision from abroad which their own land is not extensive enough to supply, the increase or decline of this carrying trade will influence the numbers of the people no less than similar changes would do in the cultivation of the soil.

---

exportation of corn or cattle, or even of wine, oil, tobacco, madder, indigo, timber; because these last articles take up that surface which ought to be covered with the materials of human subsistence." This must be understood with limitations.

CHAPTER V.

OF EMIGRATION.

EMIGRATION may be either the overflowing of a country, or the desertion. As the increase of the species is indefinite, and the number of inhabitants which any given tract or surface can support finite, it is evident that great numbers may be constantly leaving a country, and yet the country remain constantly full. Or whatever be the cause which invincibly limits the population of a country, when the number of the people has arrived at that limit, the progress of generation, beside continuing the succession, will supply multitudes for foreign emigration. In these two cases, emigration neither indicates any political decay, nor in truth diminishes the number of the people; nor ought to be prohibited or discouraged. But emigrants may relinquish their country from a state of insecurity, oppression, annoyance, and inconveniency. Neither, again, *here* is it emigration which wastes the people, but the evils that occasion it. It would be in vain, if it were practicable, to confine the inhabitants at home; for the same causes which drive them out of the country, would prevent their multiplication if they remained in it. Lastly, men may be tempted to change their situation by the allurement of a better climate, of a more refined or luxurious manner of living; by the prospect of wealth; or sometimes by the mere nominal advantage of higher wages and prices. This class of emigrants, with whom alone the laws can interfere with effect, will never, I think, be numerous. With the generality of a people, the attachment of mankind to their homes and country, the irksomeness of seeking new habitations, and of living among strangers, will outweigh, so long as men possess the necessaries of life in safety, or at least so long as they can obtain a provision for that mode of subsistence which the class of citizens to which they belong are accustomed to enjoy, all the inducements that the advantages of a foreign land can offer. There appear, therefore, to be few cases in which emigration can be prohibited with advantage to the state. It appears also that emigration is an equivocal symptom, which will probably accompany the decline of the political body, but which *may* likewise attend a condition of perfect health and vigour.

But though there are few, if any, cases in which any discouragement should be offered to emigration, there are many in which it becomes the duty of a state to give it every possible encouragement.

The condition in which our own country is at present (1851), and will probably remain for many years, is an instance in point. With a population far from being excessive, regard being had to the capabilities of the country, it is yet so distributed, and its circumstances are so complicated by the joint effects of competition, commercial restrictions, laws but partially reformed, and over-crowding in great cities, that the removal of millions would become an equal advantage to those who left, and to those who remained.

The first effect would be to take off somewhat of the heavy taxation of poor-rates; and the next would be, that labour, if not better remunerated, would be at least more easy to obtain. Another advantage attending emigration, when carried on in a right spirit, is, that the due proportion between the sexes, unequal both at home and in the colonies, would be restored. Here, females are in excess; there, in demand: and this inequality being one of the causes, and not a small one, of the moral and social evils of the age, requires especial attention. Voluntary emigration takes an unusually large proportion of young adult males out of the country. Government acting in aid, *and not in place of,* a wholesome popular feeling, should do that which the popular feeling has left undone.

But this subject will be treated of more fully in the chapter which treats of COLONIZATION.

CHAPTER VI.

COLONIZATION.

EMIGRATION regards solely the removing from one land to another, and, in political economy, is conversant only with the benefits which accrue to the person who escapes from certain known social evils, and to the land whose burden is relieved by his removal. Colonization regards the land to which he is removed, the benefits which accrue to him from becoming one of its inhabitants, and to the land from his skill and labour.

The first thing to be noticed is the contrast between the late and present condition of the colonist newly arrived. He has left an over-peopled country, he has reached an under-peopled one; he has left a land where the labourer is redundant; he has come to one in which he is eagerly sought and largely remunerated; he has left an artificial state of society; he has found one in which mere external refinement is thrown into the back-ground.

In such a state there are, no doubt, many advantages; there are also some few draw-backs: yet, on the whole, the advantages greatly preponderate, and thousands, to whom a bare and often precarious subsistence was all that the mother country had to offer, may obtain comfort, affluence, and security, in the colonies.

A colony is not a mere collection of emigrants. Our colonists are British subjects; they are under the protection of British laws, and have a right to the full benefits of the British constitution. But as they are at a distance from the seat of government, so there must be some modifications made, in order to make the constitution applicable to them. Hitherto our colonies have been prosperous, rather in spite of, than in consequence of, the kind of government to which they have been subjected; but the plan which makes them, in fact, ill-regulated despotisms, governed from the Colonial Office, is not likely to survive much longer.

There are two ways in which the colonies may be made sharers in the benefits of the constitution. One way is by giving them the right of sending representatives to the British Parliament, and treating them in all respects as parts of an undivided empire. Another, of considering each dependency as a separate state, and making provision for its local self-government.

The one *alone* would have many draw-backs, in the distance of many colonies from the mother country, the separation of the member from his constituents, the want of opportunities of frequent communion with them.

The other *alone* keeps up a feeling of distinction from the mother country among the colonists, which is productive of many evil results.

If their local affairs were regulated by a local representative assembly, under a governor appointed by the crown, and a voice were given them in the general government by representatives in the Imperial Parliament, most of the evils under which they now labour would soon be removed. A body of men in Parliament would watch over the interests of the colonies, while an additional bond of union would exist

---

* Paley treats colonies only as capable of adding to the population of the mother country.

II. COLONIZATION.—The only view under which our subject will permit us to consider *colonization*, is in its tendency to augment the population of the parent state. Suppose a fertile but empty island to lie within reach of a country in which arts and manufactures are already established; suppose a colony sent out from such a country to take possession of the island, and to live there under the protection and authority of their native government: the new settlers will naturally convert their labour to the cultivation of the vacant soil, and with the produce of that soil will draw a supply of manufactures from their countrymen at home. Whilst the inhabitants continue few, and lands cheap and fresh, the colonists will find it easier and more profitable to raise corn, or rear cattle, and with corn and cattle to purchase woollen cloth, for instance, or linen, than to spin or weave these articles for themselves. The mother country, meanwhile, derives from this connection an increase both of provision and employment. It promotes at once the two great requisites upon which the facility of subsistence, and by consequence the state of population, depend—*produc-*

between the home and out-lying portions of the empire. Colonists would be better satisfied, the Colonial Office made more responsible, and a process like that of American annexation would go on, with every new territory subject to the British crown*.

---

tion and *distribution;* and this in a manner the most direct and beneficial. No situation can be imagined more favorable to population than that of a country which works up goods for others, whilst these others are cultivating new tracts of land for them: for as, in a genial climate, and from a fresh soil, the labour of one man will raise provision enough for ten, it is manifest that, where all are employed in agriculture, much the greater part of the produce will be spared from the consumption; and that three out of four, at least, of those who are maintained by it will reside in the country which receives the redundancy. When the new country does not remit *provision* to the old one, the advantage is less; but still the exportation of wrought goods, by whatever return they are paid for, advances population in that secondary way in which those trades promote it that are not employed in the production of provision. Whatever prejudice, therefore, some late events have excited against schemes of colonization, the system itself is founded in apparent national utility; and what is more, upon principles favorable to the common interest of human nature; for it does not appear by what other method newly discovered and unfrequented countries can be peopled, or, during the infancy of their establishment, be protected or supplied. The error which we of this nation at present lament, seems to have consisted not so much in the original formation of colonies, as in the subsequent management; in imposing restrictions too rigorous, or in continuing them too long; in not perceiving the point of time when the irresistible order and progress of human affairs demanded a change of laws and policy.

CHAPTER VII.

OF MONEY AND CURRENCY*.

THERE are few questions connected with political economy more surrounded with difficulties than what is called the "currency question," and there are few about which greater errors prevail. Of these, one of

---

* Where *money* abounds, says Paley, the people are generally numerous; yet gold and silver neither feed nor clothe mankind; nor are they in all countries converted into provision, by purchasing the necessaries of life at foreign markets; nor do they, in any country, compose those articles of personal or domestic ornament, which certain orders of the community have learnt to regard as necessaries of life, and without the means of procuring which they will not enter into family establishments; at least, this property of the precious metals obtains in a very small degree. The effect of money upon the number of the people, though visible to observation, is not explained without some difficulty. To understand this connexion properly, we must return to the proposition with which we concluded our reasoning upon the subject: "that population is chiefly promoted by employment." Now, of employment, money is partly the indication, and partly the cause. The only way in which money regularly and spontaneously *flows into* a country, is in return for the goods that are sent out of it, or the work

the greatest, perhaps the greatest of all, is that which confounds wealth with money; an error all the more serious, from its almost universal diffusion. A little

---

that is performed by it; and the only way in which money is *retained* in a country, is by the country supplying, in a great measure, its own consumption of manufactures. Consequently, the quantity of money found in a country denotes the amount of labour and employment; but still, employment, not money, is the cause of population; the accumulation of money being merely a collateral effect of the same cause, or a circumstance which accompanies the existence and measures the operation of that cause. And this is true of money, only whilst it is acquired by the industry of the inhabitants. The treasures which belong to a country by the possession of mines, or by the exaction of tribute from foreign dependencies, afford no conclusion concerning the state of population. The influx from these sources may be immense, and yet the country remain poor and ill-peopled; of which we see an egregious example in the condition of Spain, after the acquisition of its South American dominions.

But, secondly, money may become also a real and an operative *cause* of population, by acting as a stimulus to industry, and by facilitating the means of subsistence. The ease of subsistence, and the encouragement of industry, depend neither upon the price of labour nor upon the price of provision, but upon the proportion which one bears to the other. Now, the influx of money into a country naturally tends to advance this proportion; that is, every fresh accession of money raises the price of labour before it raises the price of provision. When money is brought from abroad, the persons, be they who they will, into whose hands it first arrives, do not buy up provision with it, but apply it to the purpose and payment of labour.

attention to the etymological meaning of words would help us greatly in this and many other matters. Wealth is a Saxon word, and signifies that which

---

If the state receives it, the state dispenses what it receives amongst soldiers, sailors, artificers, engineers, ship-wrights, workmen; if private persons bring home treasures of gold and silver, they usually expend them in the building of houses, the improvement of estates, the purchase of furniture, dress, equipage in articles of luxury or splendour; if the merchant be enriched by returns of his foreign commerce, he applies his increased capital to the enlargement of his business at home. The money ere long comes to market for provision; but it comes thither through the hands of the manufacturer, the artist, the husbandman, and labourer. Its effect, therefore, upon the price of art and labour will *precede* its effect upon the price of provision; and during the interval between one effect and the other, the means of subsistence will be multiplied and facilitated, as well as industry be excited, by new rewards. When the great plenty of money in circulation has produced an advance in the price of provision, corresponding to the advanced price of labour, its effect ceases. The labourer no longer gains any thing by the increase of his wages. It is not, therefore, the quantity of specie collected into a country, but the continual increase of that quantity, from which the advantage arises to employment and population. It is only the *accession* of money which produces the effect; and it is only by money constantly flowing into a country that the effect can be constant. Now, whatever consequence arises to the country from the influx of money, the contrary may be expected to follow from the diminution of its quantity; and accordingly we find, that whatever cause draws off the specie of a country faster than the streams which feed it can supply, not only impoverishes the country,

constitutes our *well-being;* hence, we speak of the *commonwealth* or common *weal,* which is a more comprehensive term than the Roman res-publica or republic, and applies not only to the possession, but also to the happiness of the body politic. Another phrase shows us that the opposite of weal or wealth is not poverty, but *woe.* Riches and poverty are correlative terms, but wealth and poverty are not so. But neither may riches be confounded with money, or the want of money be considered synonymous with poverty. What then is money? Money is the circulating medium; it may be gold, silver, and copper, as in civilized Europe; it may be tin, as in the Birman Empire; it may be shells, as on the coast of Africa, or it may be salt, as in the interior of the same continent; but whatever form it may assume, it is the current representative of value. Were there no such thing as money, all the products of the earth would have to be bartered one for the other; the division of labour would be all but impossible, and trade could

---

but depopulates it. The knowledge and experience of this effect has given occasion to a phrase which occurs in almost every discourse upon commerce or politics. The *balance of trade* with any foreign nation is said to be against or in favour of a country, simply as it tends to carry money out or to bring it in; that is, according as the price of the imports exceeds or falls short of the price of the exports. So invariably is the increase or diminution of the specie of a country regarded as a test of public advantage or detriment which arises from any branch of its commerce.

hardly exist. Let us take a familiar instance: a boat-builder has constructed a boat, he wants boots, a boot-maker can supply him with the boots, but he does not want the boat, which is all the builder has to offer, nor does the builder require so many boots as will make up the value of the boat; both, then, must wait till they find other parties with other goods by means of which, through a series of barters, the builder may dispose of his boat and obtain his boots. Now all this is done by a simple transaction when money is used. It acts, in the first place, as a universal measure of value; so that, instead of saying one boat is equal to thirty pairs of boots, and one leg of mutton is equal to ten and a half 4-lbs loaves, we say the boat is worth £30 sterling, the pair of boots is worth one pound, the leg of mutton is worth seven shillings, and the 4-lb loaf is worth eight-pence; secondly—it renders ordinary barter needless, for the boat-builder is able to sell his boat at once to the person who requires it, and with the *money* to buy boots, and whatever else he requires, instead. Yet this is but a new and more convenient kind of barter, after all; instead of obtaining bread, meat, boots, coats, and a cottage, directly in exchange for so many boats, he obtains a certain amount of silver and gold, which, in his turn, he barters for the necessaries of life. Or, to take a step deeper still, the money is a common measure, which, in the great division of productive labour, enables him to barter his own for that of his fellows.

Any thing which will thus answer the purpose of a common measure may become *money*. Yet there are some peculiar advantages in a metallic currency, and especially in that which consists of silver and gold, commonly called the precious metals; they are subject to little fluctuation of value, they are durable, extremely divisible, and of small bulk, they readily take and long retain the impress of any stamp made upon them, and thus may easily be rendered representatives of any amount of current value. Again, they are not a merely fictitious standard; the coin which I call a sovereign does not derive its value solely from the amount at which it is fixed by the government; for if I melt it or cut it in pieces, I can procure with it nearly as much of any commodity. It is intrinsically worth what I buy with it, and the same may be said of all the coins of this realm; they are, in fact, valuables, capable of being bartered for other valuables, and, by their divisions and subdivisions, extremely convenient for the purpose.

But a new element is to be taken into consideration: I give my tailor, in exchange for a suit of clothes, a piece of fine paper, the intrinsic value of which is too small to be easily expressed, and he not only accepts this, but gives me, in addition to my suit of clothes, many pieces of intrinsically valuable gold and silver. How is this? The paper is a bank-note, and the tailor knows that by presenting it to its issuers, he shall receive as many sovereigns as it is stated to be worth; it is, in fact, a token or pledge, and its value must manifestly depend upon the credit of those who issue it. Were it known that the Bank could not redeem it, it would no longer have any marketable value; if any doubt arose on the subject, and those doubts could not at once be satisfied, it would be depreciated in proportion; it is a promissory note, payable on demand. The advantages of a paper currency are, its portability and convenience of transmission, and its enabling large masses of specie to be advantageously employed in other directions. A paper currency is of two kinds, convertible and inconvertible; it is convertible, when those who issue it are bound to exchange it for specie on demand; and it is inconvertible, when they are not so bound. An inconvertible currency prevailed for many years in this country; but, after many struggles and much discussion, the principle was abandoned as an unsound one, and the convertible paper substituted.

The arguments on both sides would require too much space to be admissible in an elementary treatise like the present, and may be found, moreover, considered at length in "*Mills' Political Economy.*" We come now to the consideration of what used to be called "the *balance of trade.*" This theory taught, as we have seen, that the advantage of foreign commerce lay chiefly in exports; and that in proportion as these exceeded the imports, in like manner did the country become rich; just in the same way as a man who sells much and buys little accumulates money. But this fallacy depends on that already noticed, that money is wealth; were this the case, any government might become rich *ad libitum*, by simply increasing an inconvertible paper currency; but such a government would be soon taught that

> "The value of a thing
> Is just as much as it will bring,"

and that they could not grow rich by multiplying money.

Setting aside, for the present, all the higher advantages of commerce, its power of civilizing and refining, we must look to the actual benefits which it confers upon a country; and these will be found to consist in what it brings in, not what it takes out: bullion must be regarded just as any other commodity, and if the whole value of the imports be greater than the whole value of the exports, the country must be necessarily a gainer. And here, a few words as to the way in which foreign business is transacted, may help the reader to a more accurate understanding of this question. In large operations, there is often little, if any, cash payments. A sends, from Bordeaux, wine to the value of 1000 francs to B in London; B has sent a quantity of cotton cloth to C at Bordeaux, worth £40, A receives the 1000 francs from C, and the transaction is closed: or B may send bills, that is, promises to pay money in France, and A is paid with that which has in like manner been given in payment to B: thus a mercantile transaction in one land is made to balance a similar transaction in another. Even travellers for pleasure often regulate their payments unconsciously in the same way. I go to spend a month with my friends in Spain; I pay £50 into the hands of my banker who furnishes me with circular notes; thus I take out of the country neither gold nor silver, but only pieces of paper; for these, I receive Spanish gold at Madrid, or Cadiz, or Barcelona, and my pieces of paper are made circuitously to pay for British manufactures exported into Spain.

CHAPTER VIII.

OF TAXATION.

THE necessity of government has been already shown. No government can exist without support, and the only mode in which that support can be fairly given, so that the cost shall press equally upon all classes of the community, is by a pecuniary tax.

The right of taxation is proved to the Christian sufficiently by the example of our LORD, who paid taxes for himself and one, at least, of his disciples, actually working a miracle to provide the requisite sum; and, on another occasion, commanding his disciples to "render unto Cæsar the things which are Cæsar's."

But, inasmuch as there are few who would deny the abstract legality of taxation, we pass to consider those points in which doubts may arise; viz. the manner in which taxation should be levied, and the persons on whom its burden ought to fall.

But there is a preliminary topic which claims our attention; viz. the purpose for which taxes are raised. In this, and most civilized countries, taxes are raised for two purposes; first, to supply the wants of the state itself, i. e. to pay those expenses incurred in maintaining the peace and order of the commonwealth; and, secondly, to satisfy the public creditor.

The *first* of these purposes will need no discussion. The *second* opens many and most important ones.

Who is the public creditor?

What is the nature of his claim?

Is it, or is it not, founded in strict justice?

Is there any probability of liquidating the debt incurred?

National debts, our own among the number, are contracted in the manner following:

Some cause requiring larger expenditure than usual, generally war, renders the income of a government inadequate to its requirements, and that to so great an extent that additional taxes cannot be imposed to meet the urgency of the case. Under these circumstances, the government negotiates a loan, the state borrows money precisely in the same way as any private individual would, offering that rate of interest requisite to ensure the obtaining the needful sum, and giving the creditor security on the public revenue.

The sum thus borrowed, and for which interest is paid, is usually called " the funds," or " government securities," neither of which terms are precisely applicable; for the money itself does not exist, and the securities bear the same relation to that for which they *are* securities, as do other documents bearing the same name.

The national debt of this country amounts to upwards of 750,000,000 sterling. A large part of this enormous sum was expended in the struggle with France, under Napoleon, the result of which was the destruction of the French empire, the restoration of the French monarchy, and the settlement of Europe upon what were called legitimate principles.

Whatever opinions may be held now concerning those events, I think it can hardly be denied that they were at the time deemed absolutely necessary to the safety of this country, and that they were carried on in conformity with the public will, if not in direct obedience to it.

The persons who, at any period of our history, have for public purposes advanced money to the government, or, if it be thought a better mode of expression, have invested money in government securities, *were* the public creditors; those on whom, by purchase or descent, their claims have devolved, *are* the public creditors.

The justice of the claim made and allowed at this time must depend on the joint conduct of the debtor and creditor; and, in order to get at this, we must examine the way in which the debt has increased or diminished, and the faith which has been kept in matter of payment of interest to the creditor.

It will be seen that the claim itself is one of very simple character. A says, my father lent the government in his day £10,000, for which he covenanted to receive 5 per cent. interest; he bequeathed that claim to me, and it has been allowed, but I am only receiving 3½ per cent. for the same. But, on further inquiry, we shall find that at a particular period the government stated to A's father, and to all who were in his position, "the value of money is less now than it was when we borrowed it from you; we shall, therefore, only pay 4 instead of 5 per cent.; but as we are bound by our contract with you, we propose to you either to continue your loan to us on this reduced interest, or to receive back the sum originally paid, and this we will effect by a new loan." A's father accepted the first of the two alternatives; and, by a subsequent reduction made in the same way, he found his interest brought down to 3½ per cent. at which rate an income is now paid to A. Nothing can be fairer than this; some portions of the debt have been paid off, and it is still rather diminishing than increasing.

But some persons, who fancy that the abolition of the debt would place England in a higher position than that which she at present occupies, have endeavoured to persuade themselves and others that the claim of the fund-holder is not founded in justice; and their arguments take the following form: "The money borrowed was borrowed for the defence of the nation; but as the nation was bound to defend itself, the money ought not to have been *lent*, but *given*; and as the *property* of the nation was what was in danger, so the defence of it was the especial duty of those who possessed that property; i. e. *the rich*, or, in other words, those who advanced the money in question." The inference from this curiously fallacious argument is, that we have been wrong in paying any interest at all, and shall be still more wrong if we continue to pay it. It amounts, in fact, to this: that A, the nation, borrowed from B, the individual, money to pay B's debts; that, having done this, A pays B a perpetual interest for the money so borrowed. Whereas B ought to have paid the debt, or liquidated the obligation himself, and so terminated the matter.

All this supposes—I. That property was the only thing at stake—the keeping of our national freedom, the preservation of our old laws and religion, our commercial independence, and our colonial empire, all being entirely overlooked, or regarded only as interesting to the comparatively small body of fundholders.

II. It entirely mis-states the case; if the money were borrowed for *national* purposes, the *nation* was bound to repay it, or at least to pay the stipulated interest; and the fund-holders, as a portion of the nation, pays a portion of the taxes whereby their own claim is satisfied. Thus, as it was the nation which borrowed, so it is the nation which pays. The case may be rendered still clearer by an illustration: a community of thirty persons have need, for their common use, of a sum of thirty thousand pounds; i. e.

they want one thousand pounds each. The natural solution of the question is, that each should pay the sum of one thousand pounds, and the common interest be consulted by the common sacrifice.

But when the proposition is made, it is found that twenty-eight out of the thirty are not in a condition to furnish their quota. The business or enterprise in which they are engaged is prosperous, and will well reward them for this necessary outlay; but, though the share of each in it is worth much more than a thousand pounds, only two of the thirty are able to furnish the sum in money.

Under these circumstances, the two rich members say, "we will advance fifteen thousand pounds each; but as we are not legally bound to advance more than the fifteenth part of that sum, and our money is worth to us five per cent. so the community, i. e. the thirty persons, must tax themselves to furnish the fifteen hundred pounds which will be annually required for interest. In that taxation, we, the advancers of the whole sum, thus take our part; all interests are consulted, the credit of the community saved, and a species of mutual assurance is effected."

This is the exact case with the nation at large and the national creditor.

From this it will appear that the application of the sponge to the national debt, a favourite nostrum of some political quacks, or the applying the annual interest to liquidate the principal, both of which would constitute a national bankruptcy, can be justified only by the same circumstances which justify any private bankruptcy : viz. the ascertained inability to pay either principal or interest.

We have now arrived at the conclusion, that the purposes for which, among ourselves, taxation is imposed, are just and right. We come next to the questions, in what manner these public contributions should be levied? and who are the persons on whom the burden ought to fall?

Of these two questions, the latter must take precedence; because the manner of raising the public income is wholly determined by the consideration upon what classes it is intended to lay the burden. If I wish to tax solely the rich, I must lay an impost on all articles of luxury, and establish a property tax of such a nature as to leave untouched small sums and small incomes. If I wish to tax chiefly the poor, I must tax the necessaries of life, and the wages of the workman. But it may be remarked, that no system of mere taxation can be devised by which the wealthy can be altogether exempted, and the poor alone burdened.

All that can be done towards this iniquitous and impolitic end, is to make the poor man pay as much as the rich; and this would be effectually accomplished by taxing simply the *necessaries* of life; for as the rich man cannot consume more than the poor, so he would not be called upon to pay more.

I think it will hardly be denied, that, as government exists for the welfare of all, so it has a claim upon all for support; and this will be the more evident in proportion as the right is recognized of universal *representation* (universal *suffrage* is another thing). No man is exempt from this claim simply because he is poor; for he in return makes his claim upon government for protection in life and limb, in the exercise of his civil rights and his religious duties. He requires to be sure of his wages, to be defended against invasions from abroad and riots at home; and for these advantages he looks to the rulers of his country.

Universal taxation, therefore, *must* follow universal representation; and if the principles of pure justice were applied to the question, none would be more easily solved; for each would then be called upon to contribute in proportion to his ability. Not simply because he who has ten thousand pounds receives ten times as much protection as he who has but one thousand, nor solely on account of any arithmetical proportion whatever; but also because all men are stewards of that wealth which God has given, and which is *His;* they are bound, as such, therefore, to distribute it. The duty of supporting government is of divine authority, and men are under obligation to fulfil it according to what they have, and not according to what they have not.

The object of taxation, then, is to raise, by the contributions of every member of the community, a sum requisite for, and adequate to, the public service, and to arrange these contributions so that no one shall pay more or less than his share.

This is attempted to be done by two modes of taxation—direct and indirect.

Taxation is *direct* when a specific sum of money is demanded of the citizen for the use of government. An income tax, a property tax, a land tax, a poll or capitation tax, assessed taxes, legacy duties, poor-rates, and rates of all kinds, are instances of direct taxation.

Corn laws, excise, customs, and stamp duties, are instances of indirect taxation.

It has been contended, by some, that all taxation ought to be direct; by others, that it ought to be wholly indirect.

The advocates of direct taxation say that, as property and person alone require government protection, so an income tax which repays the one, and a capitation tax which defrays the expenses of the other, would be at once the fairest, the easiest to collect, and the least expensive in the collection, of all imposts; and that therefore into these all taxes should be commuted.

They further observe that direct taxation is by no means so unpopular as it is sometimes supposed; that men are willing enough to pay their contributions, when they are satisfied of the necessity, which all are now, and when they see the fairness of the assessment, which all then would see.

They also contend that the negative benefits of direct taxation are yet greater than the positive; for in all indirect taxation the expense of collection is doubled; the interests of particular classes or trades are consulted, to the disadvantage of the rest; a new crime is created—that of smuggling, the moral evil of which it is very difficult to exhibit to the uneducated classes in its true light; and that the public revenues are diminished, without any corresponding benefit in return. Besides all these objections, indirect taxation interferes with the freedom of trade, and, by its restrictions, limits and sometimes neutralizes the advantages which the industry of a country may obtain for its inhabitants.

The advocates for indirect taxation rest their defence on these points: they contend that—

1. It reaches most easily all incomes, securing the contributions of all to the public need. It may be very difficult to obtain the payment of a few shillings by way of direct taxation from the labouring man; but it is very easy to lay a tax upon his bread, his beer, and his tea; which tax he cannot avoid paying, and does indeed pay unconsciously, and without a murmur.

2. That it avoids the unpopular and apparently oppressive measure of demanding so much money as

a direct payment for government protection, and at the same time is free from the objection of encouraging falsehood and concealment, which an income tax is sure more or less to occasion.

3. That it involves the principle of protection, without which the agriculturist and manufacturer of our own country has no chance of success in contending with the more lightly taxed foreigner.

Now, as all these arguments have their weight, and require to be taken into the account (save the last, which is to be decided on other grounds, and will be considered in a separate chapter), we have to strike a balance of benefits and evils, and decide accordingly.

The theory which would commute all taxes into an income tax and a capitation tax, would be a perfectly true one, were it possible for an income tax to be levied on perfectly fair principles, and to reach accurately the incomes it professes to assess: but the first of these desiderata has not yet been so much as attempted; and all experience shows us that the latter is not to be expected.

Let it be supposed, however, that a fairly graduated income tax were established, reaching *all* incomes, and enabling employers to pay for their workmen, while it did not press too heavily upon the larger incomes; it would still be necessary to create supplementary taxes, to supply the deficiency, a growing deficiency too, occasioned by the evasions of the tax.

Should this deficiency be made good by direct or by indirect taxation? Partly, without doubt, by the former; a few direct taxes on articles of luxury or ostentation, such as carriages, horses, dogs, armorial bearings, servants not employed in business, would be expedient, both as supplying the required sum and equalizing the irregularities of the greater and more universal tax.

A house tax, if equitably levied, is perhaps as fair as any of these supplementary imposts; for few more accurate means exist of ascertaining the amount of any man's income than the manner in which he chooses to be lodged. Few taxes are, on the other hand, more noxious than a window tax; its results being equally injurious to health, to taste, to art, to trade, and to comfort.

If, after all, any mode of indirect taxation should be considered needful in aid of the more direct mode, it should be levied on such objects as are of sufficiently general use to produce a sum large enough for the purpose required, and which are yet not the absolute necessaries of life.

The argument against the *principle* of direct taxation, on the ground of its unpopularity, may be speedily disposed of. Men for the most part regard the matter in a purely utilitarian point of view, and are keen enough to perceive which system is really the most oppressive. If a government which obliges me to pay seven pounds per annum in direct taxes does at the same time enable me to save ten pounds every year in the necessaries of life, I shall hardly be so foolish as to clamour against direct taxation; nor is it likely that the real state of the case can be hidden from the great mass of the nation. On the whole, the balance of argument is really in favour of the more direct method; while, at the same time, direct taxation could not be imposed to the extent which our necessities require; and there are also limits within which indirect taxation may, at all times, be permitted without disadvantage.

The last question is—whether there be any probability of liquidating this debt? That it is desirable, no one can doubt; although, as its desirability consists in the decrease of taxation, every tax, either direct or indirect, which is remitted, has precisely the same effect on the amount demanded from the public, as though a portion of the debt with its consequent burdens were removed. There is, moreover, this advantage attending the removal of taxes, instead of liquidating portions of the debt; that those imposts which are most objectionable may be taken off in succession, and when no obnoxious taxes remain, then the surplus may be applied to the liquidation of the debt.

Unquestionably there seems but small prospect of speedily paying off so gigantic an incumbrance; yet, as it was, during the long peace, steadily diminishing, and as the falling in of the long annuities will at no very distant time greatly reduce it, there is nothing really terrible to this country in the aspect of a debt under which every other government in the world would be crushed.

Paley treats the subject of taxation with special reference to population, and in accordance with the theory, that whatever augments population is favourable to a country, and whatever diminishes it is prejudicial. So far as this theory is true, so far the observations of Paley are pertinent; but they stand or fall with the theory which they support. He observes: As *taxes* take nothing out of a country, as they do not diminish the public stock, only vary the distribution of it, they are not necessarily prejudicial to population. If the State exact money from certain members of the community, she dispenses it also amongst other members of the same community. They who contribute to the revenue, and they who are supported or benefited by the expenses of government, are to be placed one against the other; and whilst what the subsistence of one part is profited by receiving, compensates for what that of the other suffers by paying, the common fund of the society is not lessened*. This is true; but it must be observed, that although the sum distributed by the state be always *equal* to the sum

---

* It must be observed that this argument has, in reality, little to do with taxation. More persons, by hundreds of thousands, are taxed than receive any *direct benefit* by the impost. Government *employés* form a very small fraction of the people, even if the army and navy be included.

collected from the people, yet the gain and loss to the means of subsistence may be very *unequal;* and the balance will remain on the wrong or the right side of the account, according as the money passes by taxation from the industrious to the idle, from the many to the few, from those who want to those who abound, or in a contrary direction. For instance, a tax upon coaches, to be laid out in the repair of roads, would probably improve the population of a neighbourhood; a tax upon cottages, to be ultimately expended in the purchase and support of coaches, would certainly diminish it. In like manner, a tax upon wine or tea distributed in bounties to fishermen or husbandmen, would augment the provision of a country; a tax upon fisheries and husbandry, however indirect or concealed, to be converted, when raised, to the procuring of wine or tea for the idle and opulent, would naturally impair the public stock*. The effect, therefore, of taxes upon the means of subsistence depends, not so much upon the amount of the sum levied, as upon the object of the tax, and the application. Taxes likewise may be so adjusted, as to conduce to the restraint of luxury, and the correction of vice; to the encouragement of industry, trade, agriculture, and marriage.

---

* There appears some confusion in this argument: those who are engaged to do the necessary work of government, live as the majority of their fellow-subjects; such conversions as those of which Paley speaks, do not, in fact, take place at all.

Taxes thus contrived become rewards and penalties; not only sources of revenue, but instruments of police. Vices, indeed, themselves cannot be taxed, without holding forth such a conditional toleration of them as to destroy men's perception of their guilt; a tax comes to be considered as a commutation; the materials, however, and incentives of vice may. Although, for instance, drunkenness would be, on this account, an unfit object of taxation; yet public houses and spirituous liquors are very properly subject to heavy imposts.

Nevertheless, although it may be true that taxes cannot be pronounced to be detrimental to population, by any absolute necessity in their nature; and though, under some modifications, and when urged only to a certain extent, they may even operate in favour of it; yet it will be found, in a great plurality of instances, that their tendency is noxious. Let it be supposed that nine families inhabit a neighbourhood, each possessing barely the means of subsistence, or of that mode of subsistence which custom hath established among them; let a tenth family be quartered upon these, to be supported by a tax raised from the nine; or rather, let one of the nine have his income augmented by a similar deduction from the incomes of the rest; in either of these cases, it is evident that the whole district would be broken up; for, as the entire income of each is supposed to be barely sufficient for the establishment which it maintains, a deduction of any part destroys that establishment. Now it is no answer to this objection, it is no apology for the grievance, to say, that nothing is taken out of the neighbourhood, that the stock is not diminished; the mischief is done by deranging the distribution. Nor, again, is the luxury of one family, or even the maintenance of an additional family, a recompense to the country for the ruin of nine others. Nor, lastly, will it alter the effect, though it may conceal the cause, that the contribution, instead of being levied directly upon each day's wages, is mixed up in the price of some article of constant use and consumption, as in a tax upon candles, malt, leather, or fuel. This example illustrates the tendency of taxes to obstruct subsistence; and the minutest degree of this obstruction will be felt in the formation of families. The example, indeed, forms an extreme case; the evil is magnified, in order to render its operation distinct and visible. In real life, families may not be broken up, or forced from their habitation, houses be quitted, or countries suddenly deserted, in consequence of any new imposition whatever; but marriages will become gradually less frequent.

It seems necessary, however, to distinguish between the operation of a new tax and the effect of taxes which have been long established. In the course of circulation, the money may flow back to the hands from which it was taken. The proportion between the supply and the expense of subsistence, which had been disturbed by the tax, may at length recover itself again. In the instance just now stated, the addition of a tenth family to the neighbourhood, or the enlarged expenses of one of the nine, may, in some shape or other, so advance the profits or increase the employment of the rest, as to make full restitution for the share of their property of which it deprives them; or, what is more likely to happen, a reduction may take place in their mode of living, suited to the abridgment of their incomes. Yet still the ultimate and permanent effect of taxation, though distinguishable from the impression of a new tax, is generally adverse to population. The *proportion* above spoken of can only be restored by one side or other of the following alternative: by the people either contracting their wants, which at the same time diminishes consumption and employment; or by raising the price of labour, which, necessarily adding to the price of the productions and manufactures of the country, checks their sale at foreign markets. A nation which is burdened with taxes must always be undersold by a nation which is free from them; unless the difference be made up by some singular advantage of climate, soil, skill, or industry. This quality belongs to all taxes which affect the mass of the community, even when imposed upon the properest objects, and applied to the fairest purposes. But abuses are inseparable from the disposal of public money. As governments are usually administered, the produce of public taxes is expended upon a train of gentry, in the maintaining of pomp, or in the purchase of influence. The conversion of property which taxes effectuate, when they are employed in this manner, is attended with obvious evils. It takes from the industrious to give to the idle; it increases the number of the latter; it tends to accumulation, it sacrifices the conveniency of many to the luxury of a few; it makes no return to the people, from whom the tax is drawn, that is satisfactory or intelligible; it encourages no activity which is useful or productive*.

The sum to be raised being settled, a wise statesman will contrive his taxes principally with a view to their effect upon *population*; that is, he will so adjust them, as to give the least possible obstruction to those means of subsistence by which the mass of the community is maintained. We are accustomed to an opinion that a tax, to be just, ought to be accurately proportioned to the circumstances of the persons who pay it. But upon what, it might be asked, is this opinion founded, unless it could be shown that such a proportion interferes the least with the general conveniency of subsistence? Whereas, I should rather believe that a tax, constructed with a view to that con-

---

* This will hardly be the case in any well-ordered government; there is too much reason to believe that in Paley's time his statement was true; happily for us, it is no longer applicable, or, at least, in a small and rapidly decreasing proportion.

veniency, ought to rise upon the different classes of the community in a much higher ratio than the simple proportion of their incomes. The point to be regarded, is not what men have, but what they can spare; and it is evident that a man who possesses a thousand pounds a year can more easily give up a hundred, than a man with a hundred pounds a year can part with ten; that is, those habits of life which are reasonable and innocent, and upon the ability to continue which the formation of families depends, will be much less affected by the one deduction than the other. It is still more evident that a man of a hundred pounds a year would not be so much distressed in his subsistence by a demand from him of ten pounds, as a man of ten pounds a year would be by the loss of one; to which we must add, that the population of every country being replenished by the marriages of the lowest ranks of the society, their accommodation and relief become of more importance to the state than the conveniency of any higher but less numerous order of the citizens. But whatever be the proportion which public expediency directs, whether the simple, the duplicate, or any higher or intermediate proportion of men's incomes, it can never be attained by any *single* tax; as no single object of taxation can be found which measures the ability of the subject with sufficient generality and exactness. It is only by a system and variety of taxes, mutually balancing and equalizing one another, that a due proportion can be preserved. For instance, if a tax upon lands press with greater hardship upon those who live in the country, it may be properly counterpoised by a tax upon the rent of houses, which will affect principally the inhabitants of large towns.

Distinctions* may also be framed in some taxes which shall allow abatements or exemptions to married persons; to the parents of a certain number of legitimate children; to improvers of the soil; to particular modes of cultivation, as to tillage in preference to pasturage; and in general to that industry which is immediately *productive*, in preference to that which is only *instrumental;* but, above all, which may leave the heaviest part of the burden upon the methods, whatever they be, of acquiring wealth without industry, or even of subsisting in idleness.

---

* All these distinctions are now admitted to be either mischievous or impracticable. It is understood that the common sense of mankind will prompt them what to do for their own interests; that the aggregate interest of individuals make up the interest of the community; and that the best way to *favour* any branch of industry, is to leave it entirely unfettered.

As to population, at a season when emigration is looked upon, and with reason, as the only effectual relief for the too great multitudes that throng our markets, and clog our operations at home, bounties upon large families will be felt to be worse than ridiculous.

CHAPTER IX.*

OF THE EXPORTATION OF PROVISIONS.

NOTHING can have a more positive tendency to reduce the number of the people, than the sending abroad part of the provision by which they are maintained; yet this has been the policy of legislators very studious of the improvement of their country. In order to reconcile ourselves to a practice which appears to militate against the chief interest, that is, against

---

* The argument of this chapter is somewhat vitiated by the continued reference to population as the supreme good of a country. It may also be said, that where there is not corn to spare, there will of necessity be no exportation; but this is not necessarily true, for a people may grow corn and export it, living themselves on food of an inferior quality. Not more than a century ago, the people of the Balearic Isles exported to Barcelona nearly all the corn grown in the province; the poorer classes in the islands eating a coarse kind of bread made of the pods of the carob tree. Other similar cases may be adduced, in which the exportation of corn from countries long settled, and where there is no superfluity, may take place without lowering the number of inhabitants, or arguing any defect of population. It does, however, in such cases, prove a low degree of comfort and civilization.

the population of the country that adopts it, we must be reminded of a maxim which belongs to the productions both of nature and art, "that it is impossible to have enough without a superfluity." The point of sufficiency cannot in any case be so exactly hit upon, as to have nothing to spare, yet never to want. This is peculiarly true of bread-corn, of which the annual increase is extremely variable. As it is necessary that the crop be adequate to the consumption in a year of scarcity, it must of consequence greatly exceed it in a year of plenty. A redundancy, therefore, will occasionally arise from the care that is taken to secure the people against the danger of want: and it is manifest that the exportation of this redundancy subtracts nothing from the number that can regularly be maintained by the produce of the soil. Moreover, as the exportation of corn, under these circumstances, is attended with no direct injury to population, so the benefits which indirectly arise to population from foreign commerce belong to this, in common with other species of trade; together with the peculiar advantage of presenting a constant incitement to the skill and industry of the husbandman, by the promise of a certain sale and an adequate price, under every contingency of season and produce. There is another situation, in which corn may not only be exported, but in which the people can thrive by no other means; that is, of a newly settled country with a fertile soil. The exportation of a large proportion of the corn which a country produces, proves, it is true, that the inhabitants have not yet attained to the number which the country is capable of maintaining; but it does not prove but that they may be hastening to this limit with the utmost practicable celerity; which is the perfection to be sought for in a young establishment. In all cases, except these two, and in the former of them to any greater degree than what is necessary to take off occasional redundancies, the exportation of corn is either itself noxious to population, or argues a defect of population, arising from some other cause.

CHAPTER X.

OF LABOUR.

It has long been made a question, whether those mechanical contrivances which *abridge labour*, by performing the same work by fewer hands, be detrimental or not to the population of a country? From what has been delivered in preceding parts of this work, it will be evident that this question is equivalent to another: whether such contrivances diminish or not the quantity of employment? And this question must not be treated as though labour itself were the thing desired; but rather the *result* of labour. Labour was in the first place inflicted as a curse; employment need not be laborious; and though idleness would be a far greater curse than even the amount of labour now required from mankind, still, in proportion as toil diminishes, so is the curse alleviated; and if it were possible that all the heavier and more exhausting kinds of labour could be altogether laid aside, mankind would undoubtedly benefit by the change. Now this is the natural effect of machinery. It diminishes labour. Does it therefore diminish employment, and deprive a number of men of the means of support? Its first and most obvious effect undoubtedly is this; because, if one man be made to do what three men did before, two are immediately discharged: but if, by some more general and remoter consequence, they increase the demand for work, or, what is the same thing, prevent the diminution of that demand, in a greater proportion than they contract the number of hands by which it is performed, the quantity of employment, upon the whole, will gain an addition. Upon which principle, it may be observed, first, that whenever a mechanical invention succeeds in one place, it is necessary that it be imitated in every other where the same manufacture is carried on; for it is manifest that he who has the benefit of a conciser operation will soon outvie and undersell a competitor who continues to use a more circuitous labour. It is also true, in the second place, that whoever *first* discover or adopt a mechanical improvement, will, for some time, draw to themselves an increase of employment; and that this preference may continue even after the improvement has become general: for, in every kind of trade, it is not only a great, but permanent advantage, to have once pre-occupied the public reputation. Thirdly—after every superiority which might be derived from the possession of a secret has ceased, it may be well questioned whether even then any loss can accrue to employment. The same money will be spared to the same article still. Wherefore, in proportion as the article can be afforded at a lower price, by reason of an easier or shorter process in the manufacture, it will either grow into more general use, or an improvement will take place in the quality and fabric, which will demand a proportionable addition of hands. The number of persons employed in the manufactory of stockings has not decreased since the invention of stocking-mills. The amount of what is expended upon the article, after subtracting from it the price of the raw material, and consequently what is paid for work in this branch of our manufactories, is not less than it was before. Goods of a finer texture are worn in place of coarser. This is the change which the invention has produced, and which compensates to the manufactory for every other inconveniency. Add to which, that in the above, and almost in every instance, an improvement which conduces to the recommendation of a manufactory, either by the cheapness or the quality of the goods, draws up after it many dependent employments, in which no abbreviation has taken place. In conclusion, then, the sparing of human labour in any one direction, is but setting it free to act more effectually in another. The less the labour employed on any article, the cheaper and more universally accessible it becomes, the more rapid the advance in civilization, and the greater the diffusion of what are justly called the comforts of life. Hence the necessity that labour should be free and unrestricted, that it should be able to take all the advantages which soil, climate, and situation present; that it should not be obliged to act under circumstances of depression: it requires a fair field and no favour.

CHAPTER XI.

OF LAWS AND CUSTOMS RELATING TO LAND.

From the reasoning that has been pursued, and the various considerations suggested in the former chapters, a judgment may, in some sort, be formed, how far regulations of law are in their nature capable of contributing to the support and advancement of population. I say *how far;* for, as in many subjects, so especially in those which relate to commerce, to plenty, to riches, and to the number of people, more is wont to be expected from laws than laws can do. Laws can only imperfectly restrain that dissoluteness of manners, which, by diminishing the frequency of marriages, impairs the very source of population. Laws cannot regulate the wants of mankind, their mode of living, or their desire of those superfluities which fashion, more irresistible than laws, has once introduced into general usage; or, in other words, has erected into necessaries of life. Laws cannot induce men to enter into marriages when the expenses of a family must deprive them of that system of accommodation to which they have habituated their expectations. Laws, by their protection, by assuring to the labourer the fruit and profit of his labour, may help to make a people industrious; but, without industry, the laws cannot provide either subsistence or employment; laws cannot make corn grow without toil and care; or trade flourish without art and diligence. In spite of all laws, the expert, laborious, honest workman will be *employed*, in preference to the lazy, the unskilful, the fraudulent, and evasive; and this is not more true of two inhabitants of the same village, than it is of the people of two different countries, which communicate either with each other, or with the rest of the world. The natural basis of trade is rivalship of quality and price; or, which is the same thing, of skill and industry. Every attempt to *force* trade by operation of law, that is, by compelling persons to buy goods at one market which they can obtain cheaper and better from another, is sure to be either eluded by the quick-sightedness and incessant activity of private interest, or to be frustrated by retaliation. One half of the commercial laws of many states are calculated merely to counteract the restrictions which have been imposed by other states. Perhaps the only way in which the interposition of law is salutary in trade, is in the prevention of frauds*.

Next to the indispensable requisites of internal

---

* Paley considers some interference necessary for this end, grounding his opinions on his untenable theory of population.

peace and security, we have to consider the interference of law in the encouragement of *agriculture*, the object of which, if it exist at all, should be to increase the quantity of provision raised for the use of the country. Now, the principal expedient by which such a purpose can be promoted, is to adjust the laws of property as nearly as possible to the following rules: first—"to give to the occupier all the power over the soil which is necessary for its perfect cultivation;" secondly—"to assign the whole profit of every improvement to the persons by whose activity it is carried on." What we call property in land, as hath been observed above, is power over it. Now it is indifferent to the public in whose hands this power resides, if it be rightly used; it matters not to whom the land belongs, if it be well cultivated. When we lament that great estates are often united in the same hand, or complain that one man possesses what would be sufficient for a thousand, we suffer ourselves to be misled by words. The owner of ten thousand pounds a year *consumes* little more of the produce of the soil than the owner of ten pounds a year. If the cultivation be equal, the estate in the hands of one great lord affords subsistence and employment to the same number of persons as it would do if it were divided amongst a hundred proprietors. In like manner we ought to judge of the effect upon the public interest which may arise from lands being holden by the king, or by the subject; by private persons, or by corporations;

by laymen, or ecclesiastics; in fee, or for life; by virtue of office; or in right of inheritance. I do not mean that these varieties make no difference; but I mean that all the difference they do make, respects the cultivation of the lands which are so holden.

There exists in this country conditions of tenure which condemn the land itself to perpetual sterility. Of this kind is the right of *common**, which precludes each propietor from the improvement, or even the convenient occupation, of his estate, without (what seldom can be obtained) the consent of many others. This tenure is also usually embarrassed by the interference of *manorial* claims, under which it often happens that the surface belongs to one owner, and the soil to another; so that neither owner can stir a clod without the concurrence of his partner in the property. In many manors, the tenant is restrained from granting leases beyond a short term of years; which renders every plan of solid improvement impracticable. In these cases, the owner wants, what the first rule of rational policy requires, " sufficient power over the soil for its perfect cultivation." This power ought to be extended to him by some easy and general law of enfranchisement, partition, and enclo-

---

* The right of common in the vicinity of large cities is more beneficial than hurtful, inasmuch as it provides open spaces which cannot be built upon, forming what have been well called the "*lungs*" of our great towns.

sure; which, though compulsory upon the lord or the rest of the tenants, whilst it has in view the melioration of the soil, and tenders an equitable compensation for every right that it takes away, is neither more arbitrary, nor more dangerous to the stability of property, than that which is done in the construction of roads, bridges, embankments, navigable canals, and indeed in almost every public work, in which private owners of land are obliged to accept that price for their property which an indifferent jury may award. It may here, however, be proper to observe, that although the enclosure of wastes and pastures be generally beneficial to population, yet the enclosure of lands in tillage, in order to convert them into pastures, is as generally hurtful.

But, secondly, agriculture is discouraged by every constitution of landed property which lets in those who have no concern in the improvement to a participation of the profit. This objection is applicable to all such customs of manors as subject the proprietor, upon the death of the lord or tenant, or the alienation of the estate, to a fine apportioned to the improved value of the land. But of all institutions which are in this way adverse to cultivation and improvement, none is so noxious as that of *tithes*. A claimant here enters into the produce who contributed no assistance whatever to the production. When years, perhaps, of care and toil have matured an improvement; when the husbandman sees new crops ripening to his skill and industry; the moment he is ready to put his sickle to the grain, he finds himself compelled to divide his harvest with a stranger. Tithes are a tax not only upon industry, but upon that industry which feeds mankind; upon that species of exertion which it is the aim of all wise laws to cherish and promote; and to uphold and excite which, composes, as we have seen, the main benefit that the community receives from the whole system of trade, and the success of commerce*.

---

* Paley adds, in conformity with his theory of agriculture: "And, together with the more general inconveniency that attends the exaction of tithes, there is this additional evil, in the mode at least according to which they are collected at present, that they operate as a bounty upon pasturage. The burden of the tax falls with its chief, if not with its whole weight, upon tillage; that is to say, upon that precise mode of cultivation which, as hath been shown above, is the business of the state to relieve and remunerate, in preference to any other. No measure of such extensive concern appears to me so practicable, nor any single alteration so beneficial, as the conversion of tithes into corn-rents. This commutation, I am convinced, might be so adjusted, as to secure to the tithe-holder a complete and perpetual equivalent for his interest, and to leave to industry its full operation and entire reward†."

† This desire of Paley's has been now long since accomplished, and the beneficial results which his wisdom foresaw have followed the change.

CHAPTER XII.

OF FREE TRADE AND RESTRICTION.

By freedom of commerce is meant that all who wish to buy shall buy where they find the best and cheapest articles; and that all who wish to sell shall have the liberty of selling where they find the most advantageous market. I want oil, wine, and furs: A merchant at Lucca will supply me with the first, one at Bordeaux with the second, and one at St. Petersburgh with the third. I may have them all of home growth; but the one will be thick and coarse, the other poor and unwholesome, and the last-named neither fine nor durable: those which are offered to me from abroad are all excellent in their kind. On the other hand, the Lucca merchant wants cotton cloth, the French farmer wants machinery, and the Russian fur-dealer wants cutlery. All these things I can supply much better and cheaper than each of my foreign correspondents can make for himself; why should we not exchange? I send abroad, therefore, my home-grown or home-made productions, and receive in return the produce of foreign lands. Now, that this should be done with regard to all commodities, is the theory of free trade. Founded on nature, it is obviously for the *general* advancement of mankind; but when the theory comes to be applied to practice, we are met with many difficulties and much opposition. First, the government says: We must have money for the service of the public; direct taxation, though best in principle, will not serve us; for no government would be able to raise by direct taxation the amount required for that purpose in England; we must, therefore, have customs, duties, and excise duties. This demand is one which is both expedient and just; let us see how it acts. Suppose that I can buy at Florence a quart of olive oil for sixpence, and suppose that the freight, land carriage, and profit to merchant and retainer, amount to as much more, then, if trade were quite free, I should pay one shilling for the same article in London; but there is a duty levied of three pence, which goes to the government here, and I pay one shilling and three pence to the Italian warehouse-keeper for my bottle of oil. But it may be also that the Tuscan government imposes an export duty; that is, does not allow oil to leave the country without first paying somewhat for the permission; let us call this export duty another three pence; I then pay one shilling and sixpence for my bottle of oil, and the payment may be divided somewhat in this manner: sixpence goes to the Florentine cultivator, and is the return for his labour and capital; sixpence goes to the shipowners, carriers, merchants, and retailers; three pence, minus the expense of collecting, goes to the British government, and may be expended in gun-powder and scarlet cloth, or it may help to make up the salary of the Lord Chancellor, or the pay of the policeman, B 22. While the remaining three pence may, in like manner, when the expense of collection is deducted, go towards keeping in prison some unfortunate nobleman who has been detected in reading the Bible. With the uses to which the Tuscan government may put their funds we have, however, no concern here. No government can be carried on without money, nor can any nation be left without government. So long as the duty is a moderate one, it will have little or no effect upon consumption; the foreign grower will find his market, the consumer here the required commodity, and the civil authorities the sums necessary for the public service. But now let us suppose that the grower of oil at Valencia and Malaga can supply the same article at the same price, and that the Spanish government imposes no export duty: then the Spanish oil can be sold for fifteen pence. When the Florentine oil costs eighteen pence, one fifth—that is, 20 per cent.—is added by the Tuscan government to the price of this oil, and the article is excluded from the market by legislative restriction. Let us further suppose that, in consequence of a commercial treaty with Tuscany, a duty is laid on Spanish oil, greater than that paid by the produce of Florence, or that the duty is remitted on the latter and not on the former; the value of the two articles would then be equalized, and they would divide the market; but Spain would immediately impose some retaliative duty on British produce, which would counterbalance, and probably more than counterbalance, the advantages gained by the treaty.

From this it will appear that the imposition of a duty does not necessarily interfere with the freedom of commerce, but only in those cases where the amount imposed excludes desirable commodities. At the same time, it is almost a maxim of political economy, that a low rate of duty (on articles of common use) is more productive than a high one; thus there appears reason to believe that were the present duties on tea and French wines very greatly reduced, a larger sum would be paid to the government, and the comfort and welfare of the people materially augmented. Articles of mere luxury are fair objects of heavy import duties. It matters nothing to the nation at large, and very little either to the foreign producer or the home consumer, that the rich man should pay two or three hundred per cent. duty on his bottle of *curaçoa* or *maraschino;* the state is a gainer, and no one is a loser.

From the consideration of import duties simply as means of raising a revenue, we come to regard them in the light of protective enactments. A single stocking-frame was set up some twenty years ago in

Santiago, the capital of Chili; the Chilian authorities, forthwith to protect their home manufacturers, imposed upon all foreign stockings an almost prohibitive duty. This was done with a view to *protect* home interests. What was the result? The Nottingham stocking-weaver wanted Chilian produce; but he was unable to pay for it, because his payment, that is, his manufactured goods, would not be taken; the Chilian farmer lost his market, and the inhabitants of Santiago were obliged to go without stockings; at least, this would have been the effect, had so absurd a regulation been persisted in.

But to take a familiar instance: let it be supposed that, under his present circumstances of rental, the English farmer cannot grow corn to remunerate him at less than 45 shillings a quarter; let it be also supposed that from Poland and Russia corn of equal quality can be sent into the market at 40 shillings; the foreigner, in this case, undersells the home grower by five shillings per quarter. Government lays on a protecting duty of five shillings, and thus equalizes the two articles for the benefit of the English producer. Let us then investigate this transaction: First, we see that the state takes five shillings from the foreigner, in order that the farmers may take five shillings from the British consumer; the weight then falls on the public, who are thus taxed because the conditions of farmers are unprosperous. The artisan says to the government, you make me pay ten pence for the loaf, which, were it not for your enactment, I should get for eight pence; and, as other commodities follow, to a great extent, the price of bread, your corn law makes my coat, my tools, and my cottage, all dearer to me, while my wages are not in any way raised by it. Now, as the object of this protection duty is to secure the interest of the farmer, *under his present circumstances*, it would clearly be the same thing, so far as he is concerned, to tax the public by a corn law, or to give him direct bounty out of the proceeds of the other taxes to the extent of five shillings per quarter; in each case, *all* the public would pay it; in each case, the object would be the same; in each case, it would be equally effectual; but in the latter, stripped of its indirect character, it would be an odious and iniquitous piece of favouritism.

But hitherto we have seen the matter only in one light; two questions remain: Is it so impossible to compete with the foreigner, even under present circumstances? and secondly, if so, why? The rate at which land continues to be sold, and the continuing eagerness to possess it, would seem to indicate that the impossibility itself is not by any means a self-evident proposition. No one contends that the soil of England and Ireland is less fertile than that of Poland or Russia: the increasing knowledge of agricultural chemistry, a science as yet in its infancy, will probably make our harvests more than sufficient for our wants. In fine, the problem of competition has yet to be solved.

But supposing that it be solved, and solved unfavourably,—then comes the other question: why cannot the English farmer compete with him of Poland or Lithuania? The reply is, he does not live in the same manner, subsist on the same fare, he is more taxed, and, above all, *he pays a higher rent*. Now, no one would wish to degrade the English farmer to the condition of the Polish serf or the Russian slave; the equalization cannot be made in that manner; and besides, it is to be hoped, on the contrary, that the *less* civilized will gradually be brought up to the level of the *more* civilized; and the equalization of condition will thus be effected. Again, it is not true, to any extent worthy of notice, that the English farmer is more heavily taxed than the foreigner. If direct and indirect taxation be taken together into consideration, it will appear that this country is not more burdened than the generality of continental nations. The third objection is a true and valid one: *he pays a higher rent*. This is a matter which will soon rectify itself; and with its rectification will disappear all the inconveniences which have been supposed indissolubly connected with free trade in corn. It has been strangely forgotten, by many writers, that land is a commodity as well as corn, and that its price, whether for sale or hire, must depend on what can be gained by means of it. If brooms fetch three pence each in the market, the man must be mad who buys the materials for three pence half-penny, and then says to the state—I cannot sell my produce, save at a loss, to speak nothing of my own support: make up to me the deficiency out of the taxes.

Another case supposed to require protection duties, is that of colonial produce. Other nations and their colonies may undersell us; we must, it is said, protect our colonists, by imposing a duty on produce similar to theirs when it reaches us from other sources; but it is by no means clear that we have a right to lay an extraordinary tax on our home population for the benefit of our colonies. Colonies are established to be an aid, not a burden, to the parent state; and, if rightly managed, would be so. Besides which, it is difficult to assign any irremediable cause by which our colonists are undersold; and the wiser plan is not to bolster up a corrupt system by protection duties, but to remove those causes which make free trade unprofitable. It is said that slave labour is so much cheaper than free labour, that our West India colonies cannot sell their produce at the same rate as Cuba and Brazil. If this indeed be so, I would not remedy the matter by a protection duty, which treats negro slavery as an element in prices; but I would absolutely prohibit all importation of slave-labour produce, on the ground that the system itself is bad, unchristian, and unlawful.

This principle will find its natural limitations. Where an article is *necessary,* and is only to be obtained in sufficient quantities from states employing slave labour, then the old maxim, " necessitas non habet leges," is applicable. But even then, a Christian state will make no small exertion to procure a sufficient supply from the produce of free labour, and will use the other only so long as the absolute necessity remains.

It must never be forgotten that *all* duties fall on the consumer: so long as they do not materially reduce the amount of the article imported, they are a tax on the home population—more or less justifiable in proportion as they affect the necessaries of life. If they do reduce to any considerable extent the amount of importations, then they do to the same extent affect the comfort of the people, the prosperity of merchants, and the welfare of foreign producers.

Commerce, to be really free, must be free in *all* its branches; that enactment is but a deliberate injustice which sets only one class of producers free, and holds back the rest by a system of restrictions. If the English farmer be made to stand on a commercial equality with the Pole and the Russian, he ought to be compensated by free access to *all* the products of the known world: whatever he can gain by free trade, is the return made to him for his otherwise reduced profits. The only lawful reason for any import duty is that the support of the state renders it necessary; and then it should be so arranged, so levied, and so collected, as to interfere in the slightest possible degree with the freedom of trade.

CHAPTER XIII.

OF THE LAWFULNESS OF WAR.

The lawfulness of war is one of those questions which particularly occupy the public mind at this time, and must continue unceasingly to do so, in proportion as men become more really civilized. There are some who maintain it to be in itself and altogether unlawful; and they contend that even defensive warfare is prohibited by the command to turn the other cheek to him who smiteth us on the one. Others again admit the necessity, and consequently the lawfulness, of defensive war; but deny that of aggressive war: while a third party admit the propriety of both, on sufficient cause. To the first-named reasoners, it may be sufficient to oppose the arguments of Paley.

Because the Christian Scriptures describe wars as what they are—as crimes or judgments, some have been led to believe that it is unlawful for a Christian to bear arms. But it should be remembered that it may be necessary for individuals to unite their force, and for this end to resign themselves to the direction of a common will; and yet it may be true that the will is often actuated by criminal motives, and often determined to destructive purposes. Hence, although the origin of wars be ascribed, in the Scriptures, to the operation of lawless and malignant passions*, and though war itself be enumerated among the sorest calamities with which a land can be visited, the profession of a soldier is no where forbidden or condemned. When the soldiers demanded of John the Baptist, " And what shall we do?" he said unto them, " Do " violence to no man, neither accuse any falsely, and " be content with your wages†." In which answer we do not find, that, in order to prepare themselves for the reception of the kingdom of God, it was required of soldiers to relinquish their profession, but only that they should beware of the vices of which that profession, it may be presumed, was justly accused. The precept, "Be content with your wages," supposed them to continue in their situation. It was of a Roman centurion that Christ pronounced that memorable eulogy, " I have not found so great faith, " no, not in Israel‡." The first Gentile convert§ who was received into the Christian church, and to whom the Gospel was imparted by the immediate and especial direction of Heaven, held the same station; and in the history of this transaction we discover not the smallest intimation that Cornelius, upon becoming a Christian, quitted the service of the Roman legion,

---

* James, iv, 1.   † Luke, iii, 14.   ‡ Luke, vii, 9.
§ Acts, x, 1.

that his profession was objected to, or his continuance in it considered as in any wise inconsistent with his new character.

But as the institution of slavery is treated by the Christian Scriptures with precisely the same forbearance, we are not hereby entitled to argue for the continued lawfulness of war. It appears to be in the same category with slavery and capital punishment: so long as each or all are *necessary*, so long each or all are lawful; but few will now deny that in each case the lawfulness expires with the necessity.

In applying the principles of morality to the affairs of nations, the difficulty which meets us arises from hence: " that the particular consequence sometimes "*appears* to exceed the value of the general rule." In this circumstance is founded the only distinction that exists between the case of independent states and of independent individuals. In the transactions of private persons, no advantage that results from the breach of a general law of justice can compensate to the public for the violation of the law; in the concerns of empire, this may sometimes be doubted. Thus, that the faith of promises ought to be maintained, as far as is lawful, and as far as was intended by the parties, whatever inconveniency either of them may suffer by his fidelity, in the intercourse of private life, is seldom disputed; because it is evident to almost every man who reflects upon the subject, that the common happiness gains more by the preservation of the rule than it could do by the removal of the inconveniency. But, when the adherence to a public treaty would enslave a whole people; would block up seas, rivers, or harbours; depopulate cities; condemn fertile regions to eternal desolation; cut off a country from its sources of provision, or deprive it of those commercial advantages to which its climate, produce, or situation naturally entitle it; the magnitude of the particular evil induces us to call in question the obligation of the general rule. Moral Philosophy furnishes no precise solution to these doubts. She cannot pronounce that any rule of morality is so rigid as to bend to *no* exceptions; nor, on the other hand, can she comprise those exceptions within any previous description. She confesses that the obligation of every law depends upon its ultimate utility; that this utility having a finite and determinate value, situations may be feigned, and consequently may possibly arise, in which the general tendency is outweighed by the enormity of the particular mischief; but she recalls, at the same time, to the consideration of the inquirer, the almost inestimable importance, as of other general rules of relative justice, so especially of national and personal fidelity; the unseen, if not unbounded, extent of the mischief which must follow from the want of it; the danger of leaving it to the sufferer to decide upon the comparison of particular and general consequences; and the still greater danger of such decisions being drawn into future precedents. If treaties, for instance, be no longer binding than whilst they are convenient, or until the inconveniency ascend to a certain point, which point must be fixed by the judgment, or rather by the feelings, of the complaining party; or, if such an opinion, after being authorized by a few examples, come at length to prevail; one and almost the only method of averting or closing the calamities of war, of either preventing or putting a stop to the destruction of mankind, is lost to the world for ever. We do not say that no evil can exceed this, nor any possible advantage compensate it; but we say, that a loss which affected *all* will scarcely be made up to the common stock of human happiness by any benefit that can be procured to a single nation, which, however respectable when compared with any other single nation, bears an inconsiderable proportion to the whole. These, however, are the principles upon which the calculation is to be formed. It is enough, in this place, to remark the cause which produces the hesitation that we sometimes feel, in applying rules of personal probity to the conduct of nations.

As between individuals it is found impossible to ascertain every duty by an immediate reference to public utility, not only because such reference is oftentimes too remote or obscure for the direction of private consciences, but because a multitude of cases arise in which it is indifferent to the general interest by what rule men act, though it be absolutely necessary that they act by some constant and known rule or other; and as, for these reasons, certain positive constitutions are wont to be established in every society, which, when established, become as obligatory as the original principles of natural justice themselves; so, likewise, it is between independent communities. Together with those maxims of universal equity which are common to states and to individuals, and by which the rights and conduct of the one, as well as of the other, ought to be adjusted, when they fall within the scope and application of such maxims; there exists also amongst sovereigns a system of artificial jurisprudence, under the name of the *law of nations*. In this code are found the rules which determine the right to vacant or newly discovered countries; those which relate to the protection of fugitives; the privileges of ambassadors; the condition and duties of neutrality; the immunities of neutral ships, ports, and coasts; the distance from shore to which these immunities extend; the distinction between free and contraband goods; and a variety of subjects of the same kind. Concerning which examples, and indeed the principal part of what is called the *jus gentium*, it may be observed, that the rules derive their moral force (by which I mean the regard that ought to be paid to them by the consciences of sovereigns), not from their internal reasonableness or justice, for many of them are perfectly arbitrary; nor yet from the authority by which they were established, for the greater part have grown insensibly into usage, without any public compact, formal acknowledgment, or even known original; but simply from the fact of their being established, and the general duty of conforming to established rules upon questions and between parties where nothing but positive regulations can prevent disputes, and where disputes are followed by such destructive consequences. The first of the instances which we have just now enumerated may be selected for the illustration of this remark. The nations of Europe consider the sovereignty of newly discovered countries as belonging to the prince or state whose subjects make the discovery; and, in pursuance of this rule, it is usual for a navigator who falls upon an unknown shore, to take possession of it, in the name of his sovereign at home, by erecting his standard or displaying his flag upon a desert coast. Now, nothing can be more fanciful, or less substantiated by any considerations of reason or justice, than the right which such discovery, or the transient occupation and idle ceremony that accompany it, confer on the country of the discoverer. Nor can any stipulation be produced by which the rest of the world have bound themselves to submit to this pretension. Yet, when we reflect that the claims to newly discovered countries can hardly be settled between the different nations that frequent them, without some positive rule or other; that such claims, if left unsettled, would prove sources of ruinous and fatal contentions; that the rule already proposed, however arbitrary, possesses one principal quality of a rule—determination and certainty; above all, that it is acquiesced in, and that no one has power to substitute another, however he might contrive a better, in its place; when we reflect upon these properties of the rule, or rather upon these consequences of rejecting its authority, we are led to ascribe to it the virtue and obligation of a precept of natural justice, because we perceive in it that which is the foundation of justice itself—public importance and utility. And a prince who should dispute this rule, for the want of regularity in its formation, or of intelligible justice in its principle, and by such dispute disturb the tranquillity of nations, and at the same time lay the foundation of further disturbance in future, would be little less criminal than he who breaks the public peace by a violation of engagements to which he had himself consented, or by an attack upon those national rights which are founded immediately in the law of nature, and in the first perceptions of equity. The same thing may be repeated of the rules which the law of nations prescribes in the other instances that were mentioned; namely, that the obscurity of their origin, or the arbitrariness of their principle, subtracts nothing from the respect that is due to them, when once established.

War may be considered with a view to its *causes* and to its *conduct*.

The *justifying* causes of war are deliberate invasions of right*. The objects of just war are pre-

---

* Paley adds another cause, but one which cannot be acquiesced in; he continues—and the necessity of maintaining

caution, defence, or reparation. In a larger sense, every just war is a *defensive* war; inasmuch as every just war supposes an injury perpetrated or attempted*. Many writers have added to the justifying causes of war, such ill-behaviour on the part of any foreign power towards *its own* dependencies as manifestly tends to the detriment of the whole human race. The conduct of Russia towards Poland, of Austria towards Hungary, have been cited as instances in point.

I am much inclined to doubt this theory. It is difficult for any foreign nation to be a fair judge in such cases; and were the principle once admitted, there would never be wanting occasions of war; every local discontent, every provincial insurrection, would become a chance of embroiling the whole civilized world. Again, if it be lawful for one person to interfere on *one* side, it is undoubtedly as lawful for another person to interfere on the other side; if tyranny be a crime in the eye of the Christian, so is rebellion; and these names will be often applied differently by persons differently situated for judging.

Remonstrance may without question be resorted to; and the remonstrances of a powerful nation will rarely or ever be treated with disrespect.

---

such a balance of power amongst neighbouring nations, as that no single state, or confederacy of states, be strong enough to overwhelm the rest.

* Paley here adds, but not rightly (or feared).

The *insufficient* causes, or *unjustifiable* motives of war, are the family alliances, the personal friendships, or the personal quarrels of princes; the internal disputes which are carried on in other nations; the justice of other wars, the extension of territory or of trade; the misfortunes or accidental weakness of a neighbouring or rival nation.

Another unjustifiable cause of war is the maintaining what used to be called "the balance of power," of which Paley's description will be found in a note. It will be obvious to every Christian politician that the prosperity and consequent *power* of any nation can be no grounds of an attack on the part of others, however great that power may become. Did there exist any such rights as this, a coalition of all the powers of Europe against Great Britain, without provocation, would be a lawful league.

Nor is war justified by an injury which we only fear may be inflicted upon us. Nations, like courts of justice, can only proceed upon overt acts; mere suspected intentions furnish no grounds for war.

It may be lawful for a nation which suspects the intentions of a neighbouring power to *prepare* for war; but even this right should be exercised with extreme caution, for it is liable to great abuse.

There are *two* lessons of a rational and sober policy, which, if it were possible to inculcate into the councils of princes, would exclude many of the motives of war, and allay that restless ambition which is constantly stirring up one part of mankind against another. The first of these lessons admonishes princes "to place "their glory and their emulation, not in extent of "territory, but in raising the greatest quantity of hap- "piness out of a given territory." The enlargement of a territory by conquests is not only not a just object of war, but, in the greater part of the instances in which it is attempted, not even desirable. It is certainly not desirable, where it adds nothing to the numbers, the enjoyments, or the security of the conquerors. What commonly is gained to a nation, by the annexing of new dependencies, or the subjugation of other countries to its dominion, but a wider frontier to defend; more interfering claims to vindicate; more quarrels, more enemies, more rebellions to encounter; a greater force to keep up by sea and land; more services to provide for, and more establishments to pay? And, in order to draw from these acquisitions something that may make up for the charge of keeping them, a revenue is to be extorted, or a monopoly to be enforced and watched, at an expense which costs half their produce. Thus the provinces are oppressed, in order to pay for being ill-governed; and the original state is exhausted in maintaining a feeble authority over discontented subjects. No assignable portion of country is benefited by the change; and if the sovereign appear to himself to be enriched or strengthened, when every part of his dominion is made poorer and weaker than it was, it is probable that he is deceived by appearances. Or were it true that the grandeur of the prince is magnified by these exploits, the glory which is purchased, and the ambition which is gratified, by the distress of one country, without adding to the happiness of another, which at the same time enslaves the new and impoverishes the ancient part of the empire, by whatever names it may be known or flattered, is an object of universal execration; and not more so to the vanquished, than it is oftentimes to the very people whose armies or whose treasures have achieved the victory.

There are, indeed, two cases in which the extension of territory may be of real advantage, and to both parties; and this may reconcile us to an event after it has taken place, though it would not justify the steps which led to it. Aggressive war is not lawful because the object to be obtained by it may be as beneficial to the conquered as to the conqueror; for this would be to do evil that good may come of it—a principle, the unchristian character of which is now almost universally admitted. Of the two cases, the first is, where an empire thereby reaches to the natural boundaries which divide it from the rest of the world. Thus we account the British Channel the natural boundary which separates the nations of England and France; and if France possessed any countries on this, or England any cities or provinces on that, side of the sea, the recovery of such towns and districts to what may be called their natural sovereign, though it might not be a just reason for commencing war, would be a proper use to make of victory. The other case is, where neighbouring states, being severally too small and weak to defend themselves against the dangers that surround them, can only be safe by a strict and constant junction of their strength; here conquest will effect the purposes of confederation and alliance; and the union which it produces is often more close and permanent than that which results from voluntary association. Thus, if the heptarchy had continued in England, the different kingdoms of it might have separately fallen a prey to foreign invasion; and although the interest and danger of one part of the island was in truth common to every other part, it might have been difficult to have circulated this persuasion amongst independent nations, or to have united them in any regular steady opposition to their continental enemies, had not the valour and fortune of an enterprising prince incorporated the whole into a single monarchy. Here, the conquered gained as much by the revolution as the conquerors. In like manner and for the same reason, when the two royal families of Spain were met together in one race of princes, and the several provinces of France had devolved into the possession of a single sovereign, it became unsafe for the inhabitants of Great Britain any longer to remain under separate governments. The union of England and Scotland, which transformed two quarrelsome neighbours into one powerful empire, and which was first brought about by the course of succession, and afterwards completed by amicable convention, would have been a fortunate conclusion of hostilities, had it been effected by the operations of war. These two cases being admitted—namely, the obtaining of natural boundaries and barriers, and the including under the same government those who have a common danger and a common enemy to guard against,—I know not whether a third can be thought of, in which the extension of empire by conquest is useful even to the conquerors.

It is necessary to note, however, that the way to judge of the lawfulness of any particular war, is to ascertain whether it were really *necessary*. No expected advantages can justify an appeal to arms, unless, first, the object sought to be obtained is one to which we have an undoubted right; and when, secondly, it can be obtained in no other way.

The second rule of prudence which ought to be recommended to those who conduct the affairs of nations, is, "never to pursue national *honor* as distinct " from national *interest*." This rule acknowledges that it is often necessary to assert the honor of a nation for the sake of its interest. The spirit and courage of a people are supported by flattering their pride. Concessions which betray too much fear or weakness, though they relate to points of mere ceremony, invite demands and attacks of more serious importance. Our rule allows this; and directs only, that when points of honor become subjects of contention between sovereigns, or are likely to be made the occasions of war, they be estimated with reference to utility, and not *by themselves*. " The dignity of his crown," " the " honor of his flag," "the glory of his arms," in the mouth of a prince, are stately and imposing terms; but the ideas they inspire are insatiable. It may be always glorious to conquer, whatever be the justice of the war, or the price of the victory. The dignity of a sovereign may not permit him to recede from claims of homage and respect, at whatever expense of national peace and happiness they are to be maintained, however unjust they may have been in their original, or in their continuance, however useless to the possessor, or mortifying and vexatious to other states. The pursuit of honor, when let loose from the admonitions of prudence, becomes, in kings, a wild and romantic passion: eager to engage, and gathering fury in its progress, it is checked by no difficulties, repelled by no dangers; it forgets or despises those considerations of safety, ease, wealth, and plenty, which, in the eye of true public wisdom, compose the objects to which the renown of arms, the fame of victory, are only instrumental and subordinate. The pursuit of interest, on the other hand, is a sober principle; computes costs and consequences; is cautious of entering into war; stops in time; when regulated by those universal maxims of relative justice which belong to the affairs of communities as well as of private persons, it is the right principle for nations to proceed by: even when it trespasses upon these regulations, it is much less dangerous, because much more temperate, than the other.

From what has been said, it will follow that war is lawful only so far as it is necessary. If the territory of a nation be invaded by the armies of an alien power,—if her subjects are oppressed and maltreated by foreign authorities,—if peaceful remonstrances are disregarded, and undoubted rights are violated,—if the offer of arbitration be refused,—and a determination manifested to continue or to aggravate the offence,—then war becomes defensive, necessary, and lawful. Under all other circumstances, it is unchristian, needless, and to be condemned.

CHAPTER XIV.

OF THE CONDUCT OF WAR.

If the cause and end of war be justifiable, all the means that appear necessary to the end are justifiable also. This is the principle which defends those extremities to which the violence of war usually proceeds: for, since war is a contest by *force* between parties who acknowledge no common superior, and since it includes not in its idea the supposition of any convention which should place limits to the operation of force, it has naturally no boundary but that in which force terminates—the destruction of the life against which the force is directed. Let it be observed, however, that the licence of war authorizes no acts of hostility but what are necessary or conducive to the end and object of the war. Gratuitous barbarities borrow no excuse from this plea: of which kind is every cruelty and every insult that serves only to exasperate the sufferings or to increase the hatred of an enemy, without weakening his strength, or in any manner tending to procure his submission; such as the slaughter of captives, the subjecting them to indignities of torture, the violation of women, the profanation of temples, the demolition of public buildings, libraries, statues, and in general the destruction or defacing of works that conduce nothing to annoyance and defence. These enormities are prohibited, not only by the practice of civilized nations, but by the law of nature itself, as having no proper tendency to accelerate the termination or accomplish the object of the war; and as containing that which, in peace and war, is equally unjustifiable—ultimate and gratuitous mischief.

There are other restrictions imposed upon the conduct of war, not by the law of nature primarily, but by the *laws of war* first, and by the law of nature as seconding and ratifying the laws of war. The laws of war are part of the law of nations; and founded, as to their authority, upon the same principle with the rest of that code; namely, upon the fact of their being established, no matter when or by whom, upon the expectation of their being mutually observed, in consequence of that establishment; and upon the general utility which results from that observance. The binding force of these rules is the greater, because the regard that is paid to them must be universal, or none. The breach of the rule can only be punished by the subversion of the rule itself: on which account, the whole mischief that ensues from the loss of those salutary restrictions which such rules prescribe, is justly chargeable upon the first aggressor. To this consideration may be referred the duty of refraining, in war, from poison and from assassination. If the law of nature simply be consulted, it may be difficult to distinguish between these and other methods of destruction which are practised without scruple by nations at war. If it be lawful to kill an enemy at all, it seems lawful to do so by one mode of death as well as by another; by a dose of poison as by the point of a sword; by the hand of an assassin as by the attack of an army: for if it be said that one species of assault leaves to an enemy the power of defending himself against it, and that the other does not,—it may be answered, that we possess at least the same right to cut off an enemy's defence, that we have to seek his destruction. In this manner might the question be debated, if there existed no rule or law of war upon the subject. But when we observe that such practices are at present excluded by the usage and opinions of civilized nations; that the first recourse to them would be followed by instant retaliation; that the mutual licence which such attempts must introduce, would fill both sides with the misery of continual dread and suspicion, without adding to the strength or success of either; that, when the example came to be more generally imitated, which it soon would be after the sentiment which condemns it had been once broken in upon, it would greatly aggravate the horrors and calamities of war, yet procure no superiority to any of the nations engaged in it: when we view these effects, we join in the public reprobation of such fatal expedients, as of the admission amongst mankind of new and enormous evils, without necessity or advantage. The law of nature, we see at length, forbids those innovations, as so many transgressions of a beneficial general rule actually subsisting.

The licence of war then acknowledges *two* limitations: it authorizes no hostilities which have not an apparent tendency to effectuate the object of the war; it respects those positive laws which the custom of nations hath sanctified, and which, whilst they are mutually conformed to, mitigate the calamities of war, without weakening its operations, or diminishing the power or safety of belligerent states.

CHAPTER XV.

OF STANDING ARMIES.

LONG and various experience seems to have convinced the nations of Europe that nothing but a *standing army* can oppose a standing army, where the numbers on each side bear any moderate proportion to one another. The first standing army that appeared in Europe after the fall of the Roman legion, was that which was erected in France by Charles VII, about the middle of the fifteenth century; and that the institution has since become general, can only be attributed to the superiority and success which are every where observed to attend it. The truth is, the closeness, regularity, and quickness of their movements; the unreserved, instantaneous, and almost mechanical obedience to orders; the sense of personal honor, and the familiarity with danger, which belong to a disciplined, veteran, and embodied soldiery, give such firmness and intrepidity to their approach, such weight and execution to their attack, as are not to be understood by loose ranks of occasional and newly levied troops, who are liable by their inexperience to disorder and confusion, and in whom fear is constantly augmented by novelty and surprise. It is not impossible that a *militia*, with a great access of numbers and a ready supply of recruits, may sustain a defensive or a flying war against regular troops: it is also true that any service which keeps soldiers for a while together, and inures them by little and little to the habits of war and the dangers of action, transforms them in effect into a standing army. But, upon this plan, it may be necessary for almost a whole nation to go out to war to repel an invader; beside that, a people so unprepared must always have the seat, and with it the miseries, of war at home—being utterly incapable of carrying their operations into a foreign country.

From the acknowledged superiority of standing armies, it follows, not only that it is unsafe for a nation to disband its regular troops, whilst neighbouring kingdoms retain theirs, but also that regular troops provide for the public service at the least possible expense. I suppose a certain quantity of military strength to be necessary, and I say that a standing army costs the community less than any other establishment which presents to an enemy the same force. The constant drudgery of low employments is not only incompatible with any great degree of perfection or expertness in the profession of a soldier, but the profession of a soldier almost always unfits men for the business of regular occupations. Of three inhabitants of a village, it is better that one should addict himself entirely to arms, and the other two stay constantly at home to cultivate the ground, than that all three should mix the avocations of a camp with the business of husbandry. By the former arrangement, the country gains one complete soldier and two industrious husbandmen; from the latter, it receives three raw military men, who are at the same time three idle and profligate peasants. It should be considered also, that the emergencies of war wait not for seasons. Where there is no standing army ready for immediate service, it may be necessary to call the reaper from the fields in harvest, or the plowman in seed time; and the provision of a whole year may perish by the interruption of one month's labour. A standing army, therefore, is not only a more effectual, but a cheaper method of providing for the public safety than any other; because it adds more than any other to the common strength, and takes less from that which composes the wealth of a nation—its stock of productive industry.

There is yet another distinction between standing armies and militias, which deserves a more attentive consideration than any that has been mentioned. When the state relies for its defence upon a militia, it is necessary that arms be put into the hands of the people at large. The militia itself must be numerous, in proportion to the want or inferiority of its discipline, and the imbecilities or defects of its constitution. Moreover, as such a militia must be supplied by rotation, allotment, or some mode of successions, whereby they who have served a certain time are replaced by fresh draughts from the country, a much greater number will be instructed in the use of arms, and will have been occasionally embodied together, than are actually employed, or than are supposed to be wanted at the same time. Now, what effects upon the civil condition of the country may be looked for from this general diffusion of the military character, becomes an inquiry of great importance and delicacy. To me it appears doubtful whether any government can be long secure, where the people are acquainted with the use of arms and accustomed to resort to them. Every faction will find itself at the head of an army; every disgust will excite commotion, and every commotion become a civil war. Nothing, perhaps, can govern a nation of armed citizens but that which governs an army—despotism. I do not mean that a regular government would become despotic by training up its subjects to the knowledge and exercise of arms, but that it would ere long be forced to give way to despotism in some other shape; and that the country would be liable to what is even worse than a settled and constitutional despotism—to perpetual rebellions, and to perpetual revolutions; to short and violent usurpations; to the successive tyranny of governors, rendered cruel and jealous by the danger and instability of their situation.

The jealousy of military interference, which characterizes the English people, seems much founded on this idea. Even the attempt to quell a riot by the exhibition of troops is unpopular, not only because it is looked upon as an exercise of a power necessarily despotic and therefore unconstitutional, but because it tends to bring into conflict those who should have their distinct and separate offices of action. A wise government, deeming it necessary to employ the military to prevent disturbances, has sagaciously kept the troops employed out of sight; ready to act, but not to be seen, unless called for by urgent necessity.

The same purposes of stength and efficacy which make a standing army necessary at all, make it necessary, in mixed governments, that this army be submitted to the management and direction of the executive; for however well a popular council may be qualified for the offices of legislation, it is altogether unfit for the conduct of war: in which success usually depends upon vigour and enterprise; upon secrecy, despatch, and unanimity; upon a quick perception of opportunities, and the power of seizing every opportunity immediately. It is likewise necessary that the obedience of an army be as prompt and active as possible; for which reason, it ought to be made an obedience of will and emulation. Upon this consideration is founded the expediency of leaving to the executive, not only the government and destination of the army, but the appointment and promotion of its officers: because a design is then alone likely to be executed with zeal and fidelity, when the authority which issues the order, chooses the instruments and rewards the service*.

Whilst we describe, however, the advantages of standing armies, we must not conceal the danger. These properties of their constitution—the soldiery being separated in a great degree from the rest of the community, their being closely linked amongst themselves by habits of society and subordination, and the dependency of the whole chain upon the will and favour of the executive—however essential they may be to the purposes for which armies are kept up, give them an aspect in no wise favourable to public liberty. The danger, however, is diminished by maintaining, upon all occasions, as much alliance of interest, and as much intercourse of sentiment, between the military part of the nation and the other orders of the people,

---

* Paley adds: To which we may subjoin, that, in governments like ours, if the direction and *officering* of the army were placed in the hands of the democratic part of the constitution, this power, added to what they already possess, would so overbalance all that would be left of regal prerogative, that little would remain of monarchy in the constitution, but the name and expense; nor would they probably remain long.

Circumstances do not appear to justify this apprehension. No military undertaking of consequence could take place without the concurrence of the House of Commons; and officers in the army do for the most part purchase their appointments, so that in reality the sovereign neither directs the operations, nor appoints the officers of the British army.

as are consistent with the union and discipline of an army*.

The steps recently taken towards the education of the soldiery, the care manifested in promoting their comforts, the gradual disuse of corporeal punishments, the rendering the soldier more amenable to civil law in time of peace, rather than to mere martial law, are all means to this end; they are links of connexion with the nation at large, which give the soldiers such a share in the general rights of the people, and so engage their inclinations on the side of public liberty, as to afford a reasonable security that they cannot be brought, by any promises of personal aggrandizement, to assist in the execution of measures which might enslave their posterity, their kindred, and the country.

---

* "For which purpose," says Paley, "the officers of an army, upon whose disposition towards the commonwealth a great deal may depend, should be taken from the principal families of the country; and, at the same time, also be encouraged to establish in it families of their own, as well as to be admitted to seats in the senate, to hereditary distinctions, and to all the civil honours and privileges that are compatible with their profession." This, so far as it is an advantage, is, and has been for nearly two centuries, the case.

FINIS.